Taxcafe.co.uk Tax Guides

How to Save Property Tax

By Carl Bayley BSc ACA

through marriage, inheritance or other changes in personal circumstances.

Others move into the property sector quite deliberately, seeing it as a safe haven providing long-term security and perhaps an income in retirement. Still others see the property market as a means to generate a second income during their working life.

An ever-growing proportion of landlords are choosing to enter the property business as a professional career.

In fact, given the ever-increasing volume of rules and regulations which the private rented sector has to contend with, a professional approach to property investment has now become essential: whatever reasons you may have for entering the property market in the first place.

This is no bad thing: a professional approach has always been desirable. Those who are prepared to devote substantial time and resources to their business are generally rewarded with better results – including those who plan their tax affairs carefully.

The last decade has, of course, seen enormous changes in the property market and in the economy as a whole and previously held views on the certainty of capital growth and the whole philosophy of 'you can't lose' have been questioned and found wanting.

Whilst these changes have been disastrous for some, they have created opportunities for others and the lower level of interest rates enjoyed by many investors over the last few years have brought healthy rental profits to many.

In effect, the economic difficulties created by the 2008/9 banking crisis and its aftermath can be seen as part of an evolutionary process. The fittest property businesses have survived to become part of a stronger property sector.

Now, the property sector faces a new challenge: a challenge which I can only describe as an unprecedented level of attacks via the tax system from a Government that would appear to be hell-bent on the sector's destruction. Quite where the Government expects to house all the former tenants that are likely to be made homeless as a result is a mystery to me!

Nonetheless, despite the difficulties which it continues to face, I personally believe that the property investment sector as we know it today is here to stay. Naturally, the sector will have its ups and downs, as any other business sector does, but the philosophy of property investment as a 'career move' is now so well entrenched that it has become impossible to imagine it could ever disappear altogether.

- Very limited scope for loss relief (both for capital losses and for rental losses)
- Accounting periods ended 5th April each year are generally necessary
- Difficulty in transferring business without incurring tax charges

Tax Advantages of Property Trades

- Greater scope for claiming indirect or abortive expenses relating to property purchases and sales
- Full relief for interest and finance costs
- Long-term assets of the business may be eligible for entrepreneurs' relief or rollover relief for CGT purposes
- Losses can be set off against any income arising in the same tax year or the previous tax year (subject to the limitations explained in Section 5.12)
- Any date may be chosen for the accounting year end
- The value of a property development or property management business will usually be exempt from IHT on death
- Businesses may usually be transferred (e.g. to a company or to another individual) without any significant tax charges

Tax Disadvantages of Property Trades

- Profits arising on property sales are subject to both Income Tax and NI
- Non-UK residents are fully taxable on all profits derived from a property trade based in the UK. From 5th July 2016 they are also taxable on any trading profits arising on the disposal of property, or an interest in property, located in the UK.
- VAT registration will become compulsory if annual turnover from taxable activities for VAT purposes exceeds £85,000

2.9   THE BOUNDARY BETWEEN INVESTMENT AND TRADING

After reading the previous section, you've probably got a fair idea of how you would *like* your property business to be treated for tax purposes. However, as I have already pointed out, it is not a question of choice, but is determined by how you conduct your business.

Furthermore, not only is it a matter of how you actually behave, very often it will hinge on what your intentions were at the beginning of any particular project.

Until recently, a property disposal was treated as a capital gain unless the **sole or main purpose** behind the acquisition of the property was to realise a profit on its disposal.

New legislation applying from 5th July 2016, however, states that the profit on disposal of UK property will be **treated** as trading profit whenever the main purpose, **or one of the main purposes**, behind its acquisition was to realise a profit on its disposal.

This broadens the scope of what might be considered to be a **trading profit** quite considerably. It does not, however, alter the basic principles which determine when a **trade** actually exists. In other words, a middle ground has been created where there is no actual trade, but where profits are simply **treated** as trading profits.

The situation applying for property disposals made after 4th July 2016 can therefore be summed up as follows:

1. **Where the sole or main purpose behind the acquisition was to make a profit on disposal:** a property trade exists, the profit on disposal is trading income subject to both Income Tax and NI, and the business will be taxed as set out in Sections 2.4 or 2.5 (depending on whether any development activity is taking place).

2. **Where one of the main purposes behind the acquisition (but not the only, or dominant, purpose) was to make a profit on disposal:** the profit on disposal will be treated as trading income and will be subject to Income Tax (but not NI). For all other purposes, the business will be treated as a property investment business, as set out in Section 2.3.

3. **Where making a profit on disposal was not a main purpose behind the acquisition:** the profit on disposal will be a capital gain subject to CGT and, if a business does exist, it will be a property investment business, treated as set out in Section 2.3.

The principles used in determining whether a business falls under Category 1 above are well established and have been discussed already in this chapter.

The dividing line between Categories 2 and 3 is yet to be established: it is dependent on new legislation which has yet to be tested in court. It may therefore be many years before the practical implications of this new legislation are fully understood.

2.11 'MIXED' PROPERTY BUSINESSES

"What if my business doesn't happen to fit neatly into one of these categories?" you may be asking.

If you have a 'mixed' property business, involving more than one of the different types of property business described in this chapter, to a degree which is more than merely incidental, then, for tax purposes, each of the business types should be dealt with separately, in the usual manner applicable to that type.

However, having said that, there is a great danger that any property development or property trading may effectively 'taint' what would otherwise be a property investment business, with the result that HMRC might attempt to deny you CGT treatment on all of your property transactions. (Property management will generally stand alone without too much difficulty, as it does not involve any property ownership.)

Tax Tip
To avoid the danger of a property investment business being 'tainted' by development or trading activities, you should take whatever steps you can to separate the businesses, such as:

i)   Drawing up separate accounts for the different businesses
ii)   Using a different business name for the different activities
iii) Reporting the non-investment activities as a different business in your tax return
iv)   Consider a different legal ownership structure for the non-investment activities (e.g. put them in a company or a partnership with your spouse, partner or adult children)
(On the other hand, it is also worth noting that combining a property investment business with a property development business may produce IHT savings: see the Taxcafe.co.uk guide *'How to Save Inheritance Tax'*.)

2.12 OTHER PROPERTY-BASED TRADES

As discussed previously, there are a number of trades which are inextricably linked with the business's underlying property but which are quite distinct from simple property investment. Such trades include:

- Hotels and Guest Houses
- Nursing Homes and Private Hospitals
- Hostels
- Serviced Offices
- Warehouses
- Holiday Parks

The key difference between these trades and the property businesses which we have examined previously in this chapter is the fact that the property's owners actually occupy the property for use in their own trade.

Tax Treatment

The profits derived from running these business activities are treated as trading profits subject to Income Tax and NI.

Most of these businesses will need to be registered for VAT when their gross annual sales income exceeds £85,000.

Gains arising on disposal of the properties held by these businesses will be subject to CGT, with the full range of attendant reliefs available to business property, including entrepreneurs' relief and rollover relief (see Sections 6.28 and 8.29 respectively).

Most properties used in these types of business will also be eligible for business property relief for IHT purposes. Dangers arise, however, where the business confers some long-term rights of occupation to its customers, as is sometimes the case with nursing homes or caravan parks, for example.

2.13   SPOUSES AND CIVIL PARTNERS

Throughout this guide, you will see me refer many times to 'married couples', spouses, or husbands and wives. In each case, the tax treatment being outlined applies equally to:

- Married couples of opposite sexes,
- Married couples of the same sex, and
- Registered civil partners

Hence, any references to 'married couples' throughout this guide should be taken to also include registered civil partnerships; any reference to the taxpayer's 'spouse' will also include their civil partner where relevant; and any reference to 'husbands' or 'wives' will include spouses of the same gender and civil partners.

However, it remains important to remember that, unless specified to the contrary, the tax treatment being outlined applies to legally married couples and legally registered civil partners only. Unmarried couples are subject to entirely different rules.

2.14   JOINT OWNERSHIP & PROPERTY PARTNERSHIPS

Before we move on to look at the detailed tax treatment of property businesses, it is worth pausing to think about the potential impact of joint ownership.

The first point to note is that joint ownership itself does not alter the nature of your property business.

In England and Wales, joint ownership comes in two varieties:

- Joint Tenancy, and
- Tenancy in Common.

Don't be confused by the word 'tenancy' here, this is terminology only and doesn't affect the fact you jointly own the freehold, leasehold, etc.

In Scotland, joint ownership of property comes predominantly in one major form called 'Pro Indivisio' ownership and, as far as the tax position is concerned, this is more or less the same as a Tenancy in Common.

Joint Tenancy

Under a joint tenancy ownership of each person's share passes automatically on death to the other joint tenant. This is known as 'survivorship'. Furthermore, neither joint owner is normally able to sell their share of the property without the consent of the other.

Each joint owner under a joint tenancy is treated as having an equal share in the property. In effect, joint tenants are regarded as joint owners of the whole property.

Tenancy in Common

Under a tenancy in common, the joint owners are each free to do as they wish with their own share of the property and there is no right of survivorship. The joint owners' shares in the property under a tenancy in common do not necessarily have to be equal. In effect, tenants in common each own their own separate share in the property.

The same considerations apply equally to joint 'Pro Indivisio' owners in Scotland.

Tax Tip
A tenancy in common provides far more scope for tax planning than a joint tenancy. We will see much more on the potential benefits of tenancies in common in the following chapters.

Property Investment & Joint Ownership

When it comes to a property investment business, all that joint ownership means is that each individual has their own property investment business and is taxed on their own share of rental profits and capital gains accordingly. The joint ownership does not affect the nature of the underlying business.

Joint owners carrying on a property investment business will not generally constitute a business partnership unless they also formally create such a partnership.

Property Development

Joint owners engaged in property development will generally form a business partnership under basic legal principles. This is because two or more individuals engaged in the mutual pursuit of commercial trading profits are, in law, generally deemed to constitute a partnership.

Example

Ingrid and Lenny buy an old barn and some disused farm land as tenants in common. They convert the barn into a pair of semi-detached dwellings and build two new houses on the disused land. They then sell all of the newly developed properties and share the profit equally. Ingrid and Lenny are in a trading partnership.

It nevertheless does remain possible for joint owners of a property used in a property development trade to be engaged in a 'joint venture', rather than a business partnership, if the terms of the arrangements between the parties do not amount to the mutual pursuit of profit.

Example

Luke owns an old farm. At the edge of the farm there is a small field which Luke is no longer able to farm profitably.

Ives comes to Luke with a proposition which goes like this: "If you sell me a half interest in your small field for its current agricultural value, I'll get planning permission to build some houses and then, after I've built and sold them, I'll pay you the residential use value for your remaining half interest."

Whilst this proposition does involve joint ownership of some development land, it does not amount to a trading partnership as Luke is not participating in Ives' development profit.

A property trading partnership may also exist without joint ownership.

Not only does Meera have a considerable amount of tax to pay for 2017/18, her liability is too great for her to be eligible to pay her tax through her PAYE coding and she must make payments on account in respect of 2018/19. Hence, unless Meera has reasonable grounds for claiming that her 2018/19 tax liability will be less than that for 2017/18, she will have to make tax payments as follows:

By 31st January 2019:
      Tax due for 2017/18:   £3,800
      First Instalment for 2018/19:   £1,900
      Total payment due: £5,700

By 31st July 2019:
      Second Instalment for 2018/19:   £1,900

By 31st January 2020:
      Balancing payment (or repayment) for 2018/19
      First Instalment for 2019/20

And so on, every six months thereafter for as long as her self-assessment tax liability exceeds £1,000 per annum.

The example has also demonstrated another very important fact. When you begin to receive any significant level of income that is not taxed at source, such as property rental or trading profits, the tax liabilities arising in the first year can be quite severe. You will need to find the tax on two years' worth of profits within the space of only six months – most of it on one single day. This is what I call the 'double whammy' effect of self assessment!

Of course, once you are 'in the system' and things settle down a bit, you should just be paying fairly similar levels of tax every six months.

Nevertheless, every time your rental or trading income increases significantly, you will be hit by this 'double whammy' effect again!

Wealth Warning
Where an individual is already paying tax under PAYE and also has property rental income, HMRC often attempts to collect the tax due on the property business through the PAYE system. At best, this vastly accelerates the date of collection of the tax due, at worst it can lead to overpayments. Whilst such overpayments may eventually be reclaimed, there will be no compensatory payment of interest. Fortunately, taxpayers have the right to appeal against any PAYE codings which attempt to include their rental income in this way and hence continue to pay the tax on this income via the self-assessment system.

Turn to Section 5.5 to see the example in this section revisited where Meera has a property trade and is thus also subject to NI on her profits.

3.5   TAX RETURNS

Nowadays, most people submit their tax returns online and many use specialised software for the purpose, so you may be less aware of which boxes or pages your entries will actually appear in on the final return. However, the way in which property businesses should be reported on the self assessment return (or returns) is summarised below.

Rental income from UK land and property should be detailed on pages UKP1 and UKP2 of the tax return. This is referred to as the 'UK Property Supplement'.

Page UKP1 begins with a few general questions, including the number of UK rental properties which you had during the relevant tax year (Box 1).

This may seem like a pretty trivial and innocent question, but it is important to get it right as HMRC will compare this figure with the details of the properties you hold at the land registry.

When completing Box 1, remember to include:

i)   UK properties only (subject to point (iii) below)
ii)   Rental properties that you hold jointly with another person
iii)   UK properties and other properties within the EEA let as qualifying furnished holiday lets (see Section 8.17 for details)
iv)   Properties not let on arm's length commercial terms (see Section 4.16)
v)   Any property on which you are claiming 'rent-a-room relief' (see Section 4.11)
vi)   All your UK rental properties (see Section 4.3), including any properties from which you actually received no rental income during the year

If you hold any of these properties jointly with another person you should put an 'X' in Box 3. (We will look at joint lettings and some of their potential benefits in more detail in Section 8.2.)

We will deal with the significance of Boxes 2 and 4 later, in Chapter 4.

The rest of page UKP1 deals with income from the commercial letting of furnished holiday accommodation in the UK or elsewhere in the EEA (see Section 1.4). See Section 8.17 for further details.

Details of all other UK property rental income should be entered on page UKP2.

Income from land and property located overseas is treated as a different source of income. With the exception of income from qualifying furnished holiday lets in the EEA, this income should be detailed on pages F4 and F5 which form part of the 'Foreign Supplement'. Any foreign tax suffered on this income should also be detailed on pages F4 and F5. Any foreign tax suffered on qualifying furnished holiday lets within the EEA should be detailed on page F6.

To claim relief for the foreign tax suffered on all of your overseas property income, you should include the total eligible amount in the sum entered at Box 2 on page F1.

Where your property business is deemed to be a trade for tax purposes, you will instead need to complete the 'Self-Employment Supplement'. A short, two page version of this supplement can be completed in certain restricted circumstances. In most cases, however, you will need to complete the full six page version, including any cases where gross sales income exceeds the VAT registration threshold for the relevant tax year (the current threshold for 2017/18 is £85,000; see Section 7.12 for further details), or you are claiming any capital allowances (see Section 3.10).

If you have both investment and trading activities then you will need to complete both the UK Property Supplement (and/or the Foreign Supplement, as appropriate) and the Self-Employment Supplement.

Where property is held jointly, but not as a partnership (see Section 2.14), each joint owner must include their own share of property income and expenses on their own tax return each year, as appropriate.

For any form of income received from a partnership, the Partnership Supplement should be used. The full version of this supplement will be required where there is partnership rental income but the short version can be used where there is only partnership trading income.

A separate partnership tax return must also be completed on behalf of the partnership in addition to each of the partners' own tax returns.

Short Returns

HMRC issues short returns to selected taxpayers. These are only four pages long and may detail all of a taxpayer's sources of income rather more concisely than the usual full tax return of six pages plus supplements. Some property investors whose tax affairs are relatively simple may receive a short return.

Wealth Warning
If you receive a short return, it remains your legal obligation to ensure that all of your income and capital gains are reported to

HMRC, as appropriate. In some cases, this will mean that you should revert to the normal full return and it is your responsibility to ascertain whether this is the case. In particular, you cannot use a short return if:

- Your gross business income exceeds the VAT registration threshold for the relevant tax year (see Section 7.12), or
- You have any income from furnished holiday lettings.

Completing a short return (if you are issued with one and remain eligible to use it) will make no difference whatsoever to your actual tax liability, nor its due date for payment.

3.6   REGISTERING A NEW PROPERTY BUSINESS

Guidance issued by HMRC suggests that anyone starting a new property business should register within three months. In the case of a new property trade, this is quite correct and we will take a closer look at the relevant reporting requirements in Section 5.6.

The guidance also states that landlords should 'contact Revenue and Customs for a self assessment and a land and property form, or register as self-employed'.

Wealth Warning
Landlords starting a property letting business should **not** register as 'self-employed' or as a 'business'. Self-employment income is subject to NI. Rental income is not. By registering as self-employed, landlords may incur NI liabilities which, by rights, they should not have to pay.

It is, however, advisable to follow HMRC's first suggestion and notify them of the start of your property business by registering for self-assessment. This can be done online at: www.gov.uk/register-for-self-assessment/overview.

If you are already registered for self-assessment, there is no need to register again, but you will need to ensure that your tax return includes details of your new property income and is submitted on time.

When registering for self-assessment, it is important to remember that you are **not** self-employed for tax purposes (unless you have a property trade, for which see Section 5.6). As a landlord with rental income, you should follow the link from 'If you're not self-employed' in order to get to form SA1 to register for self-assessment.

When completing form SA1, in response to the question 'Why do you need to complete a tax return?' you should tick the box for 'I'm getting income from land and property in UK': unless your rental income comes from an overseas property, in which case tick the box for 'I'm getting taxable foreign income of £300 or more'.

The law actually only requires you to register for self-assessment by 5th October following the tax year in which your letting business commences rather than within three months, as suggested by HMRC. Generally, however, it is probably better to get it done sooner rather than later, but:

> **Practical Pointer**
> Some taxpayers registering a new business with HMRC within the same tax year as they commenced their business have been issued a notice to deliver a tax return for the previous year. Once a notice has been issued, there is an obligation to complete a tax return, and hence unnecessary extra work has been created.
>
> My advice to new landlords is therefore to register for self-assessment shortly after the end of the tax year in which your business commences (see Section 4.3 regarding the date on which a new letting business is deemed to commence for tax purposes).
>
> (But see Section 5.6 regarding new property trades).

HMRC can withdraw a notice to deliver a tax return where it has been issued unnecessarily: but requesting this will also require unnecessary extra work, so it is still best avoided in the first place!

Strictly speaking, a taxpayer is always required to notify HMRC of any new source of income by 5th October following the tax year in which the 'new source' commences.

A 'new source' for this purpose means the commencement of a property business, rather than a new property within an existing business. It is not necessary to advise HMRC every time you rent out a new property!

However, as explained in Section 4.3, when someone with a UK property business rents out their first overseas property, this does amount to a new source. The same is true for anyone renting out their first UK property, including non-UK residents.

Furthermore, commencing a property trade when you already have a property investment business, or vice versa, will also constitute a new source of income. (See Section 5.6 for further requirements for new property trades.)

In practice, there are not usually any penalties for a delay in reporting a new property investment business, as long as the tax return includes the new source of income, and is completed and submitted by the normal due date.

However, for anyone not already within the self-assessment system, it is essential to report the new source of income by the 5th October deadline so that a 'Unique Taxpayer Reference' ('UTR') number can be issued in time for them to complete and file their tax return by the due date.

It is now almost impossible to file a tax return without a UTR and there is a considerable delay in issuing new numbers. If you have not reported your new source of income by the 5th October deadline, you will have no legitimate excuse for filing your tax return late just because you did not receive your UTR in time.

In Summary

In summary, to avoid any unnecessary penalties, additional paperwork, or other aggravations, my advice is to notify HMRC of the commencement of a new property business as follows:

- New property trades: within three months (following the procedure detailed in Section 5.6).
- New property investment businesses where you are **not** already within the self-assessment system: as soon as possible after the end of the tax year in which the business commenced.
- New property investment businesses where you **are** already within the self-assessment system: by 5th October after the end of the tax year in which the business commenced or by simply including the new source of income in your tax return.

3.7 NON-RESIDENTS, ETC

As explained in Section 2.15, non-UK residents remain liable for UK Income Tax on rental income receivable from property situated in the UK and on profits derived from developing, or trading in, UK property. They may also be subject to UK Income Tax on other profits from a property business which is based in the UK, such as a property management business or a UK-based property developing or property trading business dealing in overseas property.

Certain classes of non-UK resident individuals with taxable income in the UK are entitled to the same personal allowances as UK residents (see Appendix A), and may set these off against that income. These include British Nationals resident abroad, nationals of states within the EEA (see Section 1.4), Crown servants, residents of the Isle of Man or the Channel Islands and residents of other countries which have a suitable double taxation agreement with the UK.

UK residents who are also UK domiciled are liable for UK Income Tax on all worldwide income as it arises.

UK resident but non-UK domiciled individuals may choose to only pay UK Income Tax on income from property situated abroad as and when they remit it back to the UK. This option, known as the 'remittance basis', comes at a price, however. We will look at the taxation of these individuals in more detail in Section 8.25.

The tax concepts of residence and domicile can sometimes be fairly complex and are examined in detail in the Taxcafe.co.uk guides 'Tax Free Capital Gains' and 'How to Save Inheritance Tax' respectively.

Broadly, though, in most cases, it is safe to say that, if you have British parents and have lived in the UK all of your life, then you are most probably UK resident and domiciled.

3.8   CLAIMING DEDUCTIONS

Whatever type of property business you have, there will usually be expenses which may be claimed as a deduction from your profits. Some deductions are very much dependent on the type of business and we will therefore examine some of the specific types of deductible expenditure in the next two chapters.

Firstly, however, it is worth dealing with some of the basic principles which apply to deductions claimed in any type of property business.

Accruals versus Cash

The general rule under UK tax law is that expenses are deductible when they are incurred: known as the 'accruals basis'; rather than when they are paid for: known as the 'cash basis'.

For example, under the accruals basis, if a landlord has some roof repairs carried out on a rental property in March 2018, they may deduct the cost in their accounts to 5th April 2018, even if the roofer doesn't invoice them until May and they do not pay the bill until July.

The accruals basis must be used unless one of the alternative cash bases applies.

The cash basis for small trading businesses has been available since 2013/14. Qualifying taxpayers must elect to use this basis which we will examine in Section 5.13.

Under current Government proposals, a new cash basis for small landlords is to apply from 2017/18 onwards. It is proposed that, where the landlord qualifies for this new cash basis, it will apply automatically, unless the landlord elects to opt out of it.

Landlords with annual rental income of £15,000 or less have also sometimes been permitted to prepare accounts and tax returns on a cash basis for many years. This is a concessionary basis and is different to the new basis proposed for introduction from 2017/18.

We will examine both of these cash bases for landlords in Section 4.18.

The Government seems to be very keen on promoting the use of the cash basis by all small businesses and claims that this is all being done in the name of 'simplification'. However, whilst the alternative cash bases which are now available (or at least proposed) may suit some small business owners, my view is that they are generally disadvantageous for property business owners.

Hence, whilst we will examine the use of the cash bases described above in Sections 4.18 and 5.13, it is assumed throughout the rest of this guide (unless specifically stated to the contrary) that accounts and tax returns are being prepared on an accruals basis.

Wholly and Exclusively

All expenses must be incurred wholly and exclusively for the purposes of the business and, naturally, must actually be borne by the taxpayer.

The term 'wholly and exclusively' is enshrined in tax law but it is not always interpreted quite as literally as you might think.

Example
Saleema pays £50 per week for gardening services. This covers the upkeep of her own garden and that of the house next door, which she also owns and rents out. This is what we call 'mixed use'. The gardening costs are partly private expenditure and partly incurred for Saleema's property business. This does not mean that all of the gardening expenditure falls foul of the 'wholly and exclusively' rule. The correct interpretation is to say that part of the gardening expenses are incurred wholly and exclusively for business purposes and to claim an appropriate proportion.

Nevertheless, any expenditure incurred for the benefit of the taxpayer or their family will not be allowed as a business deduction. Where there is a 'dual purpose' (i.e. both business and private elements exist), the strict position is that none of the expenditure is allowable.

This contrasts with 'mixed use' expenditure, as in our example above, where a reasonable apportionment between the business and private elements is possible so that the business element may still be claimed.

The distinction between 'dual purpose' and 'mixed use' is a difficult one. The best explanation I can give you is that with 'dual purpose' expenditure, the business and private elements generally take place simultaneously. This is why most office clothing is not allowable, since it performs the personal functions of providing warmth and decency at the same time as giving the wearer the appropriate appearance for their work.

The 'Revenue versus Capital' Issue

As well as being incurred 'wholly and exclusively' for the purposes of the business, expenditure must usually also be 'revenue expenditure' if it is to be claimed for Income Tax purposes.

The term 'revenue expenditure' refers to expenditure which is incurred on an ongoing basis in order to earn revenue (i.e. income) in the business. Expenditure on the acquisition or enhancement of a long-term asset of the business will generally be 'capital expenditure' (although, as we shall see later, this does not usually extend to interest and finance costs).

In the tax world, all business expenditure will be either 'revenue' or 'capital'. Capital expenditure may not usually be claimed for Income Tax purposes, but will often be deductible in CGT calculations (though not always!) Some Income Tax relief for certain types of capital expenditure is, however, given in the form of 'capital allowances' or 'replacement furniture relief'. We will examine these reliefs further in Sections 3.10 and 4.10 respectively.

Whether expenditure is capital or revenue depends not only on the nature of the expenditure but also on the type of business you have.

Capital expenditure is a particularly significant issue in a property investment or property letting business as a great many of your expenses will be deemed to be capital for tax purposes. We will therefore cover some more specific examples relevant to property investment businesses in the next chapter.

Before that, however, let's look at a simple example to illustrate the difference between capital and revenue expenditure.

Example
Willie runs a chain of sweet shops. As part of his expansion programme, he opens two new shops, one in Midchester and one in Normingham. He buys the freehold of the Midchester shop, but rents the premises in Normingham.

The Midchester shop is a long-term capital asset of Willie's business. The cost of buying the freehold is therefore a capital expense, deductible only for CGT purposes if and when Willie decides to sell the property. This treatment also extends to all costs incurred in the purchase, such as legal fees and SDLT. (But see Section 4.4 for the treatment of interest and finance costs.)

The Normingham shop, however, is only rented and Willie does not own any long-term asset. The rent paid is a direct cost of making sales of sweets in Normingham and thus represents a revenue cost which Willie may deduct against his profits for Income Tax purposes.

Practical Pointer

Many capital expenses which you incur will be deductible in the event of a sale of the underlying property. That sale may take place many years from now. It is important, therefore, to keep the receipts and other documentary evidence of this expenditure in a safe place: as it may save you a significant amount of CGT one day!

Grants & Insurance Claims

Any grants or insurance claims received should be deducted from the underlying expense.

Tax Tip

If you incur deductible expenditure which is also the subject of an insurance claim, you may claim the expenditure as and when it is incurred and need only credit the insurance claim (as a 'negative expense') back into your accounts when it is received. This could be in a later tax year, giving you a tax cashflow advantage to partly compensate for the cashflow disadvantage you suffer whilst waiting for your claim to be sorted out.

VAT On Expenses

If you are unable to recover the VAT on any expense then, as long as the underlying expense itself is deductible, you may also include your irrecoverable VAT cost in the deduction claimed. This is a simple reflection of the fact that, in such cases, the business expense incurred is the VAT-inclusive cost. We will return to the question of when VAT may be recoverable in Chapter 7.

Commencement & Pre-Trading Expenditure

You may incur some expenses for the purposes of your property business before it even starts. Such expenses incurred within seven years before the commencement of your business will usually still be allowable if they would otherwise qualify under normal principles. In such cases, the expenses may be claimed as if they were incurred on the first day of the business.

The expenses do, however, need to relate to the same business as the one you eventually start. For property letting businesses, this means they must fall into the same one of the four categories described in Section 4.1.

3.9 ADMINISTRATIVE EXPENSES

One category of expenses which is pretty common to any type of property business is administrative expenses. This heading is very broad, and can extend to the cost of running an office, motor and travel costs and support staff's wages. As usual, the rule is that any expenditure must be incurred wholly and exclusively for the purposes of the business. Sadly though, most entertaining expenditure is specifically excluded.

Motor Expenses

The cost of running any vehicles used in your business may be claimed as a business expense. Generally, the vehicle will also have some private non-business use, so an appropriate proportion only is claimed. (Or a proportion is disallowed, depending on how you look at it and how you want to draw up your accounts.)

The appropriate proportion to claim will vary from one taxpayer to the next. Typically, for a self-employed taxpayer with a property trading business, it will fall in the range 25% to 50%; for landlords with property investment businesses it will tend to be somewhat lower, perhaps 10% to 20%; but these are only very rough guides and the appropriate claims may be considerably higher or lower in some cases.

You will need to work out the appropriate proportion applying in your own case based on the specific facts which support your claim. Keeping a mileage log to record your business journeys is the best way to do this and is highly recommended, although not everyone does this. The exact percentage of business use will vary from one year to the next, but a reasonable average rate is usually acceptable unless there is a significant change in your overall pattern of behaviour.

Most vehicles tend to have mixed business and private use but, if you were to buy a van purely for use in your business, then a 100% claim might be justifiable.

Those with property trading businesses may alternatively claim fixed mileage rates instead of the appropriate proportion of actual running costs (see Section 5.8). Strictly speaking, this option is no longer available to landlords with property investment businesses: although many people are taking the view that the mileage rate represents a reasonable approximation of the business cost and can therefore still properly be claimed. This may remain a reasonable and pragmatic approach where the overall business mileage is quite low, although HMRC may need some persuading to accept this if the landlord is unfortunate enough to be selected for enquiry.

Home Office Costs

Many people with a property business handle their business administration from a room in their own home, just like many other small businesses. In these cases, the taxpayer may claim an appropriate proportion of their household bills as a business expense.

Generally, the proportion to be used is based on the number of rooms in the house, excluding bathrooms, toilets, kitchens, landings and hallways. The claim should be further restricted where there is also some private use of the part of the house which is used in the business.

Example
Shakira spends about 30 hours per week running her property business from a small room in her house. The house also contains a living room, a kitchen, a bathroom and two bedrooms. Shakira's house therefore has four rooms which count for the purposes of our calculation. The room which Shakira uses for business also has some private use which she estimates to amount to around 10% of the room's total use. Shakira may therefore claim 90% of one quarter, or 22.5%, of her household bills as a business expense.

In practice, where the private use of the part of the house used in the business is negligible, HMRC has not usually sought a further reduction in the proportion of household expenses claimed.

> ### Wealth Warning
> Exclusive business use of part of your home can have a detrimental effect on your CGT position, as we shall see in Chapter 6.

The household expenses which may be included in the office cost calculation would generally comprise:

- Heating and lighting (electricity, gas, oil, coal, etc.)
- Cleaning (cleaners' wages and/or cleaning materials)
- Council tax
- Water rates or metered water supplies
- General repairs to the fabric of the building
- Insurance
- Mortgage interest or rent

Note that, if part of the taxpayer's mortgage interest on their own home is already being claimed on the basis that part of the mortgage has been used to fund business expenditure (e.g. the deposit on a rental property), that part must be excluded from the household expenses used to calculate the claim for business use of the home (i.e. it cannot be counted twice!)

Sections BIM 47800 to BIM 47825 of HMRC's own Business Income Manual provide instructions to tax inspectors telling them to accept reasonable claims for an appropriate proportion of the above costs. (It may be useful to refer them to these sections if you encounter any resistance to a claim.)

HMRC's instructions acknowledge that there are a variety of acceptable methods for apportioning household expenses where there is business use of the home and no method is mandatory.

The instructions do, however, draw a distinction between running costs (heating, lighting, cleaning and metered water) and fixed costs (all of the other items listed above). They then go on to suggest that running costs should be apportioned according to actual use, whereas fixed costs should be apportioned according to the room's availability: although their own examples do interpret this in different ways.

In practice, the key point is to be reasonable. Where the business use is quite extensive (say 20 hours or more per week) it will generally be reasonable to claim the same proportion of all household costs (as in Shakira's example above). Where there is only moderate business use, however, (say less than 20 hours per week) it will usually be reasonable to restrict the claim for fixed costs to a lower proportion.

One potential method for doing this is illustrated in the below example.

Example
Rhodri has five rooms in his house excluding the kitchen, bathrooms and hallway. One of these is his study which he uses for business just nine hours per week. The study is also used privately for on average just one hour per week.

Rhodri's total household costs for the year are:

Running costs: £2,500
Fixed costs: £8,000

Rhodri uses his study for business purposes for nine hours per week out of total actual usage of ten hours per week on average. He therefore claims the following proportion of his running costs:

£2,500 x 1/5 x 9/10 = £450

Rhodri also considers that his study is available for use 16 hours per day (it has no bed so cannot be used at night). This equates to 112 hours per week. He therefore claims the following proportion of his fixed costs:

£8,000 x 1/5 x 9/112 = £129

This gives him a total claim in respect of his household expenses of £579.

The 'number of rooms' allocation method is not compulsory and any other method which produces a reasonable result may be applied instead. Some consistency in the allocation method used would generally be expected, however.

Note that, from 2017/18 onwards, any mortgage interest element within a residential landlord's claim for 'use of home' needs to be separated out and treated in accordance with the regime described in Section 4.5. For example, if £6,000 out of the £8,000 of fixed costs incurred by Rhodri represents mortgage interest, and he is a residential landlord, then £96 (£6,000 x 1/5 x 9/112) of his 'use of home' claim will need to be separated out and dealt with as an interest cost subject to restricted relief as shown in Section 4.5.

Minimal Use

HMRC's instructions also suggest that small claims not exceeding £2 per week, or £104 per year, will be acceptable for even the most minimal amounts of business use. This simple claim is available to all property businesses as an alternative to the more complex calculations considered above. For those with minimal business use of their home, it will make sense to simply claim this small deduction.

Note that the claim should be restricted, as appropriate, where the business has not been running for a full year. Some actual business use of the home is also required, even if only very small.

Flat Rate Deductions

A system of flat rate deductions for business use of the taxpayer's home is available for trading businesses. (See below regarding property letting businesses.)

The flat rate deductions are an alternative method which is available **instead of** the proportionate calculation discussed above.

The amount of the deduction is calculated on a monthly basis according to the number of hours spent wholly and exclusively working on business matters at the home. The rates applying are:

Hours worked in the month	Deduction allowed for the month
25 to 50	£10
51 to 100	£18
101 or more	£26

Strictly speaking, this flat rate deduction regime is only available to trading businesses. Whether, in practice, HMRC will permit landlords with property rental income to use the regime still remains to be seen. However, their own manuals do tell their inspectors that where "there is only minor business use of the home you may accept a reasonable estimate". It is hard to see what grounds they could have for not accepting the use of the same flat rate deductions which are available to other businesses as a reasonable estimate.

Having said all that, the flat rate deductions are not exactly generous, so I find it difficult to believe that many property business owners working from home at least 25 hours per month will want to use them anyway.

Anyone who feels that it is not worthwhile performing complex calculations to arrive at a suitable proportion of household expenses can still claim the simple deduction of £2 per week described above in any case.

Telephone & Broadband

The cost of business calls and other business use of telephone lines, broadband, etc, may be claimed. Strictly, a detailed analysis of business and private use should be carried out but, in practice, a reasonable estimated allocation will usually be acceptable. A suitable proportion of line rental and other service charges can also be claimed.

Business Premises

If your property business grows to the point where you need to rent premises from which to run it, the rent, business rates and other running costs which you incur will generally be an allowable expense.

Expenditure on purchasing or improving your own business premises will always be treated as capital in nature, whatever type of business you have.

If you buy a property to run your business from, you will be able to claim any interest and other finance charges incurred. The same principles that are outlined in Section 4.4 (for rental property purchases) will apply to determine which interest and finance charges qualify for relief. For residential landlords, the restrictions in the rate of relief applying (see Section 4.5) will also apply to interest or finance charges on funds used to buy your own business premises.

The running costs, including business rates, of a property which you purchase for use as your business premises may also be claimed as annual overheads.

Travel and Subsistence

Travel costs incurred for business purposes should generally be allowable. This might include the cost of:

- Visiting existing rental properties or development sites
- Scouting for potential new properties or sites
- Visiting your bank, mortgage broker, solicitor, or accountant
- Visiting hardware stores to purchase goods for use in your business
- Visiting property shows, exhibitions, courses, etc.

Where your trip necessitates an overnight stay, you will additionally be able to claim accommodation costs and subsistence (meals, etc.). Care needs to be taken here, however, in the case of any travel which has a 'dual purpose'. Travel, subsistence and accommodation costs will only be allowable if your trip was purely for business purposes, or if any other purpose was merely incidental.

If you travel to Brighton for a day to view some properties, for example, the fact that you spend a spare hour at lunchtime sunbathing on the beach will not alter the fact that this was a business trip. If, on the other hand, you take your whole family to Brighton for a week and spend just one afternoon viewing a few properties, then the whole trip will be private and not allowable for tax purposes.

Strictly speaking, subsistence costs may only be claimed where connected with an overnight stay whilst travelling on business. However, in practice, reasonable expenditure incurred whilst some distance away from your own home and business base is usually accepted.

Staff Training

Any costs you pay to train your employees should be allowable. Different rules apply to your own training costs, however (see Chapters 4 and 5).

Staff Entertaining

Most entertaining expenditure is not allowable for Income Tax purposes. The only exception, for any business large enough to have employees, is staff entertaining. Please don't take this as carte blanche to have continual parties and meals out 'on the business', as this represents a benefit in kind on which the employees will have to pay Income Tax and you will have to pay 13.8% employer's NI

There is, however, an exemption for one or more annual staff parties or similar functions costing no more than £150 per head in total. For most businesses, this is sufficient to ensure that no-one gets taxed on the annual Xmas party. Naturally, before you can make use of this exemption, you need to have some employees!

3.10 CAPITAL ALLOWANCES

As explained in Section 3.8, capital expenditure is not usually directly eligible for an Income Tax deduction. Some capital expenditure is, however, eligible for a form of relief known as 'capital allowances'.

Capital allowances on property expenditure are dependent on both the type of business and the type of property. We will therefore return to these in Chapters 4 and 5.

In this section, we will look at the basic principles of the capital allowances regime applying both to 'plant and machinery' and to motor vehicles used wholly or partly in a property business.

Using This Section

In this section, as in the rest of this guide, I will be concentrating predominantly on property businesses run by individuals or partnerships. Whilst I will refer to companies occasionally, most of the details given in this section relate to other property businesses rather than companies.

Having said that, the capital allowances regime for companies is broadly the same: the principal difference being that allowances and rates for companies are usually changed from 1st April rather than 6th April.

For further details of the capital allowances regime applying to companies, see the Taxcafe.co.uk guide *'Using a Property Company to Save Tax'*.

The capital allowances regime has undergone several changes in recent years. To keep this section to a manageable size, and focus on current planning issues, I will largely ignore capital allowances on expenditure incurred prior to 6th April 2014 throughout this edition of this guide. (Except in a few cases where some of the old rules remain relevant.)

More details on the capital allowances regime in general, and capital allowances on expenditure within property in particular, can be found in the Taxcafe.co.uk guide *'Capital Allowances'*.

Plant and Machinery

The term 'plant and machinery' covers qualifying plant, machinery, furniture, fixtures, fittings, computers and other equipment used in a business. What qualifies as 'plant and machinery' for capital allowances purposes depends on the nature of the business, so we will look at this again in Sections 4.9 and 5.10, when the practical application of the rules set out in this section will become more apparent.

The Annual Investment Allowance ('AIA')

The AIA provides 100% tax relief for qualifying expenditure on plant and machinery up to the maximum amount of allowance available for each accounting period. It is available to sole traders, partnerships and companies.

The maximum amount of AIA available depends on what period the business's accounting period falls into, as follows:

- 6th April 2014 to 31st December 2015:   £500,000
- 1st January 2016 onwards: £200,000

Transitional rules apply to determine the maximum amount of AIA available where an accounting period straddles one of the above dates. The AIA is also restricted where there is an accounting period of less than twelve months' duration. This will often apply to a new business's first accounting period.

Example
Rebecca commences business by letting out her first rental property on 1st February 2018. Her maximum AIA for the period to 5th April 2018 will be: 64/365 x £200,000 = £35,068.

Transitional Rules

For accounting periods straddling 1st January 2016, the maximum AIA is calculated on a pro rata basis. For example, a landlord with an accounting year ended on 5th April 2016 was entitled to a maximum AIA for the whole year of:

270/366 x £500,000 =   £368,852
96/366 x £200,000 =   £52,459
Total: £421,311

But, an additional rule also applies to any expenditure incurred after 31st December 2015. The maximum amount which can be claimed in respect of expenditure incurred in the part of the accounting period falling after that date is restricted to the appropriate proportion of the new £200,000 limit. Hence, in the case of the landlord described above, the maximum AIA which could be claimed on expenditure incurred between 1st January and 5th April 2016 was £52,459.

As explained in Section 4.1, landlords generally use accounting periods ending on 5th April each year. Those with property trades may have different accounting periods. The maximum AIA applying for some other popular accounting periods straddling 1st January 2016 is as follows:

Year end in 2016:	31-Mar	30-Apr	30-Jun	30-Sep
For the year as a whole	£425,410	£400,820	£350,820	£275,410
After 31/12/2015	£49,727	£66,120	£99,454	£149,727

Enhanced Capital Allowances

Certain categories of expenditure are eligible for 'enhanced capital allowances' of 100%. These include:

- Qualifying energy-saving equipment - see etl.decc.gov.uk
- Environmentally beneficial equipment - see www.wrap.org.uk

Equipment must be new and unused to qualify for this allowance.

Enhanced capital allowance claims do not use up your AIA and are not generally subject to any monetary limit.

Writing Down Allowances

Expenditure on qualifying plant and machinery which is neither eligible for the AIA, nor for enhanced capital allowances, is eligible for 'writing down allowances'. The rate of writing down allowances on most plant and machinery is now 18%.

Expenditure qualifying for writing down allowances is pooled together with the unrelieved balance of qualifying expenditure brought forward from the previous accounting period. This pool of expenditure is known as the 'main pool'.

The writing down allowance of 18% is calculated on the total balance in the main pool. The remaining balance of expenditure is then carried forward and 18% of that balance may be claimed in the next accounting period. And so on.

However, where the balance in the main pool reduces to less than £1,000, the full balance may then be claimed immediately.

Example
During the year ending 31st March 2018, Margaret spends £201,800 on qualifying plant and machinery for her property development business. £200,000 of her expenditure is covered by the AIA and she therefore obtains immediate tax relief for the whole of this sum.

The remaining £1,800 is eligible for a writing down allowance of £324 (18%). The 'unrelieved' balance of this expenditure, £1,476, is carried forward to the year ending 31st March 2019.

Margaret's total capital allowances for the year ending 31st March 2018 are:

Annual investment allowance:	*£200,000*
Writing down allowance:	*£324*
Total allowances claimed:	*£200,324*

Margaret's qualifying capital expenditure in each of the next three years is fully covered by the AIA.

In the year ending 31st March 2019, she is also able to claim an 18% writing down allowance on the £1,476 balance of unrelieved expenditure brought forward from the previous year: i.e. £266. A balance of £1,210 is then carried forward again to the year ending 31st March 2020 when Margaret is able to claim a writing down allowance of 18%, or £218.

This leaves a balance of £992 carried forward. As this is less than £1,000, Margaret will be able to claim it in full in the year ending 31st March 2021.

Note that, for the sake of illustration, I have assumed throughout this example that Margaret did not have any balance on her main pool brought forward from the year ended 31st March 2017.

Note also that if Margaret had spent more than the maximum amount of the AIA on qualifying plant and machinery in any future year, the excess would be added to the main pool and the process of claiming 18% of the remainder each year would be further prolonged, perhaps indefinitely.

The Special Rate Pool

Certain types of expenditure must be allocated to a 'special rate pool' instead of the main pool. These include:

- Certain defined categories of 'integral features' (see Section 4.9).
- Expenditure of £100,000 or more on plant and machinery with an anticipated working life of 25 years or more.
- Expenditure on thermal insulation of an existing building used in a qualifying trade.

Expenditure in the special rate pool is eligible for writing down allowances at just 8%, instead of the usual 18%. This is particularly relevant to property investors letting out commercial property or qualifying furnished holiday accommodation and we will therefore return to this issue in Section 4.9.

It is worth noting, however, that the AIA may be allocated to any such expenditure in preference to expenditure qualifying for the normal rate of writing down allowance.

Where the balance on the special rate pool reduces to less than £1,000, the full balance may then be claimed immediately in the same way as for the main pool.

Motor Vehicles

Capital allowances are also available on motor vehicles used in the business. Vans and motorcycles will generally be eligible for the same allowances as plant and machinery, as described above. Most cars are not eligible for the AIA, but do have their own system of writing down allowances.

There are now effectively two different capital allowances regimes for cars. The first regime applies to:

i)   Cars provided to employees,
ii)   Cars owned by a company, and
iii)   Other cars which are wholly used for business purposes

Cars falling under headings (i) and (ii) are referred to as 'company cars'. For full details of the capital allowances regime applying to company cars, see the Taxcafe.co.uk guide *'Using a Property Company to Save Tax'*.

Cars falling under heading (iii) are pretty rare as this means that the car is owned and used by the owner of the business and there is absolutely no private use of the vehicle. In over thirty years as a tax adviser, I have never encountered such a car.

For the rest of this section, we will therefore concentrate purely on the second regime: i.e. cars owned and used by the business owner themselves which have some element of private use.

These cars must each be put in their own individual pool for capital allowances purposes. The rate of writing down allowances available depends on the car's CO_2 emissions and date of purchase, as follows:

- Cars with CO_2 emissions over the 'higher threshold' attract writing down allowances of just 8%.

- Cars with CO_2 emissions over the 'lower threshold' but not over the 'higher threshold' attract writing down allowances of 18%.

The 'higher threshold' is currently 130g/km. For cars purchased before 6th April 2013 it was 160g/km; for cars purchased after 31st March 2018 it is to be reduced to 110g/km.

The 'lower threshold' is currently 75g/km. For cars purchased between 1st April 2013 and 31st March 2015 it was 95g/km; for cars purchased before

1st April 2013 it was 110g/km; for cars purchased after 31st March 2018 it is to be reduced to 50g/km.

The allowances must be restricted to reflect the element of private use. For example, a car purchased in March 2018 for £20,000 which has 140g/km of CO_2 emissions and 75% private use will be eligible for an allowance of £400 (8% x £20,000 = £1,600 less 75%).

A car purchased in March 2018 for £10,000 which has 120g/km of CO_2 emissions and 75% private use will be eligible for an allowance of £450 (18% x £10,000 = £1,800 less 75%).

Note that the unrelieved balance of expenditure to be carried forward to the next period is calculated before the deduction in respect of private use.

'Green' Cars (I'm talking about environmentally friendly cars here, not the colour of the paintwork!)

Cars with CO_2 emissions of no more than the 'lower threshold' (see above) currently attract a 100% first year allowance. The usual restriction for private use still applies and a balancing charge (see below) will continue to apply on disposal of the car.

The 'lower threshold' is currently expected to be reduced to 50g/km for cars purchased between 1st April 2018 and 31st March 2021, after which the 100% first year allowance for low emission cars is expected to be abolished.

Balancing Allowances and Charges

When a car with private use is sold (or otherwise disposed of), a balancing allowance, or charge, will arise, reflecting the difference between the sale price (or other disposal proceeds) and the unrelieved balance of expenditure.

A balancing allowance, like any other capital allowance, is a deduction from taxable income. A balancing charge is added to taxable income. Balancing allowances and charges on cars with private use are subject to the same restriction in respect of private use as writing down allowances.

Summary of Capital Allowances on Cars with Private Use

To summarise the position, let's look at an example.

Example

In May 2017, Kenneth buys a car for £20,000 and uses it 40% for his property business and 60% privately. The car has 142g/km of CO2 emissions.

In his accounts for the year to 5th April 2018, Kenneth claims a writing down allowance of £640 (£20,000 x 8% x 40%). However, the unrelieved balance carried forward to the next year is just £18,400 (£20,000 – 8%).

For the year ending 5th April 2019, Kenneth is able to claim a writing down allowance of £589 (£18,400 x 8% x 40%). The unrelieved balance carried forward this time is £16,928 (£18,400 – 8%).

In February 2020, Kenneth sells the car for £12,000. This gives rise to a balancing allowance of £1,971 (£16,928 - £12,000 = £4,928 x 40%).

Note that, if Kenneth had sold the car for more than £16,928 (the unrelieved balance of expenditure), he would have been subject to a balancing charge. The charge in this case would have been 40% of the excess of the sale price over £16,928.

Other Assets with Private Use

The capital allowances regime for cars is echoed to some extent in the case of other assets with both business and private use which are purchased and used by a business owner.

All such assets must each be placed in their own capital allowances pool, or 'puddle', as I like to call them. The writing down allowances on these 'puddles' will be at either 8% or 18%, as appropriate. As with cars, a suitable deduction must be made in respect of the private use of the asset. The unrelieved balance on the 'puddle' carried forward to the next period is again calculated before taking account of this deduction.

Balances under £1,000 in 'puddles' cannot be written off like similar small balances in the main or special rate pools.

The AIA remains available on assets (other than cars) with an element of private use. The allowance must, however, be restricted to reflect the private use, so the AIA should be allocated to other expenditure first whenever possible.

The great advantage/disadvantage of the 'puddle' is that a balancing allowance/charge will arise when each asset is disposed of. These balancing allowances or charges are calculated in exactly the same way as for a car with private use, as explained above. Claiming the AIA on assets with private use will naturally mean that a balancing charge arises whenever any proceeds are received on the disposal of those assets.

Other Points on Capital Allowances

Both the AIA and all writing down allowances, including allowances on motor cars, are restricted if the business starts part-way through the year or, in the case of a trading business, if accounts are drawn up for a period of less than twelve months.

Writing down allowances may be claimed on used assets which the taxpayer introduces into the business, based on their market value at the date of introduction. For example, if a taxpayer has an old computer which they have had for many years and begins using it for business purposes, they may claim writing down allowances on the computer based on its value at that date. The usual deduction for private use continues to apply where appropriate.

Where a car is introduced into the business, the same principles apply, but the date of introduction is used to determine the rate of writing down allowances, rather than the original date of purchase. The 100% first year allowance for low emission cars is not available on a used car.

The AIA is not available on used assets which the taxpayer introduces into the business, or on assets acquired from connected persons (see Section 6.9).

None of the usual allowances are available in the year that a business ceases. A balancing allowance or charge will apply instead, based on the difference between the unrelieved balance of expenditure and the total value of the remaining business assets at the date of cessation.

Assets bought on hire purchase continue to be eligible for capital allowances as normal but must be brought into use in the business before the end of the accounting period.

Subject to the above points, the full allowance due is available on any business asset purchased part-way through the year – even on the last day.

Any sale proceeds received for assets used wholly in the business are deducted from the balance on the main pool or special rate pool, as appropriate. Where this gives rise to a negative balance, a balancing charge will arise.

Since the advent of the AIA, most small businesses now have little or no balance of unrelieved expenditure left in their main or special rate pools.

Hence, there is a strong chance of a balancing charge arising whenever any asset used in the business is sold: unless it is replaced by another qualifying asset of equal or greater value within the same accounting period.

Notwithstanding any of the above, where the disposal proceeds or market value of an asset which ceases to be used in the business exceeds the amount originally claimed for capital allowances purposes (before any private use deduction), the amount of proceeds or market value used in the relevant calculation is restricted to the amount originally claimed.

Capital Allowance Disclaimers

It is worth pointing out that, apart from balancing allowances and charges, capital allowances are not mandatory. The amount of allowance available is effectively a maximum which may be claimed and the taxpayer may claim any amount between zero and that maximum each year.

Why claim less than the maximum?

> **Tax Tip**
> If your total taxable income is less than your personal allowance, any capital allowances which you claim may be wasted. Instead, it will generally be better to claim a lower amount of allowances in order to fully utilise your personal allowance against your income (or as much as possible).
>
> The unrelieved balance of expenditure carried forward will then be greater, giving you higher capital allowances next year when, hopefully, they will actually save you some tax!

Some possible exceptions to the above 'tax tip' may arise where your property business is making losses and you are able to obtain tax relief for your capital allowances in a different period. See Sections 4.12 and 5.1 for further details.

3.11 THE TAX RELIEF 'CAP'

There is an annual limit on the total combined amount of Income Tax relief available under a number of different reliefs. The total amount of relief which any individual may claim under all of these reliefs taken together in any tax year is limited to the greater of:

- £50,000, or
- 25% of their 'adjusted total income' (see below)

The Affected Reliefs

Ten different reliefs are affected. The most important ones for property investors to be aware of are:

- Property loss relief
- Relief for trading losses against other income
- Qualifying loan interest
- Share loss relief

'Property loss relief' refers to your ability to set capital allowances within UK rental losses or overseas rental losses against your other income for the same tax year or the next one (see Sections 4.12 and 4.15).

Individuals with trading losses can set them off against their other income in the same tax year or the previous one. Additional relief applies in the early years of a trade. (See Section 5.12 for further details.)

'Qualifying loan interest' is the relief which is given for interest on personal borrowings used to invest funds in a qualifying company (or partnership). This relief will often be claimed by property investors who invest via a company and is covered in detail in the Taxcafe.co.uk guide *'Using a Property Company to Save Tax'*.

'Share loss relief' applies in limited circumstances and allows owners of some private companies to claim Income Tax relief for losses on their shares. Sadly, it is not usually available to property company owners.

Adjusted Total Income

Broadly speaking, 'adjusted total income' means an individual's total taxable income for the tax year in which relief is being claimed; after deducting gross pension contributions (including tax relief given at source); but before deducting any other reliefs.

3.12 MAKING TAX DIGITAL

The Government is considering making fundamental changes to the way most UK businesses must keep their business records and report their trading results to HMRC. This includes landlords with rental income. The proposed new system is called 'making tax digital', or 'MTD' for short.

Practical Pointer – The Good News!
With the exception of some new requirements for VAT registered businesses (see Section 7.12) we have now been assured that MTD will not be introduced until at least April 2020.

Until recently, the Government had been proposing to make MTD compulsory for all sole trader or partnership businesses (including landlords) with total gross income (before deducting expenses) of £10,000 or more from April 2019; and a year earlier for those with gross income over the VAT threshold (currently £85,000).

Following the recent extension to this timetable, it is difficult to predict exactly what form MTD will eventually take and who will be required to operate it. Nonetheless, it is still worth taking a brief look at the MTD proposals as it remains possible that many businesses (including landlords) may be required to operate the new system from April 2020.

What had previously been proposed was that all businesses (including landlords) to which MTD applied would be required to:

i)   Keep their accounting records in a 'digital' format
ii)   Report their results to HMRC on a quarterly basis, four times a year using an online digital reporting system. Results would have to be reported within one month of the end of the relevant calendar quarter

The Government had accepted that accounting records kept on spreadsheets (which many small businesses use) would be sufficient to meet the digital requirements of MTD: provided that specialised software was integrated into those spreadsheets and used to report the quarterly results digitally.

There was a proposal that free software would be provided to small businesses to enable them to comply, although nothing concrete has emerged as yet.

The quarterly reports required under MTD were to be simpler than a full set of accounts and would only need to be in summary format. Some accounting adjustments, such as accounting for trading stock (see Section 5.2) and accruing for costs that have not yet been paid (e.g. the roof repairs referred to in Section 3.8), would not have been mandatory for quarterly reporting, merely optional. This approach would have simplified the process but also distorted the results.

Instead of completing a tax return, each business owner would have a period of nine months after the end of their business's accounting period to finalise their accounts for the period, submit any necessary adjustments to HMRC and make a final declaration that the accounts were correct.

Under a further proposal, the Government was also considering allowing businesses to opt out of some accounting adjustments in their final accounts: although this could cause considerable difficulty with other users of business accounts, such as banks and other mortgage providers.

Whilst we may see some change to these previous proposals if and when MTD is eventually introduced, they currently remain our best guide to what any new system might look like after April 2020.

Look out for further news in the next edition of this guide.

Chapter 4

Saving Income Tax on a Property Investment Business

4.1 THE TAXATION OF RENTAL INCOME

In many respects, property letting is treated much like any other business for Income Tax purposes, but it also has many quirks which set it apart.

In essence, it is treated as a business, but not as a trade, and this leads to some fundamental differences in tax treatment, as we shall see to both our frustration and our delight.

For tax purposes, property letting needs to be divided into four categories:

- 'Normal' UK property letting
- 'Normal' overseas property letting
- UK furnished holiday letting
- Other furnished holiday letting within the EEA (see Section 1.4)

'Normal' in this context simply means anything other than furnished holiday letting in the UK or elsewhere in the EEA.

Each of these four categories is effectively treated as a separate business. Most of the rules which we will examine in this chapter apply equally to each category, but there are a few variations applying to overseas property (see Section 4.15) and furnished holiday letting (see Section 8.17).

Each of the four categories above needs to be accounted for and reported on your tax return separately. Hence, you will need to draw up accounts for each category which detail all your income and relevant expenses. However, all of the properties within each category are effectively regarded as a single business.

'Normal' UK property letting is generally referred to as a 'UK property business' and 'normal' overseas property letting is generally referred to as an 'overseas property business'. So, for example, if you are letting a number of UK properties on a commercial basis (none of which are furnished holiday lets), this will be treated as a single UK property business and one set of accounts will usually suffice (although many landlords prefer to have a separate set of accounts for each property).

Separate accounts will, however, be required for any non-commercial lettings (see Section 4.16) within any of the four categories.

All rental income must be included within the appropriate category, no matter how modest the source, unless it is fully covered by the 'rent-a-room' scheme (see Section 4.11) or, from 2017/18 onwards, the property income allowance (see Section 4.17).

Technically, landlords may draw up accounts for any period. Unlike other types of business, however, landlords must generally be taxed on the rental profits arising for the tax year running from 6th April to the following 5th April.

Hence, whilst landlords could draw up accounts for a different period and then 'time apportion' the results in order to produce appropriate figures for the tax year, this would seldom produce any significant advantages and it is far simpler to just produce accounts for the year ending 5th April. This, therefore, is what most landlords do.

Up until 2016/17, accounts generally had to be drawn up on an accruals basis. However, from 2017/18 onwards, it is proposed that some landlords will have the option to choose whether to use the accruals basis or a new cash basis. Indeed, it is currently proposed that, for those who do qualify for the new cash basis, this will be the default option and those who wish to use the accruals basis will need to opt out.

In Section 4.18, we will look at the new cash basis for landlords, who qualifies for it, and some of its advantages and disadvantages.

On balance, my view is that the cash basis will generally be disadvantageous for landlords and for this reason, unless specifically stated to the contrary, it is assumed throughout the rest of this guide, that landlords are preparing their accounts under the accruals basis.

Nonetheless, for those who qualify for the new cash basis, it is worth considering as an option, as it will be advantageous in some cases.

Landlords under the Accruals Basis

Under the accruals basis, income and expenditure is recognised when it arises, or is incurred, rather than when it is received or paid. For example, if you started renting out a property on 12th March 2018, at a monthly rent of £1,000, the income you need to recognise in your accounts for the year ending 5th April 2018 is:

$$£1,000 \times 12 \times 25/365 = £821.92$$

(You are renting it for 25 days in the 2017/18 tax year.)

Expenses should also be recognised as they are incurred (see Section 3.8).

4.2 DEDUCTIBLE EXPENDITURE

The rules on what types of expenditure may be claimed as deductions in a property letting business are generally similar to those for other types of business, although there are some important differences. Some of the main deductions include:

- Interest and finance costs (but see Section 4.5)
- Property maintenance and repair costs
- Heating and lighting costs, if borne by the landlord
- Insurance costs
- Letting agent's fees
- Advertising for tenants
- Accountancy fees
- Legal and professional fees
- The cost of cleaners, gardeners, etc, where relevant
- Ground rent, service charges, etc.
- Bad debts
- Pre-trading expenditure
- Landlord's administrative expenditure

If your tenant contributes part of an otherwise allowable expense, you may claim only the net amount which you actually bear yourself.

In the next few sections, we will take a closer look at some of the more common areas of expenditure typically encountered in property letting businesses and examine what determines whether or not these expenses may be deducted for Income Tax purposes. Please note, however, that this is not an exhaustive list and other types of expenditure which meet the general principles outlined in Section 3.8 will often be allowable.

The administrative expenses described in Section 3.9 should also not be forgotten (in my experience, they often are!)

4.3 WHEN IS A PROPERTY A RENTAL PROPERTY?

In this chapter, you will see me refer to 'rental property'. Whether a property is a 'rental property' at any given time is often crucial to determine whether (or how much of) a piece of expenditure is allowable.

Quite obviously, a property is a rental property whilst it is rented out. For most tax purposes, a property is usually also a 'rental property' when:

- It is available for letting but is currently vacant
- It is being prepared for letting
- It is being renovated between lettings, with the intention of letting it out again thereafter

In each case, however, the property's 'rental property' status would be lost if it was actually used for something else (e.g. a family holiday for the investor's spouse and children). Nevertheless, merely sleeping there overnight, whilst redecorating the property for subsequent rental, should not usually harm the property's status.

Strictly, for Income Tax purposes, a vacant property ceases to be a rental property immediately once a decision is taken to sell it. In practice, however, this rule will not usually be applied where the period between the decision and the sale is relatively brief.

HMRC generally regards the day on which your first rental property within each category (see Section 4.1) is let out for the first time as being the first day of your property letting business.

However, any eligible expenditure incurred within the seven year period before your first rental property in the category is first let should remain claimable as 'pre-trading expenditure' (see Section 3.8). This sometimes means the expenditure must be claimed in a later tax year.

Eligible expenses relating to your second, and subsequent, rental properties within each category may generally be claimed as incurred, even if the relevant property is not let by the end of that tax year.

Remember, however, that you have to treat each of the four categories described in Section 4.1 as separate businesses. Hence, a first overseas rental gets treated as a 'first property' even if you already have a portfolio of UK properties. The same goes for your first UK rental when you have a portfolio of overseas properties; your first furnished holiday let; etc.

4.4   INTEREST AND FINANCE COSTS

From 2017/18 onwards, there are restrictions on the **rate** of tax relief available to residential landlords in respect of interest and finance costs. I will look at those restrictions in detail in Section 4.5. Firstly, however, I am going to look at **which** interest and finance costs are eligible to be claimed in the first place.

When Can Interest be Claimed?

Interest is allowable and may be claimed against rental income if it is incurred for the purposes of the property business. There are two ways in which this can occur:

i)   The interest arises on capital which has been introduced into the property business
ii)   The interest arises on other funds which have been utilised in the property business

At one time, HMRC did not share the view that claims for interest relief under the first heading alone were valid. Thankfully, they now accept this view in principle, although differences of opinion over the precise interpretation of the rule sometimes still arise from time to time.

Leaving such difficulties to one side for the moment, the first heading above provides enormous scope for property investors to claim interest relief for Income Tax purposes.

When a property is rented out for the first time, the value of that property at that date represents capital introduced into the business.

Any other capital expenditure incurred on a rental property also represents capital introduced into the business, including SDLT and legal fees paid on the purchase and the cost of furnishing the property, where relevant. The fact that a deduction cannot generally be claimed for these expenses themselves does not prevent them from being capital introduced into the business.

Hence, subject to 'the catch' explained below, interest relief will generally be available on any borrowings against a rental property up to its original value when first rented out PLUS all of the other capital expenditure incurred in purchasing it and preparing it for letting. *It does not matter what the borrowed funds are used for!*

You cannot double-count the same expenditure, however. For example, if you build an extension on a property before letting it out, its value when first rented out will be increased by this expenditure, so you cannot add it on again as further capital introduced.

For borrowings in excess of the capital introduced in respect of a property, we must rely on the second heading above. In other words, interest relief on these additional borrowings will only be available if the borrowed funds are used for business purposes. (Note that some interest arising under the second heading alone may not be allowable if the landlord is using the cash basis – see Section 4.18 for further details.)

Example 1
Matthew buys an investment property for £100,000 and immediately begins to rent it out unfurnished. He finances his original purchase with a buy-to-let mortgage of £75,000 and pays the remainder in cash. He also pays SDLT of £3,000 and legal fees of £800. Naturally, he is able to claim relief for the interest on his buy-to-let mortgage against his rental income from the house.

A few years later, Matthew re-mortgages the property and borrows an additional £30,000 to bring his total borrowings up to £105,000. He spends the new funds on various personal items not related to his property business.

Despite having spent the new funds on personal items, Matthew remains entitled to interest relief against his rental income for the first £103,800 of his borrowings: i.e. an amount equal to the property's value when he first rented it out plus the SDLT and legal fees he paid on the purchase. The last £1,200 of his borrowings are not eligible for relief, however, as these are in excess of the amount of 'capital' introduced into the business and have not been used for other business purposes either.

After a few more years, Matthew borrows a further £22,000 against the property. This time, he spends £12,000 by taking his partner on a luxury cruise but uses £10,000 to improve another rental property. Matthew cannot claim any interest relief on the £12,000 used personally as this does not represent 'capital' introduced into the business. However, he can claim interest relief on the £10,000 used to improve another rental property as this has been used for business purposes.

Matthew therefore now has a total of £113,800 of eligible borrowings for interest relief purposes out of his overall total of £127,000. (We will look at how investors should calculate their interest relief in this type of situation a little later.)

Another way to look at the position for interest relief is that:

i)   Borrowings against a rental property up to a sum equal to the original value of that property when first rented out PLUS any other capital expenditure relating to that property are generally allowable (subject to avoiding any 'double-counting' and also 'the catch' described below)

ii)   Other borrowings are allowable when the funds are used for business purposes

Interest will therefore always be allowable if it arises on funds used to purchase or improve rental properties or otherwise expended for the purposes of the property business (subject to the points set out in Section 4.18 where landlords are using the cash basis).

Example 2
Mark takes out a personal loan and spends the funds on making improvements to a flat which he subsequently lets out. The interest on his loan is allowable because it has been incurred for the purpose of his property business.

Example 3
Luke has a large property rental business and employs several staff to assist him. Whilst the business is generally buoyant, Luke runs into some cashflow difficulties in January 2018 and has to borrow an extra £5,000 to pay his staff's wages. Luke's borrowings were used for business purposes and hence the interest he incurs will be allowable for tax purposes.

Example 4

John borrows an extra £50,000 by re-mortgaging his own home. He uses these funds for the deposits on two new properties which he lets out. John may claim the interest on the £50,000 of new borrowing as it has been used for business purposes.

Practical Pointer

In a case like John's in our last example here, there will usually be the practical difficulty of establishing just how much interest should be claimed. John will already have an outstanding balance on his mortgage so it would not be right for him to claim all of his interest. In practice, we have to do an apportionment.

Example 4 Resumed

Prior to re-mortgaging, John had a balance of £120,000 on the mortgage on his own home. The extra £50,000 took that balance up to £170,000. John should therefore claim 50/170ths of his mortgage interest for tax purposes.

Repayment Mortgages

Interest calculations are fairly straightforward in the case of an interest-only mortgage, but what about repayment mortgages? The first and most important point to note is that you can only ever claim relief for the interest element of your loan or mortgage payments. The capital repayment element may not be claimed. Your mortgage provider will usually send you an annual statement detailing the interest charged.

Where you have a repayment mortgage which is only partly allowable for business purposes, an apportionment must be made, as outlined above. However, as you repay capital, the total outstanding balance on the account will reduce, so how do you do your apportionment then? The usual approach is to stick with the apportionment ratio which you derived when you first did the re-mortgaging (e.g. 50/170ths in John's case).

Some, more aggressive, accountants might suggest that all repayments should be treated as repaying the original 'non-business' element of the loan. This approach may, however, be subject to challenge by HMRC.

Tax Tip

To maximise the business element within your interest payments, arrange for the new funds obtained on re-mortgaging to be allocated to a separate mortgage loan account with the bank. Make the new account interest-only, whilst leaving the original mortgage account as a repayment account.

In this way, you can put beyond doubt the fact that the capital repayment element belongs exclusively to the 'non-business' part of your mortgage.

'The Catch': What Counts as 'Capital Introduced'?

Our last example raises another important point. John was able to claim interest relief for part of the mortgage on his own home because he had spent the funds for business purposes: as deposits on rental properties.

Those deposits, however, also count as part of the capital introduced into the business. In other words, this restricts the investor's ability to obtain any further relief for additional borrowings against the rental property.

Let's say that John used £25,000 from the mortgage on his own home as a deposit on a buy-to-let property purchased for £90,000 and that the other £65,000 was made up of £5,000 in cash and £60,000 from a buy-to-let mortgage. Let's also assume that John paid a further £3,200 in purchase costs (SDLT, legal fees, etc).

Hence, at this stage, as far as this property is concerned, John has introduced 'capital' of £93,200 into his property business (i.e. the value of the rental property plus his purchase costs), but is already claiming interest relief on borrowings of £85,000 – i.e. the buy-to-let mortgage of £60,000 and £25,000 of the additional mortgage on his own home.

John can therefore only automatically claim interest relief on further borrowings against the rental property of just £8,200 – i.e. the same amount that he originally funded in cash (£5,000 + £3,200). Any further borrowings will only be eligible for interest relief if the funds are used for business purposes.

What John can do, however, is borrow further funds against his rental properties to repay some or all of the additional £50,000 mortgage on his own home. This would mean that he would be replacing one qualifying loan with another so he would continue to obtain interest relief on the new borrowings.

What Happens When Properties Are Sold Or Cease to Be Used In The Business?

Interest on borrowings used to finance the purchase or improvement of a property will generally cease to be allowable if that property ceases to be used in the rental business (e.g. if it is subsequently adopted as the owner's own residence).

However, the eligibility of the interest for tax relief will follow the use of the underlying funds. Consider this example:

Example 5
In 2017, Abel borrows £50,000 secured on his own home, Eden Cottage, and uses the money to buy a rental property, Babel Heights. At this stage, the interest on his £50,000 loan is clearly allowable.

A few years later, in 2020, Abel sells Babel Heights and uses the sale proceeds to buy a new rental property, Ark Villa. Abel's interest payments on the £50,000 loan continue to be allowable as the underlying funds have been reinvested in the business.

In 2022, Abel sells Eden Cottage and moves into a new house in Gomorrah. Abel's mortgage on the new Gomorrah property exceeds the final balance on his Eden Cottage mortgage. The new mortgage therefore includes the original £50,000 borrowing used to acquire a business property and hence the appropriate proportion of Abel's interest payments should still be allowable.

In 2023, Abel sells Ark Villa in order to finance the costs of an extension he is building on his Gomorrah home. At this point, the interest on his £50,000 borrowings ceases to be allowable for Income Tax purposes.

As well as tracking the underlying funds, there is also the possibility that interest relief may sometimes continue to be available under the 'capital introduced' principle (i.e. our first heading at the start of this section).

Example 6
Naamah owns a rental property at 22 Canaan Street which she bought for £100,000 some years ago and which has no mortgage against it.

In 2018, she takes out a mortgage of £75,000 on the Canaan Street property and uses this money to buy a second rental property in Judea Gardens. Clearly, at this stage, her mortgage interest is allowable against her rental income.

A few years later, she sells the property in Judea Gardens but the mortgage on her Canaan Street property remains outstanding.

She has sold the property which was purchased with the borrowed funds, but the interest on her Canaan Street mortgage remains allowable because it is also a rental property and the mortgage is less than its value when it was first rented out

Existing Property Introduced into the Business

The interest on any mortgage over a property which is newly introduced into the rental business becomes allowable from that point onwards. Hence, the interest on the mortgage on your own former home may be claimed from the date on which you make it available for letting.

Furthermore, as the entire value of the property at that date represents capital which you have introduced into your business, you could also re-mortgage the property and the whole amount of any interest payable on loans secured on the property, up to its value on the first day you rent it out, will be allowable for tax purposes.

Example 5 Revisited

By 2025, Abel's Gomorrah property is worth £500,000 and his outstanding mortgage is £300,000. Abel re-mortgages the Gomorrah property, realising an additional £150,000 which he uses to buy a new home in neighbouring Sodom.

Abel now starts to rent out his Gomorrah property. The entire interest payable on Abel's £450,000 mortgage will now be allowable against his rental income.

Note that, where an existing property, such as a former home, is introduced into the rental business, the 'capital introduced' will be limited to its value when first rented out only. Previous capital expenditure on the property, such as legal fees paid on the purchase, cannot also be counted in this case. The current value of any contents rented out with the property (furniture, etc) can, however, be included.

Wealth Warning

It is in this sort of situation that HMRC has recently been putting a different interpretation on the 'capital introduced' principle. In some cases, HMRC has argued that, for a person like Abel, the allowable interest should be restricted to the amount arising on funds actually expended on the property itself (e.g. £300,000 in our example above).

Whilst it remains reasonable to take the view that all of the interest on the entire outstanding mortgage should be allowable in a case like this (as, logically, it must all represent 'capital introduced'), there is unfortunately now a degree of doubt about the position.

Loans in Joint Names, etc.

Strictly, for interest to be claimed as an allowable cost, it must be a liability of the owner of the business. This generally means that the underlying loan must be in the name of the property investor themselves.

By concession, however, HMRC will allow qualifying interest paid by a property investor to still be claimed when the underlying loan is:

i) In joint names with their spouse, or
ii) In the sole name of their spouse.

Under scenario (ii), it is vital that the interest is actually paid by the property investor themselves, even though it is their spouse's liability.

Naturally, the interest is still only allowable if incurred for the purposes of the business, as detailed above.

Other Finance Costs

The treatment of other finance costs, such as loan arrangement fees, will generally follow the same principles as those applying to interest. In other words, these costs will generally be allowable where the borrowed funds either represent capital introduced into the business or are otherwise used for business purposes.

Difficulties may sometimes occur, however, over the timing of relief for such costs. Sometimes, general accounting principles may dictate that the cost should be spread over the life of the loan. In such cases, the tax treatment will follow the same principles.

Example
Eve has a large rental property portfolio and decides to consolidate her borrowings into one single 20-year loan. The bank charges her an arrangement fee of £20,000 for this new finance. Eve should therefore claim £1,000 each year over the 20-year life of the loan.

After 15 years, however, she decides to re-finance her business again and terminates the 20-year loan agreement. At this stage she may claim the remaining £5,000 of the original fee which she has not yet claimed for tax purposes. She may also claim any early redemption fee which she suffers.

In the past, HMRC tended to regard early redemption fees as a personal cost rather than a business cost and did not generally consider them to be allowable for either Income Tax or CGT.

However, it is now more generally accepted that refinancing is a normal, commercial, part of a property business and early redemption fees will generally be accepted as an allowable cost for Income Tax purposes, provided that there is a good business reason for the early redemption.

As in Eve's case, any unclaimed portion of the original arrangement fees may usually also be claimed in the event of a loan's early termination (as long as they qualified as a business cost in the first place of course).

The timing of relief for arrangement fees, etc, is unaffected by whether the investor pays them at the outset or adds them to the value of their loan. Furthermore, if fees incurred for business purposes are added to the value of a loan, there is no need to restrict the amount of the subsequent interest charges qualifying for relief.

Accelerating Relief

Spreading relief for loan arrangement fees over the life of the loan is based on generally accepted accounting principles. However, it is important to understand that those principles only require the fees to be spread over the useful life of the loan and not necessarily its full legal life.

Hence, for example, if you take out a ten year loan, but fully expect to refinance your property again after five years, then it would be quite reasonable to claim any loan arrangement fees over a five year period rather than a ten year period.

Accelerating tax relief where it is legitimate to do so is almost always a good idea, but the changes to the rate of tax relief for interest and finance costs which we will be looking at in the next section mean that the potential savings to be made by accelerating relief for finance costs are absolute ones and not mere timing differences.

Where you decide to claim relief over a shorter period than the legal term of your loan, it is important to retain some evidence of your rationale for doing so, such as a business plan which includes your financing policy, for example.

4.5 THE RATE OF TAX RELIEF FOR INTEREST AND FINANCE COSTS

In utter defiance of one of the most important basic principles under which businesses are taxed in the UK, the Government has introduced restrictions on tax relief for interest and finance costs paid by residential landlords.

Before we look at these dreadful restrictions in detail, it is worth pointing out that they do **not** affect:

- Furnished holiday letting businesses (see Section 8.17)
- Landlords renting out non-residential property
- Property investment companies

The restrictions do, however, apply to all individuals renting out 'normal' residential property (i.e. not furnished holiday lets) in the UK or overseas, including those operating:

- As an individual in their own name
- As joint owners
- Through a partnership
- Through a trust

The Restrictions in Detail

Tax relief for interest and finance costs relating to residential property lettings is to be restricted to basic rate only. This is being done by phasing out higher rate tax relief for interest and finance costs over a four year period, commencing in 2017/18. The restrictions work as follows:

- 2017/18: 75% deducted as normal, 25% relieved at basic rate
- 2018/19: 50% deducted as normal, 50% relieved at basic rate
- 2019/20: 25% deducted as normal, 75% relieved at basic rate
- 2020/21 onwards: all relieved at basic rate

Any unrelieved excesses which are eligible for relief at basic rate may be carried forward for relief in future years.

Example
Adam has a salary in excess of the higher rate tax threshold each year. He also receives annual rental profits of £40,000 from a residential property portfolio: before deduction of interest and finance costs which amount to £36,000 each year. The annual profit from Adam's rental business is just £4,000, but his tax liabilities on this income will be as follows:

	2016/17	2017/18	2018/19	2019/20	2020/21
Profit before interest	40,000	40,000	40,000	40,000	40,000
Less: Deductible interest	36,000	27,000	18,000	9,000	0
	(100%)	(75%)	(50%)	(25%)	Nil
Taxable profit	4,000	13,000	22,000	31,000	40,000
Tax thereon at 40%(A)	1,600	5,200	8,800	12,400	16,000
Basic rate tax relief on remaining interest of	0	9,000	18,000	27,000	36,000
Equals (at 20%): (B)	0	1,800	3,600	5,400	7,200
Tax payable (A-B)	£1,600	£3,400	£5,200	£7,000	£8,800

The tax bill on his rental business increases by 450%. From 2018/19 onwards, his tax bill is actually in excess of his overall profit. By 2020/21, he will be suffering a tax charge of £8,800 on a profit before tax of just £4,000: an effective tax rate of 220%!

The effect of the restriction on interest relief will be to turn a pre-tax profit into a post-tax loss! But the agony does not end there. Adam is a higher rate taxpayer making rental profits. The impact of these restrictions will also extend to many landlords who are currently basic rate taxpayers; and even to many who are making rental losses.

Example

Delilah has a salary of £30,000. She also has a portfolio of residential rental properties yielding rental profits (before interest and finance costs) of £33,000. From 2016/17 onwards, she pays interest of £35,000 on the buy-to-let mortgages on her properties. Overall, she is making a loss of £2,000, but she is able to fund this from her salary income.

In 2016/17, Delilah's overall rental loss of £2,000 is simply carried forward. The PAYE deducted from her salary covers her basic rate tax liability on that income, leaving her no further tax to pay: as one would expect where rental losses arise!

In 2017/18, Delilah may only deduct 75% of her interest costs from her rental income. This amounts to £26,250, leaving her with a taxable 'profit' of £6,750. She has a loss of £2,000 brought forward from 2016/17 which reduces this to £4,750. This £4,750 of 'profit' is added to her salary income, giving her total taxable income of £34,750. This is less than the higher rate tax threshold, so the basic rate tax relief on her remaining interest cost will cover her tax liability for this year. Once again, she has no further tax to pay. She also has £4,000 of unrelieved interest to carry forward.

In 2018/19, Delilah may deduct just 50% of her interest cost from her rental income. This amounts to £17,500 and leaves her with a taxable 'profit' of £15,500 which, when added to her salary, gives her total taxable income of £45,500. We do not yet know the higher rate tax threshold for 2018/19, but it does seem likely to be at least £45,500. So, at this stage, Delilah still doesn't have a problem. The basic rate tax relief on the other half of her interest will cover her tax liability leaving her with nothing further to pay and £6,000 of unrelieved interest to carry forward.

Crunch time for Delilah will come in 2019/20. For this year, she may deduct just 25% of her interest, or £8,750. This leaves her with a taxable 'profit' of £24,250. Adding this to her salary will push her well over the higher rate tax threshold. For the sake of illustration, we will assume her taxable income exceeds the higher rate tax threshold by £6,000.

The Income Tax payable at 40% on this top £6,000 of Delilah's income will amount to £2,400. She will be able to claim relief for her interest costs but the rate of relief will be restricted to basic rate: 20%. The tax relief for the interest set against Delilah's top £6,000 of income will thus be just £1,200, leaving her with a tax liability of £1,200 to pay (£2,400 – £1,200).

Delilah will have excess unrelieved interest costs totalling £8,000 to carry forward by this stage, but these will be of no practical help while she continues to make an overall loss.

In 2020/21 things will get even worse for Delilah. She will not be eligible to deduct any of her interest costs from her rental income and will have a taxable 'profit' of £33,000. Even if the Government makes good on its commitment to increase the higher rate tax threshold to £50,000 by this point, Delilah's taxable income will exceed it by £13,000. After deducting the basic rate tax relief for her interest costs, Delilah will have a tax liability of £2,600. To illustrate this in more detail, Delilah's tax calculation for the last two years discussed above can be summarised as follows:

	2019/20 £	2020/21 £
Rental profits before interest	33,000	33,000
Deductible interest (25%/Nil)	(8,750)	-
	----------	---------
	24,250	33,000
Salary	30,000	30,000
	----------	---------
Total taxable income	54,250	63,000
Less:		
Personal allowance (say)	(12,000)	(12,500)
	----------	---------
	42,250	50,500
	=====	=====
Income Tax at 20% on basic rate band of £36,250/£37,500 (say)	7,250	7,500
Income Tax at 40% on remaining £6,000/£13,000	2,400	5,200
	----------	---------
	9,650	12,700
Less:		
Tax deducted under PAYE (basic rate tax on salary less personal allowance)	(3,600)	(3,500)
Interest relief against property income at 20%on £24,250/£33,000 (as above)	(4,850)	(6,600)
	----------	---------
Income Tax due	1,200	2,600
	=====	=====

Interest Relief Summary

	2019/20	2020/21
Unrelieved interest brought forward	6,000	8,000
Allowable interest cost for the year	35,000	35,000
	----------	--------
	41,000	43,000
Current year interest allowed as a deduction £35,000 x 25%/Nil	(8,750)	-
Interest relieved at basic rate (as above)	(24,250)	(33,000)
	----------	---------
Unrelieved interest carried forward	8,000	10,000
	======	=====

In summary, by 2020/21, when the Government's vicious attack on landlords has been fully implemented, Delilah will have a tax liability of £2,600 despite making a loss of £2,000 and having £10,000 of unrelieved interest costs carried forward.

How anyone can call such an outcome 'fair' defies belief!

How Much Interest Attracts Basic Rate Tax Relief?

The amount of interest and finance costs on residential property which attracts basic rate tax relief from 2017/18 onwards is the lowest of the following three amounts:

i)   The total qualifying interest and finance costs on residential property for the year (as established under the principles set out in Section 4.4), less (for 2017/18 to 2019/20) the proportion allowed as a direct deduction against rental profits, plus any unrelieved interest brought forward

ii)   The taxable residential rental profits for the year

iii)   The landlord's total taxable income for the year, excluding interest income, other savings income, and dividends; and after deducting their personal allowance

The unrelieved interest brought forward under (i) means interest which can only be relieved at basic rate; it does not include interest which is fully deductible and is included within rental losses brought forward.

Let's look at these three amounts for Delilah in 2019/20. Her total qualifying finance costs for the year are £35,000. From this, we deduct the 25% allowed as a direct deduction against rental profits for that year, i.e. £8,750, leaving £26,250. We then add the unrelieved interest of £6,000 brought forward, to give a total of £32,250 for amount (i).

Amount number (ii), Delilah's taxable residential rental profits for the year, is £24,250 (as calculated above). This is after deducting the 25% proportion of her qualifying interest and finance costs for the year which is allowed as a direct deduction in 2019/20.

Delilah's total taxable income for the year is £54,250. Deducting her personal allowance of (say) £12,000 gives us £42,250 for number (iii).

So, in this case, the three amounts are:

i)   £32,250
ii) £24,250
iii) £42,250

Delilah can claim basic rate tax relief on the lowest amount (£24,250).

If we go back to the earlier example of Adam, we can see that amount number (i) (his total qualifying interest and finance costs, less the proportion allowed as a direct deduction against his rental income) was always the lowest amount and was thus the amount on which he claimed basic rate tax relief. This will generally be the case for most profitable property rental businesses.

Exceptions may arise for landlords with little or no other income.

Example
In 2017/18, Sheba has residential rental profits of £30,000 before deduction of interest and finance costs which total £24,000. She has no other income.

75% of Sheba's interest costs, or £18,000, is deducted directly from her rental income, leaving her with £12,000 of taxable income. This exceeds the 2017/18 personal allowance of £11,500 by just £500.

Sheba has a further £6,000 of interest and finance costs eligible for relief at basic rate (i.e. 25% of her total cost for the year). However, the amount eligible for relief is restricted to just £500: the amount by which her taxable income exceeds the personal allowance.

Sheba therefore has no tax to pay and unrelieved interest and finance costs of £5,500 to carry forward. These carried forward costs could save her £1,100 in a later year when her rental profits are higher.

This example illustrates the only bit of good news about the new restrictions: landlords like Sheba, whose overall income is quite low, are now able to carry forward some of their interest and finance costs rather than set them against income which is covered by their personal allowance.

In other words, such landlords will get effective tax relief for their interest and finance costs (albeit in the future and restricted to basic rate only) rather than wasting them as a deduction against income which would not have been taxed anyway.

Further Implications

Changing allowable interest and finance costs from a deduction to a relief (at basic rate) means that the landlord's total taxable income increases. We have already seen how this impacts on the use of the personal allowance and basic rate band, but the increase in total taxable income will also impact on:

- The High Income Child Benefit Charge (see Section 3.3)
- Withdrawal of personal allowances where income exceeds £100,000 (see Section 3.3)
- The additional rate threshold (see Appendix A)
- CGT rates (see Section 6.4)

Example

Job has residential rental profits of £200,000 before deduction of interest costs totalling £150,000. He has no other income. He and his wife have three small children, so his wife claims child benefit of £2,501. Job's Income Tax calculation for 2016/17 was as follows:

	£
Taxable income (£200,000 - £150,000)	50,000
Less: personal allowance	(11,000)
	39,000
Income Tax at 20% on £32,000	6,400
Income Tax at 40% on £7,000	2,800
Total tax due	9,200

From 2017/18 onwards, Job's interest deduction will gradually change into interest relief at basic rate only. This will increase his taxable income by £37,500 (25% of his interest deduction) each year for four years. In 2017/18, Job's taxable income will be £87,500 and he will be subject to the HICBC. In 2018/19, his taxable income will be £125,000 and his personal allowance will be withdrawn. In 2019/20, Job's taxable income will be £162,500 and he will be subject to additional rate tax. By 2020/21, Job's Income Tax calculation will be as follows:

	£
Taxable income	200,000
Income Tax at 20% on £37,500 (say)	7,500
Income Tax at 40% on £112,500	45,000
Income Tax at 45% on £50,000	22,500
HICBC	2,501
	77,501
Less: Basic rate relief on interest £150,000 @ 20%	(30,000)
Total tax due	47,501

Unlike Adam (our first example in this section), Job does at least have (just about) enough profit to cover his tax bill. Nonetheless, his effective tax rate is still a whopping 95% - and he has no other income to pay it from!

(For ease of illustration, I have used 2017/18 rates for child benefit throughout this example)

Which Costs are Affected?

The restrictions described in this section apply to interest and finance costs on any amount borrowed for the purposes of generating income from residential lettings. Finance costs include incidental costs of obtaining finance. The restrictions will therefore apply to most of the interest and finance costs incurred by a residential landlord, including:

- Buy-to-let mortgages
- Other mortgages and loans used to fund deposits or other business expenditure
- Personal loans or credit cards used to fund furnishings, refurbishment work or other business expenditure
- Hire purchase agreements for the purchase of cars or other assets used in the business
- Business overdrafts

The types of cost affected will include:

- Interest
- Other charges which are equivalent to interest
- Loan arrangement fees
- Early repayment penalties
- Facility arrangement fees
- Guarantee fees
- Professional fees incurred for the purposes of obtaining loan finance (see Section 4.6)

However, as the restrictions only apply to costs related to borrowings, it would appear that some items might not be affected: such as bank charges on a business current account, for example.

It is also important to remember that any costs relating to non-residential property or to furnished holiday lettings are exempt from the restrictions. In the case of a landlord with a portfolio which includes different types of property, some costs will need to be apportioned.

Example
Isaac borrows £1m to refinance his property portfolio. The portfolio consists of furnished holiday lets worth £300,000, commercial property worth £800,000 and residential property worth £700,000: a total of £2m.

The restrictions on tax relief for interest and finance costs will only apply to the element of the loan relating to Isaac's residential property. In this case, it would be reasonable to apply the restrictions to 35% of the costs arising (£700,000/£2m = 35%).

In 2017/18, the total interest and finance costs relating to Isaac's loan amount to £60,000. The amount which Isaac can deduct in the normal way, as a direct expense, is as follows:

Residential lettings:	*£60,000 x 35% x 75% =*	*£15,750*
Other lettings:	*£60,000 x 65% =*	*£39,000*
Total		*£54,750*

Isaac may also claim basic rate tax relief on the remaining costs of £5,250 (£60,000 x 35% x 25%).

The basis for apportioning costs used by Isaac in this example is not the only possible method. He might perhaps, instead, look at the borrowing history prior to the refinancing. Other alternative methods might be available in other cases: all that is required is that the apportionment is carried out on a 'just and reasonable' basis.

If Isaac had other costs on borrowings which were wholly related to his residential lettings, then these would be wholly subject to the restrictions on relief. Conversely, if he had other costs wholly related to his non-residential or furnished holiday lettings then none of these would be subject to those restrictions.

4.6   LEGAL AND PROFESSIONAL FEES

Legal fees and other professional costs incurred for the purposes of the business may fall into one of four categories for tax purposes:

i)   Revenue expenditure
ii)   Capital expenditure
iii)   Costs of obtaining loan finance
iv)   Abortive capital expenditure

See Section 3.8 for an explanation of the difference between revenue expenditure and capital expenditure.

Revenue Expenditure

Revenue expenditure may be claimed as a deduction against rental income. These are the costs which are incurred year in, year out, in earning the rental profits. They will include items such as debt collection expenses, agent's fees and accountancy fees for the preparation of your annual accounts and the business part of your tax return.

Legal and professional costs relating to a tenants' lease of a year or less are also generally allowable (e.g. legal fees for preparing the lease).

However, HMRC regards any expenses connected with the first letting of a property for more than one year as a capital expense which cannot be claimed. Costs relating to subsequent long leases will generally be allowable provided that the new lease is on broadly similar terms and for a period of less than 50 years and the property has not been used for some other purpose in the interim.

Capital Expenses

Legal fees and other professional costs incurred for the purchase or sale of properties cannot be claimed for Income Tax purposes within a property letting or investment business. As long as the purchase or sale in question goes through, however, all is not lost, as these items may then be claimed as allowable deductions for CGT purposes when the property is disposed of (see Chapter 6).

This category would include:

- Legal fees
- Estate agent's fees
- SDLT or LBTT
- Survey fees
- Valuation fees
- Professional costs incurred on a successful planning application

Costs of Obtaining Loan Finance

When purchasing a property, it is important to note that it is only the purchase costs which must be regarded as capital expenditure and which therefore cannot be claimed for Income Tax purposes.

Any costs relating to obtaining finance (typically a mortgage) may be claimed over the useful life of the relevant loan, mortgage, etc, in the same way as loan arrangement fees (see Section 4.4).

Sadly, this means that these costs will also be subject to the restrictions described in Section 4.5, but even basic rate Income Tax relief will often be preferable to a CGT deduction at some uncertain time in the future. Furthermore, since HMRC has been known to deny CGT relief for costs which could have been claimed for Income Tax purposes, it will generally be sensible to claim Income Tax relief when you can.

In addition to the loan arrangement fees discussed in Section 4.4, costs of obtaining loan finance will typically also include:

- Mortgage broker's fees
- Lender's survey or valuation fees
- Land registry fees for registering the charge over the property
- A portion of the legal fees for the purchase

Your own survey fees remain a capital expense: it is only additional lender's survey or valuation fees which can be treated as a finance cost.

Land registry fees are typically paid by the purchaser's lawyer and then passed on to the purchaser through the final settlement: so watch out for these in the settlement statement.

Whilst it is perfectly reasonable to claim a portion of the legal fees related to dealing with the lender, registering the security, etc; not everyone does this as it is not always apparent what a suitable proportion might be.

Tax Tip
Part of the legal fees arising on the purchase of a property will often relate to the raising of finance – i.e. the mortgage.

It may therefore be worth arranging to have this element of the fees invoiced separately so that they can be claimed for Income Tax purposes, in the same way as loan arrangement fees.

Alternatively, a reasonable estimate of the appropriate proportion may be used instead. This will typically be in the region of a quarter to a third, although it very much depends on the precise circumstances of each case.

(Whilst this course of action will generally be beneficial, there are some potential drawbacks, as we shall discuss later, in Section 8.27.)

Costs such as survey or valuation fees incurred when re-mortgaging a property (for business purposes) should also be treated in the same way as loan arrangement fees.

Abortive Capital Expenditure

As we all know, sometimes a purchase or sale will not go through. In these cases, the investor will often incur costs such as survey or legal fees. Unfortunately, HMRC takes the view that costs related to purchases or sales which do not proceed are not generally allowable for Income Tax and neither will they be allowable for CGT purposes. These are what we sometimes call 'tax nothings'.

There is, however, an argument that any costs incurred <u>before</u> making a decision to purchase or sell a property are part of the regular overhead costs of the property business and are therefore properly claimable as revenue expenditure.

Example
Noah is considering buying an investment property in the Newcastle area. He spots a potential purchase in Gosforth and has a survey done on the property. However, he is unhappy with the result and decides not to pursue this purchase. Noah may claim the cost of the survey as an allowable business expense.

Noah moves his attention to Durham and finds another potential investment property. He has a survey carried out and, happy with the results, this time he decides to proceed with the purchase. Things go well until the owner of the Durham property is made redundant and is forced to take it back off the market. By this time, Noah has incurred substantial legal fees.

Noah's legal fees were incurred after he decided to purchase the Durham property. These fees are therefore abortive capital expenditure which Noah is unable to claim. Noah will, however, still be able to claim the cost of the survey fees for the Durham property as, once again, these were incurred before he made a decision to purchase the property.

To assist any claims for 'pre-decision' expenditure of this nature, it is useful to retain documentary evidence which shows that the decision to purchase or sell had not yet been taken.

Whilst I believe that claims for abortive 'pre-decision' expenditure incurred for the purposes of a property business are perfectly valid, this is a view which HMRC may not necessarily share. Some dispute over claims of this nature may therefore arise.

Professional costs incurred on an unsuccessful application for planning permission are also regarded as 'tax nothings' which generally cannot be claimed for either Income Tax or CGT purposes. However, if you can show that the same costs led to a later, successful, application they may still be regarded as part of the capital cost of the project for CGT purposes.

Even after accounting for the ability to claim 'pre-decision' expenditure, there are still some property investors incurring substantial costs which end up being classed as 'tax nothings'. This situation is a constant source of frustration to property investors and I would agree that it is very unfair.

Tax Tip
If you are incurring very significant costs of this nature, you might sometimes be better off being treated as a property trader. Whilst, as explained in Section 2.3, your tax status is not a matter of choice, if your situation is already pretty borderline, a small shift in your investment strategy may be enough to tip the

balance. Having said that, with effective tax rates on trading profits of up to 62%, the instances where investors will be better off as a property trader will be pretty rare!

Abortive capital expenditure is not allowable when the landlord is using the cash basis. See Section 4.18 for further details.

4.7   REPAIRS AND MAINTENANCE

Nowhere in the field of taxation is the question of 'capital or revenue' more difficult than in the area of repairs and maintenance and/or capital improvements. In this section, we will look at some of the general principles applying to this type of expenditure on all rental properties. Other aspects specific to commercial property and to furnished residential lettings are covered in more detail in Sections 4.9 and 4.10 respectively.

Fundamental Principles

There are two main fundamental principles which we must consider in order to determine whether any expenditure represents a repair (i.e. revenue expenditure) or a capital improvement (capital expenditure):

i)   When a property is first brought into the rental business, any expenditure which is necessary to make it fit for use will be capital expenditure. In most cases, a property will first be brought into use when purchased but the same rule applies when the taxpayer's own former home becomes a rental property.

ii) Subject to (i) above, expenditure which merely restores the property to its previous condition (at a time earlier in the same ownership) will be a repair. Conversely, any expenditure which enhances the property beyond its previous condition within the same ownership will be capital improvement expenditure.

It is always important to bear these fundamental principles in mind: they lie at the heart of the whole 'capital or revenue' question for any expenditure on a property. Fortunately, however, as we shall see later in this section, they are subject to a little more 'leeway' in practice than one might imagine!

The question of what constitutes an 'enhancement' to the property is determined as a question of fact, not opinion. Just because you think that a new extension on a building is hideous does not stop it from being classed as a capital improvement for tax purposes.

Repairs are deductible for Income Tax purposes (as long as the property is a rental property at the time) whereas capital improvements **may** be deductible for CGT purposes (see Chapter 6).

The treatment of any incidental expenditure incurred as part of a building project, such as skip hire for example, will follow the treatment of the project itself. This does not extend to interest and finance costs, however, which continue to be treated as set out in Sections 4.4 and 4.5.

Some Illustrative Examples

I could write an entirely separate book covering umpteen different examples of repairs or capital improvements. Here, however, I have tried to set out a few cases which will hopefully serve to illustrate how the principles outlined above apply in practice. Where a new principle emerges in the course of these examples, I have highlighted it for your attention as an 'Emerging Principle'.

Example 1
Melanie buys an old farmhouse intending to rent it out for furnished holiday lettings. However, when she buys the property, it has no mains electricity, no mains sewerage and a large hole in the roof. She spends £75,000 getting the property into a fit state to let it out, including £5,000 on redecoration.

The whole of Melanie's expenditure of £75,000 will be treated as capital expenditure and no Income Tax deduction will be available. The fact that part of the expenditure was for decorating is likely to be regarded as merely incidental to the overall capital nature of the work in this case.

> ### Emerging Principle
> Expenditure which might normally be regarded as revenue will be treated as capital where it forms an incidental part of a predominantly capital project. Until 2001 HMRC was prepared to allow some deduction for the 'notional repair' element within capital improvements, but sadly this is no longer the case.

Example 2
Geri has a small townhouse in Kensington which she rents out. She decides to have a conservatory built on the back of the house at a cost of £40,000, including £2,000 to redecorate the room adjoining the new conservatory. Geri's conservatory is a capital improvement and no Income Tax deduction will be available for this expenditure. Once again, the capital nature of this work also extends to the cost of redecorating the adjoining room, as this was necessitated by the major building work.

Example 3
Emma owns a row of shops which she has been renting to a number of sole traders. A massive storm severely damages the roofs of the shops and Emma has these repaired at a cost of £50,000. Emma's expenditure represents an allowable repair cost which she can claim against her rental income.

The same storm also damaged several windows in Emma's shops. The glazier advises her that it will actually be cheaper to replace the original wooden frames with new UPVC double glazing and she agrees to do this. This expenditure remains revenue expenditure despite the fact that the new windows represent an improvement on the old ones.

Emerging Principle
When, due to changes in fashion, or technological advances, it becomes cheaper or more efficient to replace something with the nearest modern equivalent, the fact that this represents an improvement may be disregarded and the expenditure may still be classed as a repair. Replacing single-glazed windows with equivalent double-glazing has been specifically highlighted as meeting this criterion by HMRC.

Example 3 Continued
At the same time, Emma also decides to have bay windows fitted in two of the shops. This element of her expenditure is a capital improvement and will have to be added to the capital value of her shops rather than claimed as a repair.

Emerging Principle
Both capital improvements and repairs may sometimes be carried out simultaneously. In such cases, the expenditure must be apportioned between the two elements on a reasonable basis.

Readers may wonder why this apportionment is allowed here, when it was denied for both Melanie and Geri above. The key difference is that both Melanie and Geri **had to** do the redecoration at the same time as the other work, whereas Emma simply **chose** to install the bay windows. It is the element of choice which makes the difference.

Tax Tip
Where an apportionment of expenditure is necessary, it would be wise to obtain evidence of the allocation made in support of your claim. This can be achieved by asking the builder to separately itemise the repairs and capital improvement elements of the work on their invoices.

Example 4
Victoria has a flat which she has been renting to students for several years. She decides to upgrade the flat to make it more suitable for letting to young professionals. She incurs the following expenditure:

i)   *£16,000 on a new kitchen, including £4,500 on equipment*
ii) *£7,000 redecorating the bathroom, including £2,000 to replace existing fittings and £1,000 to install a shower (there was only a bath before)*
iii) *£5,000 redecorating the rest of the flat*
iv) *£3,000 on rewiring*

New Kitchen

The new kitchen expenditure needs to be examined on a detailed 'item by item' basis. The treatment of each item depends on whether it is:

a) An integral part of a fitted kitchen or a free-standing item, and
b) A direct replacement or an improvement

Any items which represent improvements cannot be claimed as repairs. Hence, for example, installing a new extractor fan within a fitted kitchen, where no such fan had existed before, would be a capital improvement. As the fan is an integral part of a fitted kitchen, this would represent an improvement to the property as a whole and could thus be added to the cost of the property for CGT purposes (subject to the points discussed in Section 6.10).

Similarly, buying a fridge-freezer to replace a fridge would also be an improvement which could not be claimed as a repair. Where the new fridge-freezer is a free-standing item, it would represent a separate asset and so could not be added to the cost of the property for CGT purposes.

Fitted Kitchen Units and Integrated Equipment

A fitted kitchen is treated as part of the fabric of the building. The cost of a new fitted kitchen replacing a previous, broadly similar, set of units, work tops, sink, etc, would therefore be accepted as a repair expense. This treatment extends to the replacement of any equipment which is an integral part of a fitted kitchen, such as an integrated cooker or fridge. It does not, however, extend to free-standing items (which are considered below).

Where the replacement of a fitted kitchen can be claimed as a repair, this treatment should also include the necessary additional costs of re-tiling, re-plastering, plumbing, etc.

The usual exemption for 'nearest modern equivalent' continues to apply when considering whether items have been improved or merely replaced. If, however, Victoria's new fitted kitchen incorporates extra storage space or other extra features, then an appropriate proportion of the expenditure will need to be treated as a capital improvement. This would include any new integrated equipment which replaced an old free-standing item.

In an extreme case, where fairly standard units are replaced by expensive customised items using much higher quality materials, then the whole cost of the new kitchen will need to be regarded as a capital improvement.

Free-Standing Items

Free-standing, moveable items are not part of the fabric of the building for tax purposes. This generally includes most free-standing 'white goods' such as fridges, dishwashers, cookers, etc; as well as other moveable items such as tables, chairs, etc.

The treatment of these items where the expenditure was incurred before 6th April 2016 was highly complex and is explained in the previous edition of this guide.

For expenditure incurred **after** 5th April 2016, Victoria will be able to claim the cost of any equipment which is a direct replacement for the old equipment that she previously had in the flat. She may also be able to claim part of the cost of any equipment which represents more than a simple direct replacement. See Section 4.10 for further details.

Anything which is an entirely new item of equipment will be capital expenditure and not allowable for Income Tax purposes.

Bathroom Fittings
Replacing the existing bathroom fittings should usually be allowable repairs expenditure. Toilets, baths and washbasins are all regarded as part of the fabric of the building, so repairing or replacing them is generally allowable for Income Tax purposes.

Once again, however, replacing the existing fittings with expensive customised items using much higher quality materials would amount to a capital improvement.

Fitting the new shower will definitely be a capital improvement if this is an extra new item in **addition** to the bath. If, however, the shower **replaces** the existing bath then it might qualify as a repair under the 'nearest modern equivalent' principle.

Assuming that the shower is an additional item, however, then the remaining bathroom redecoration costs will need to be apportioned between the repair element and capital improvement element. Any expense arising due to the installation of the new shower would have to be treated as part of the capital element.

Redecorating the Flat
Most of the redecoration work, in the absence of any building work in the rooms concerned, should be fairly straightforward repairs expenditure. As usual, we need to be on the lookout for any improvement element, but a great deal of redecorating cost will always fall into the 'nearest modern equivalent' category.

Carpets, curtains and other similar items need to be considered separately. These are classed as 'furnishings' and will be dealt with under the principles set out in Section 4.10.

In this context, it makes no difference if you are replacing carpets or curtains which you yourself fitted previously or which you acquired when you purchased the property.

Rewiring

The rewiring cost will be fully allowable if it is simply 'new for old'. If, on the other hand, Victoria took the opportunity to fit a few new sockets then there would be an improvement element and, as usual, an apportionment would be required. Such an apportionment would probably also necessitate an apportionment of the redecorating costs, as some of these would also be incurred due to the electrical improvements.

Emerging Principles

The cost of replacing fixtures on a 'like for like' basis, or with their nearest modern equivalents, is regarded as a repair to the property. This includes fitted kitchens and integrated equipment.

Moveable items, such as carpets, curtains and free-standing kitchen equipment, are not regarded as part of the fabric of the building and are therefore subject to different rules (see Section 4.10).

In complex cases, the question of 'repairs or capital improvements' will need to be examined room by room, or even item by item. The tax treatment of one item may have a knock-on effect on the tax treatment of another item.

Example 5

Mel buys a rather dilapidated house in Sunderland hoping to rent it out to a family or young couple. She gets the house at a very good price owing to its current state of repair but knows that safety regulations would bar her from letting it out to anyone in its current condition.

The house desperately needs rewiring and also some urgent plumbing work, which Mel carries out at a cost of £5,000. This expenditure will have to be treated as part of her capital cost.

At this point the house is basically habitable and will meet all necessary safety regulations, but it could really do with redecorating to make it attractive to the type of tenants that Mel is ideally looking for. However, if Mel redecorates at this point then this expenditure too is also likely to be regarded as part of the capital cost of the property, especially since part of the redecorating will have been necessitated by the plumbing and rewiring work.

What Mel does instead, therefore, is to first let the house to a group of students for nine months. After that, she is able to redecorate the property and to claim this as a revenue expense deductible for Income Tax purposes.

Tax Tip

Where there is a danger that repairs or maintenance expenditure might be regarded as an incidental part of a capital project, it will be beneficial to delay this element of the work, if possible, until after an intermediate period of letting. In this way, the expenditure becomes an allowable revenue expense. Naturally, any health and safety requirements will have to be observed before undertaking the initial letting period.

Example 6

Danni buys a flat from an elderly couple, intending to rent it out. The elderly couple lived in the flat right up to the date of completion. Although it was a bit 'run down' and the decor was very old-fashioned, it was perfectly habitable and met all applicable safety requirements for a rental property.

Immediately after completion, Danni redecorates the flat in a modern style and then begins to rent it out. Danni's redecoration costs are an allowable maintenance cost for Income Tax purposes, even though she did the work straight away after buying the flat. The flat was already completely habitable and the redecoration work was purely a matter of choice or taste.

Emerging Principle

Normal routine repairs and redecoration work on newly acquired properties is usually considered allowable. Such expenditure will generally be regarded as 'normal' if the property could have been used without it and the price of the property was not significantly affected by its condition.

HMRC's View on Expenditure on Newly Acquired Properties

HMRC's view is that expenditure to rectify 'normal wear and tear' on a newly acquired rental property remains allowable as a deduction from rental income for Income Tax purposes. They take the view that there is only 'normal' wear and tear if the property's condition does not significantly affect its purchase price.

HMRC's manuals also specifically state that any expenditure on a newly acquired rental property which is not allowed for Income Tax purposes on the grounds that it represents capital expenditure should then be allowed for CGT purposes on a disposal of that same property.

Accounting Treatment

Where there are no statutory rules to the contrary, HMRC will generally expect the tax treatment of an expense to mirror its treatment in the accounts.

Wealth Warning
It is important to ensure that valid repairs expenditure is not treated as a capital item in your accounts, as this could prevent you from claiming that expenditure for Income Tax purposes.

See Section 8.27 for further important tax planning implications.

Repair Cost Provisions

In accounting terms, a 'provision' is a charge made in your accounts in respect of a future cost. Provisions for future costs are not generally allowable until the costs have actually been incurred.

There are a few exceptions to this rule, however, and a provision for repair costs may be allowed for tax purposes if:

i) There is a legal or contractual obligation to incur the expenditure,

ii) There is a specific programme of repair work to be undertaken, and

iii) The accounting provision has been computed with a reasonable degree of accuracy

Example 7
Kylie owns three flats in Donovan Towers, a tenement block in Glasgow. In February 2018, she receives a statutory notice from the council requiring her (and the other owners in the same block) to carry out some urgent roof repairs.

The 'Donovan Towers Owners and Residents Association' approaches Jason, a local builder, who provides them with a quotation for carrying out the work. On 4th April 2018, the association formally approves the quotation. Kylie's share of the cost will be £2,000.

Under these circumstances, Kylie may quite properly make a provision for her £2,000 share of the repair cost in her accounts for the year ending 5th April 2018, even though the work has not even started yet.

4.8   TRAINING AND RESEARCH

Many property investors these days spend a good deal of money on training and research. The first thing to note is the fact that this expenditure is often incurred before the business starts is not, in itself, a barrier to claiming it as a business expense. (Unless it was incurred more than seven years before the business started!)

The cost of books, DVDs, magazines and other information purchased for business purposes is usually allowable. This covers not only industry-specific publications, like trade magazines, but also books and other publications you buy to help you meet your legal and taxation obligations. Books like this one, and many of Taxcafe's other guides, which keep you updated with developments in the field of property taxation, will therefore generally be tax deductible.

The expenditure must be relevant to your business. If you are planning to invest in Spanish property, then the cost of an English-Spanish dictionary might be allowable. A self-help book on diet and yoga, however, would be pushing it too far, even if it does somehow make you a better landlord.

As far as seminars and courses are concerned, the rule is that expenses incurred in updating or expanding existing areas of knowledge may be claimed, but any costs relating to entirely new areas of knowledge are a personal capital expense. This can be a difficult distinction to draw, especially in a field such as property investment, where a great deal of industry knowledge is simply a blend of common sense and experience. It's not like you're training to become a brain surgeon after all!

My personal view is that property investment is a field of knowledge which most adults already have (e.g. from buying their own home) and that most such expenses are really only updating or expanding that knowledge and are therefore allowable.

In the end, the decision over any expense claims in this area will inevitably require you to use your own judgement.

4.9 CAPITAL ALLOWANCES FOR LETTING BUSINESSES

As we have seen in previous sections, the most significant amounts of disallowable expenditure in a property investment business derive from capital expenditure on property improvements and on furniture, fixtures and fittings.

As we saw in Section 3.10, however, some capital expenditure is eligible for capital allowances. The rules for capital allowances depend on the type of property being rented.

There are no longer any capital allowances available on the basic structure of the property itself. Capital allowances are, however, available on fixtures, fittings, furniture, equipment, and 'integral features' within:

- Commercial property (shops, offices, restaurants, etc.)
- Qualifying furnished holiday lets (see Section 8.17)
- Communal areas in rented residential property not falling within any individual 'dwelling'

The third category would, for example, include equipment in a utility room shared by the occupants of several self-contained flats in a rented building. As this category is fairly rare, I will not repeat it every time we discuss capital allowances in the rest of this section, but it is worth bearing in mind that the rules applying to capital allowances in rented commercial property and furnished holiday lets apply equally to communal areas in residential property.

Subject to the exceptions discussed above, residential property does not usually attract any capital allowances at all. (But see Section 4.10 regarding other forms of tax relief available in respect of furniture, equipment, etc, in residential rental property.)

Plant & Machinery in Rental Property

Qualifying expenditure within commercial property or qualifying furnished holiday lets may be classed as 'plant and machinery' for capital allowances purposes. Details of the capital allowances regime for 'plant and machinery' are given in Section 3.10.

The annual investment allowance ('AIA') can be claimed on expenditure on qualifying plant and machinery in commercial rental property or qualifying furnished holiday lets, including 'integral features'.

Wealth Warning
Landlords may lose the right to capital allowances on fixtures and fittings within a commercial property if they grant a lease of two years or more to a tenant and charge a lease premium. As such a premium is wholly or partly regarded as a capital sum for tax purposes (see Section 4.14), the landlord will be treated as having made a partial disposal of the property and may therefore lose the right to claim any capital allowances on assets within it.

A landlord may also lose the right to claim capital allowances on any items not qualifying as 'background' plant and machinery when a property is leased for more than five years. However, this should not generally apply to assets on which the landlord had been able to claim capital allowances previously, before the commencement of the lease.

Finally, landlords may also lose the right to capital allowances on any fixtures or fittings which they lease to the tenant separately under a different agreement to the lease of the property itself. However, this particular problem can often be avoided by making a joint election with the tenant. Furthermore, this can also be a useful method to enable the landlord to retain the right to capital allowances on assets within the property where a lease of two years or more has been granted at a premium as described above.

A landlord can, of course, only claim capital allowances on expenditure which they have incurred themselves. Nevertheless, investors with commercial rental property or qualifying furnished holiday lets can obtain immediate tax relief on up to £200,000 of qualifying expenditure each year. This will even include expenditure on so-called 'integral features' (see below).

Tax Tip
A couple holding investment property jointly (but not as a partnership) will each be entitled to their own AIA, meaning that up to twice as much relief will be available each year!

Qualifying Expenditure on Rental Property

Assets within commercial property and qualifying furnished holiday lets which qualify as plant and machinery for capital allowances purposes include the following:

- Integral features (see below)
- Manufacturing or processing equipment
- Furniture, furnishings, white goods, sinks, baths, showers and sanitary ware
- Sound insulation and gas or sewerage systems provided to meet the special requirements of a qualifying trading activity
- Storage or display equipment, counters and checkouts, cold stores, refrigeration and cooling equipment
- Computer, telecommunication and surveillance systems, including wiring and other links
- Fire and burglar alarms, sprinklers and fire-fighting equipment
- Strong rooms and safes
- Moveable partitioning where intended to be moved in the course of a qualifying trading activity
- Decorative assets provided for public enjoyment in hotels, restaurants and similar trades
- Advertising hoardings, signs and displays

Expenditure on the alteration of a building for the specific purpose of installing qualifying plant and machinery also qualifies for plant and machinery allowances itself.

Qualifying assets within a commercial property or qualifying furnished holiday let are eligible for the same rate of capital allowances whether they are purchased separately or as part of the purchase of the property.

Where a second-hand property is purchased, it is vital to analyse the qualifying fixtures in the property to support a capital allowances claim. The purchaser and seller generally have to agree a value for the qualifying fixtures within the property and make a joint election to that effect (known as a 'Section 198 Election'), which the purchaser has to submit to HMRC within two years of the date of purchase in support of their claim.

For purchases taking place after 5th April 2014, the purchaser will not generally be able to claim capital allowances on any fixtures where the seller would have been entitled to make a capital allowances claim, but failed to do so. Such failures to make legitimate claims are commonplace, so it is vital to check the seller's capital allowances claims history.

Tax Tip
Sellers can still make retrospective capital allowances claims right up to the time they sell the property, so it will usually be possible to ensure that the purchaser's ability to claim capital allowances on fixtures is not diminished or lost – provided that appropriate action is taken prior to the date of purchase!

Practical Pointer 1
The requirements for second-hand property detailed above only apply where the property has been in 'qualifying use' at some time after 5th April 2012.

For commercial property this will generally be the case, but for purchases of residential property the rules are only likely to apply where a previous owner has used the property as a qualifying furnished holiday let at some time since 5th April 2012, or where the property has been rented out since that date and has communal areas, as described above.

Practical Pointer 2
The requirements for second-hand property also only apply to expenditure on items for which a previous owner would have qualified for capital allowances. Where no previous owner would have qualified for capital allowances on any particular item, the rules do not apply and the purchaser may claim capital allowances based on a reasonable allocation of the property's purchase price.

Most commonly, this will apply to integral features already within the property prior to 6th April 2008 and which did not qualify for capital allowances at that time. (Provided there is no subsequent owner who purchased the property after that date and had the property in qualifying use any time after 5th April 2012)

Integral Features

Expenditure on assets within a defined list of 'integral features' falls into the special rate pool, attracting writing down allowances at 8% instead of the usual 18%.

However, these assets remain eligible for the AIA, so substantial amounts of qualifying expenditure on assets in this category can still attract immediate 100% relief.

The following items are classed as integral features:

- Electrical lighting and power systems
- Cold water systems
- Space or water heating systems, air conditioning, ventilation and air purification systems and floors or ceilings comprised in such systems
- Lifts, escalators and moving walkways
- External solar shading

In a nutshell: All the wiring, lighting, plumbing, heating and air conditioning in any commercial property or qualifying furnished holiday let qualifies for capital allowances, with immediate 100% relief for up to £200,000 spent on these items each year from 2016/17 onwards.

The integral features regime applies to all expenditure incurred after 5th April 2008, including qualifying items within second-hand buildings purchased after that date (subject to the requirements discussed above).

Any expenditure on integral features which is not covered by the AIA will fall into the special rate pool and attract writing down allowances at 8%. This includes any items which might otherwise be regarded as falling under one of the other qualifying headings for plant and machinery within rental property given above.

The integral features regime does not apply to expenditure incurred before 6th April 2008 and much of this would not have qualified for capital allowances. The following items of expenditure incurred before 6th April 2008 would, however, qualify for capital allowances:

- Electrical or cold water systems provided specifically to meet the particular requirements of a qualifying trading activity.
- Heating, ventilation, air conditioning and air purification systems, including any floor or ceiling which is an integral part of the system.
- Lifts, escalators and moving walkways.

This remains relevant because it is possible to claim writing down allowances on any qualifying expenditure incurred in earlier years, even if no allowances were claimed previously, provided the assets concerned are still used in the business. (Subject to the rules outlined above for fixtures within second-hand properties which were purchased after 5th April 2012.)

In the case of a purchaser buying a property from a previous owner who had held the property since before 6th April 2008, some of the integral features will not be subject to the rules for fixtures within second-hand properties (the beneficial implications of this were explained in 'Practical Pointer 2' above). The relevant features are:

- Electrical lighting and power systems *
- Cold water systems *
- External solar shading

* - Except to the extent that such systems were provided specifically to meet the particular requirements of a qualifying trading activity.

Integral Features Benefits

Combining the integral features regime with the AIA, we can see that many property investors will be able to benefit quite significantly.

Example
In June 2017, Lulach buys an old property and converts it into office units to rent out. The conversion work is completed by September and, although the office units are really just basic 'shells' with the absolute minimum of fixtures and fittings, Lulach's surveyors, Macbeth & Co., nevertheless calculate that he has spent £140,000 on 'integral features' and other fixtures qualifying as plant and machinery. Lulach can therefore claim an AIA of £140,000 against his rental income in 2017/18.

Furthermore, as we shall see in Section 4.12, property investors may be able to claim any capital allowances in excess of their rental profits against their other income for the same tax year, or the next one (although this relief is now subject to certain limitations).

Remember also, that a couple buying property jointly (but not as a partnership) could claim AIAs of up to £200,000 ***each*** every year from 2016/17 onwards. Such a couple could potentially benefit from a total tax saving of up to £184,200 in 2017/18 alone: simply by buying the right property! (Based on income of £300,000 each before claiming AIAs)

Thermal Insulation of Commercial Property

Expenditure on thermal insulation of an existing commercial building used in a qualifying business also falls into the special rate pool. The AIA is again available on this expenditure.

Landlord's Own Assets

A landlord is unable to claim capital allowances on any assets, such as furniture and equipment, within his or her residential lettings (apart from assets in communal areas not within any individual 'dwelling'). Any landlord may however claim 'plant and machinery' allowances, as detailed in Section 3.10, on equipment purchased for their own business use, such as computers and office furniture.

Capital allowances are available on motor vehicles used in the business, again as detailed in Section 3.10.

4.10 FURNISHED LETTINGS

For details of the tax relief available on furnished residential lettings for tax years up to and including 2015/16, see the previous edition of this guide. In this edition, I will be focussing solely on the tax relief available from 2016/17 onwards. From 2016/17 onwards, it is no longer necessary to distinguish between fully and partly furnished residential lettings.

Furnished holiday lettings are, however, subject to an entirely different regime: the key difference being that qualifying items within furnished holiday lettings are eligible for capital allowances (see Section 8.17).

It should also be noted that any items within 'communal areas' lying outside any individual dwelling (e.g. the common parts of a house divided into self-contained flats) will also be subject to a different regime and may be eligible for capital allowances (see Section 4.9 for details).

Before we look at the tax relief available for furnishings, it is important to stress that nothing in this section affects the landlord's ability to claim repairs expenditure under the principles examined in Section 4.7.

What Are Furnishings?

The first, and most important, thing to understand is that fixtures, fittings, and anything else which is part of the fabric of the building, are not classed as furnishings for tax purposes. Generally speaking, anything which is permanently fixed to the building is not classed as a 'furnishing' and replacing these items will often be claimable as a repair expense, as discussed in Section 4.7.

Hence, items which are classed as 'furnishings' for tax purposes include:

- Furniture
- Electrical equipment
- Free-standing 'white goods', such as fridges, dishwashers, etc.
- Carpets and other floor coverings
- Curtains, blinds, etc.
- 'Soft furnishings' (cushions, lampshades, etc.) and bed linen
- Cutlery, crockery and cooking utensils

Carpets often cause a lot of confusion as many people see them as a 'fitting' rather than a 'furnishing'. For tax purposes, however, they are classed as furnishings.

Items classed as fixtures and fittings for tax purposes include:

- Baths, toilets, sinks, showers, etc.
- Fitted kitchens, including fitted (not free-standing) equipment which is an integral part of a fitted kitchen
- Central heating equipment (boilers, radiators, etc.)
- Air conditioning
- Light fittings

Where these items are replaced, the expenditure will generally be dealt with as a repair – subject to the points outlined in Section 4.7.

The fitted equipment in a modern kitchen might include various items which would have been free-standing in a more traditional kitchen; including cookers, fridges, dishwashers and many other items. As long as both the old item and the new one replacing it are integral parts of a fitted kitchen, the cost of the replacement may be claimed as a repair (subject to the principles covered in Section 4.7).

Replacement Furniture Relief

Expenditure incurred after 5th April 2016 is eligible for 'replacement furniture relief'. This relief is available:

- To all residential landlords
- On qualifying replacement expenditure within fully furnished lets, partly furnished lets and even unfurnished lets (but not in furnished holiday lets)
- To cover replacements of all moveable items (i.e. all furnishings, as detailed above)

Any sale proceeds received on the disposal of the old item being replaced must be deducted from the replacement cost being claimed.

The relief does not cover the costs of the original furnishings when the property is first let out, or the cost of additional items.

Landlords may, however, claim part of the cost of a replacement item which performs additional functions compared to the old item which it replaces. Hence, for example, where a landlord replaces an old fridge with a fridge-freezer costing £300, but could have purchased a new fridge for £200, they will still be able to claim the £200 direct replacement cost.

Repairs to Furnishings

Landlords may also claim the cost of repairs to any items of equipment, furniture or furnishings in any rental properties.

4.11 RENT-A-ROOM RELIEF

A special relief, called 'rent-a-room relief', applies to income from letting out a part of your own home. For this purpose, the property must be your main residence (see Section 6.13) for at least part of the same tax year. The letting itself must also at least partially coincide with a period when the property is your main residence.

The relief covers income from lodgers and even extends to letting a self-contained flat, provided the division of the property is only temporary.

Complete exemption is automatically provided where the gross annual rent receivable from lettings in the property does not exceed the rent-a-room relief limit.

From 2016/17 onwards, the rent-a-room relief limit is £7,500. For earlier years it was £4,250.

The gross rent receivable for this purpose must include any contributions towards household expenses which you receive from your tenants and any balancing charges arising (see Section 3.8).

The taxpayer may elect not to claim rent-a-room relief. They might do this, for example, if the letting is actually producing a loss which, otherwise, could not be claimed. This election must be made within twelve months after the 31st January following the tax year. (E.g. for the tax year 2017/18, the election would need to be made by 31st January 2020.)

Where the gross rent receivable exceeds the rent-a-room limit, the taxpayer may nevertheless elect (within the same time limit as outlined above) for a form of partial exemption. The partial exemption operates by allowing the taxpayer to be assessed only on the amount of gross rents receivable in excess of the rent-a-room limit instead of under the normal basis for rental income.

Example
Duncan rents out a room in his house for an annual rent of £8,000. His rental profit for 2017/18, calculated on the normal basis, is £2,800. He therefore elects to use the rent-a-room basis, thus reducing his assessable rental income for 2017/18 to only £500.

The partial exemption available under rent-a-room relief has now become attractive to many more landlords renting out a part of their own home due to the restrictions in interest relief set out in Section 4.5.

Example
Isabella is a higher rate taxpayer. She rents out a room in her house for an annual rent of £9,000. Computing her rental profits in the normal way would give her allowable interest of £8,000 and other deductible expenses of £400. For 2016/17, she was better to pay tax on her actual rental profit of £600 rather than claim partial exemption under rent-a-room relief.

In 2017/18, Isabella's taxable rental profit increases to £2,600 due to the restriction in her interest relief. She will get basic rate tax relief on a further £2,000 of interest, so her tax bill on an 'actual' basis would be £640 (£2,600 x 40% - £2,000 x 20%).

Claiming partial exemption under rent-a-room relief would reduce Isabella's taxable rental profit to £1,500 (£9,000 - £7,500) giving her a tax bill, at 40%, of £600. Hence, Isabella is now better off claiming rent-a-room relief.

Isabella's savings under rent-a-room relief will increase each year up until 2020/21; by which point the claim will be saving her £1,240.

Other Points on Rent-a-Room Relief

Where the letting income is being shared with another person, the rent-a-room limit must be halved. Oddly, where the income is being shared with more than one other person, there is no further reduction. Hence, three or more joint owners can still all claim half the normal limit.

Where there is any letting income from the same property during the same tax year which does not qualify for the relief, none of the income from the property that year may be exempted.

An election to claim rent-a-room relief is deemed to remain in place for future years unless withdrawn (the same time limit applies for a withdrawal).

Rent-a-room relief continues to apply to income from lodgers where additional services are provided, such as cooking, cleaning, etc. Income in excess of the rent-a-room relief limit may, however, be regarded as trading income rather than rental income in these circumstances.

Where you are claiming complete exemption under rent-a-room relief, you should put an 'X' in Box 4 on page UKP1 of your tax return.

4.12 RENTAL LOSSES ON UK PROPERTY

As explained in Section 4.1, all your UK property lettings, apart from furnished holiday lettings, are treated as a single UK property business. For loss relief purposes, however, it is necessary to separate UK rental property into three categories:

- Non-commercial lettings (see Section 4.16)
- Furnished holiday lettings (see Section 8.17)
- Other UK rental property (which I will refer to as 'normal' rental property for the sake of illustration)

Losses arising on furnished holiday lettings or non-commercial lettings are subject to special rules we will look at in Sections 8.17 and 4.16.

Losses arising on 'normal' rental property are automatically set off against profits on other 'normal' UK rental property for the same period. Losses on 'normal' UK rental property may also be set off against profits on non-commercial lettings. Any overall net losses from 'normal' rental property remaining after this may be carried forward and set off against future profits from 'normal' UK rental property or non-commercial lettings.

Losses consisting of capital allowances may also be set off against the landlord's other income of the same tax year or the next one (subject to the tax relief 'cap' discussed in Section 3.11).

The treatment of losses from overseas lettings is covered in Section 4.15.

Example
In the tax year 2017/18, Owain has employment income of £70,000, from which he suffers deduction of tax under PAYE totalling £16,700. He also has a portfolio of rented commercial property on which he has made an overall loss of £15,000, including £10,000 of capital allowances. Owain can claim to set his capital allowances off against his employment income, which will produce a tax repayment of £4,000.

111

How Long Can Rental Losses Be Carried Forward?

Rental losses from 'normal' rental property may be carried forward for as long as you continue to have a 'normal' UK property rental business. There are two major pitfalls to watch out for here.

Firstly, rental losses are personal. They cannot be transferred to another person, not even your spouse, and they do not transfer with the properties. If you die with rental losses, they die with you.

Secondly, if your 'normal' UK property business ceases, you will lose your losses. It may therefore be vital to keep your 'normal' UK property business going. As long as you continue to have at least one 'normal' UK rental property, you still have a 'normal' UK property business.

Example
Fergus has a large UK property portfolio. Despite having made some good profits in the past, by 2017/18 he has rental losses of £1m carried forward. Fergus decides he's had enough and begins to sell off his UK property empire. Before his rental income ceases, however, he buys one small lock-up garage in Argyllshire and starts to rent it out.

Fergus's lock-up garage is enough to ensure that he still has a UK property rental business. It doesn't matter that it is tiny by comparison with his previous ventures; this one small garage keeps his rental losses alive, with the possibility of saving him up to £450,000 one day (£1m at 45%).

The only absolutely safe way to ensure that you have a continuing 'normal' UK property rental business is to ensure that you always have at least one 'normal' UK rental property let out on a commercial basis.

However, HMRC will sometimes accept that a total cessation of all 'normal' rental income is not necessarily the same as a cessation of your 'normal' UK rental business, especially where the rental properties are still held.

They will usually accept that the rental business has not ceased:

- Where you can provide evidence that you have been attempting unsuccessfully to let out your property

- Where rental has only ceased temporarily whilst repairs or alterations are carried out

They will, however, generally regard the rental business as having ceased if there is a gap of more than three years between lettings and different properties are let before and after the gap.

They may sometimes accept a gap of less than three years as not being a cessation, but not if you have clearly employed all of your capital in some other type of business, or spent it for personal purposes, such as buying yourself a new home.

If in doubt though, rent out that garage!

Wealth Warning

An overseas property will not preserve your 'normal' UK property business. A furnished holiday letting or a non-commercial letting (e.g. to your aunt for £1 a year) will not do either.

Another Wealth Warning

On page UKP1 of the tax return, you are asked to put an 'X' in Box 2 if you do not expect to receive any rental income in the next tax year. Completing this box may be seen as a strong indication that your UK property business has ceased.

I would therefore recommend leaving this box blank where you have rental losses carried forward unless you are absolutely certain that you will not have any UK rental income again in the future. (Assuming that you are completing your tax return by the normal due date, you cannot yet know that you will not have any rental income in the next tax year anyway.)

The Future of Rental Losses

One of the consequences of the changes to interest relief discussed in Section 4.5 is that landlords with 'normal' residential property are less likely to have allowable rental losses in future. They will, instead, tend to have excess interest to be carried forward for relief at basic rate. See Section 4.5 for further details.

Even those with existing rental losses are likely to see these effectively 'devalued' and turned into excess interest carried forward for relief at basic rate.

Example
Solomon is a higher rate taxpayer with annual rental profits before interest of £40,000 and interest costs of £50,000. All his rental properties are 'normal' residential property. At the beginning of 2017/18, he has rental losses brought forward of £100,000. Over the next few years, his losses are utilised as follows:

	2017/18	2018/19	2019/20	2020/21	2021/22
Profit before interest	40,000	40,000	40,000	40,000	40,000
Deductible interest	(37,500)	(25,000)	(12,500)	0	0
Taxable 'profit'	2,500	15,000	27,500	40,000	40,000
Losses					
Brought forward	100,000	97,500	82,500	55,000	15,000
Set off against profit	(2,500)	(15,000)	(27,500)	(40,000)	(15,000)
Carried forward	97,500	82,500	55,000	15,000	0
Excess Interest					
Brought forward	0	12,500	37,500	75,000	125,000
Arising in year	12,500	25,000	37,500	50,000	50,000
Relieved at basic rate	0	0	0	0	(25,000)
Carried forward	12,500	37,500	75,000	125,000	150,000

As we can see, by the end of this period, all of Solomon's rental losses have effectively been converted into excess interest carried forward for relief at basic rate only.

In 2021/22, he will have taxable income of £25,000 (£40,000 less the final £15,000 of his brought forward losses). This will be taxed at 40%, with interest relief at only 20%, giving him an Income Tax liability of £5,000.

Thereafter, he will have income of £40,000 taxed at 40%, with interest relief at 20%, giving him an Income Tax liability of £8,000 each year.

4.13 OTHER PROPERTY INVESTMENT INCOME

Most forms of income derived from investments in land and property will be subject to Income Tax under the regime outlined in this chapter. This will include tenant's deposits retained at the end of a lease and usually also any dilapidation payments received.

Since 2007, landlords in England and Wales have been required to hold tenant's deposits in escrow. A similar law was introduced in Scotland in 2012. Whatever the legal position, it is important to include deposits retained within your rental income at the end of the lease, but not before. Refunded deposits should never be included in rental income.

Dilapidation payments may sometimes be regarded as a capital receipt instead if the landlord does not rent the property out again (e.g. if the landlord sells it or adopts it as their own home). In a recent case, it was also held that, where the damage to a property is so severe as to lead to a permanent diminution in value, a dilapidation payment might again be regarded as a capital receipt. This is contrary to HMRC's usual view on this issue and it is not yet clear how widely this ruling might be interpreted. Quite possibly, it might only apply in very narrow circumstances similar to the particular case in question. Hence, the general position remains that, where the landlord does continue to rent out the property afterwards, dilapidation payments will usually be treated as additional rental income subject to Income Tax.

Where, unusually, a payment is treated as a capital receipt, this will represent a 'part disposal' of the property and will be subject to CGT in a similar way to the premium received on the grant of a long lease (see Section 6.34).

Some items are specifically excluded from property income, including:

- Any amounts taxable as trading income
- Farming and market gardening
- Income from mineral extraction rights

Wayleave (right of access) payments are sometimes included however.

4.14 LEASE PREMIUMS

Premiums received for the granting of short leases of no more than 50 years' duration are subject to Income Tax. The proportion of the premium subject to Income Tax is, however, reduced by 2% for each full year of the lease's duration in excess of one year.

The part of the premium not subject to Income Tax falls within the CGT regime (see Section 6.34) and will be treated as a part disposal of the relevant property.

Example
Alexander owns the freehold to a property and grants a 12-year lease to Kenneth for a premium of £50,000. The lease exceeds one year by eleven years and hence 22% of this sum falls within the CGT regime. Alexander is therefore subject to Income Tax on the sum of £39,000 (i.e. £50,000 less 22%).

If the tenant is running a business from the property (including sub-letting it as a landlord in their own right), the element of the premium which is taxed as income in the hands of the grantor is allowable as a deduction in the tenant's business.

The tenant must, however, claim the allowable element of the premium over the life of the lease. Hence, in Kenneth's case in the example above, he would be able to claim a deduction of £3,250 each year for the twelve years of the lease (£39,000/12 = £3,250).

4.15 OVERSEAS LETTINGS

All of a taxpayer's commercially let overseas properties (with the exception of any furnished holiday lettings within the EEA) are treated as a single business in much the same way as, but separate from, a UK property business.

Furnished holiday lettings within the EEA (see Section 1.4) are subject to the same special regime as qualifying furnished holiday lettings in the UK (see Section 8.17), although, again, these are treated as a separate business.

A UK resident and domiciled taxpayer (see Section 3.7) with overseas lettings is therefore taxed on this income under exactly the same principles as for UK lettings except:

i) Separate accounts will be required for properties in each overseas territory where any double tax relief claims are to be made
ii) Overseas furnished holiday lettings outside the EEA are not included within the special regime applying to qualifying furnished holiday accommodation (as detailed in Section 8.17)

Travelling expenses may be claimed when incurred wholly and exclusively for the purposes of the overseas letting business.

The UK tax treatment of losses arising from an overseas letting business is exactly the same as for a UK property business except, of course, that this is treated as a separate business from any UK lettings which the taxpayer has. Hence, again, for loss relief purposes, overseas property must be separated into three categories, as follows:

• Non-commercial overseas lettings (see Section 4.16)
• Furnished holiday lettings within the EEA (see Section 8.17)
• Other overseas rental property (which I will refer to as 'normal' overseas property for the sake of illustration)

As before, the special rules outlined in Sections 8.17 and 4.16 apply to qualifying furnished holiday lettings within the EEA and non-commercial overseas lettings respectively.

Losses arising on 'normal' overseas property are automatically set off against profits derived from other 'normal' overseas lettings or non-commercial overseas lettings, with the excess carried forward for set off against future 'normal' overseas rental profits. The same rule as set out in Section 4.12 applies to any capital allowances.

Where there are substantial 'normal' overseas rental losses carried forward, it will be worthwhile ensuring that this business continues. The same principles as set out in Section 4.12 will apply here, except that, to continue the business, it is necessary to continue to have 'normal' overseas rental property.

Whilst the property must be let on a commercial basis and outside the UK, it can be in any other part of the world and need not be in the same country as the property which gave rise to the original rental losses. A loss made in Albania might conceivably be set off against a profit in Zanzibar!

As before, it is essential to remember that a qualifying furnished holiday letting property within the EEA will not suffice to preserve rental losses from 'normal' overseas property.

4.16 NON-COMMERCIAL LETTINGS

Where lettings are not on a commercial or 'arm's length' basis, they cannot be regarded as part of the same UK or overseas property business as any commercial lettings which the taxpayer has. Profits remain taxable, but any losses arising may only be carried forward for set off against future profits from the same letting (i.e. the same property let to the same tenant).

Typically, this type of letting involves the lease of a property to a relative or friend of the landlord at a nominal rent, considerably less than the full market rent which the property could demand on the open market.

Where the tenant of such a non-commercial letting is a previous owner of the property (e.g. a parent of the landlord), the 'Pre-Owned Assets' Income Tax benefit-in-kind charge may apply to the benefit so received by the tenant. In many cases this will result in the tenant being charged Income Tax on the difference between the nominal rent which they pay and the full market rent.

4.17 THE PROPERTY INCOME ALLOWANCE

The Government is proposing to introduce a new allowance of £1,000 to exempt small amounts of property rental income from 2017/18 onwards. (Although the allowance is theoretically available already, the relevant legislation has yet to be enacted.)

The allowance applies to all of a landlord's property income for the tax year – not to individual properties or leases.

Where the taxpayer's total rental income for the tax year exceeds the £1,000 allowance, they may either deduct expenses as normal, or deduct the allowance from their total income.

This is unlikely to be of any use to most landlords with genuine property businesses, but may be useful to someone who:

- Rents out a second home for a short period;
- Starts a property business shortly before the end of the tax year: but bear in mind the ability to deduct 'pre-trading expenditure' when the business starts (see Section 3.8) – this ability would be lost if the property income allowance were used; or
- Has very few allowable costs

As far as the last heading is concerned, any landlord with allowable costs of less than £1,000 would be better off claiming the property income allowance unless computing their results on a normal, actual, basis would lead to a loss which they might be able to utilise in future years. Any capital allowances within such a loss could also be set off against other income in the same tax year or the next.

For higher rate taxpayers with residential lettings who have total allowable costs only a little over £1,000, including some interest and finance costs, it is worth bearing in mind that the property income allowance will be fully deductible whereas their interest and finance costs are not (see Section 4.5).

The property income allowance may not be used against income from your own company, or a partnership in which you are a partner. The restriction on income from a company extends to any 'close company' in which you are a 'participator'. See the Taxcafe.co.uk guide *Using a Property Company to Save Tax* for an explanation of these terms.

4.18 THE CASH BASIS FOR LANDLORDS

The Government proposes to introduce a new 'cash basis' of accounting for landlords, which is to be made available from 2017/18 onwards.

Although the new basis theoretically applies already, at the time of writing, the relevant legislation is still to be enacted (having been delayed due to the 'snap' General Election in June 2017).

In this section, I will set out the current proposals for the new cash basis. As it is not seen as a politically sensitive issue, it seems likely that the measure will go ahead in its current form. Nonetheless, the reader must bear in mind that the scheme has not yet been finalised and may therefore be subject to change before it is formally enacted.

The new cash basis is to be open to 'unincorporated property businesses' – i.e. landlords operating as individuals or partnerships. However, it will not be available to:

- Property businesses with total gross annual rental income exceeding £150,000
- Companies
- Trusts
- LLPs
- Other partnerships with one or more corporate partners

Under current proposals, the new cash basis will become the 'default' option for all eligible landlords from 6th April 2017 onwards. In other words, if you are eligible for the cash basis, it will automatically apply each year from 2017/18 onwards unless you elect to opt out of it. An election to opt out of the cash basis must be made within one year after the 31st January following the relevant tax year. For example, to elect out of the cash basis for 2017/18, you must make your election by 31st January 2020. It is currently anticipated that the election will be made through your tax return.

Electing out of the cash basis will ensure that you are able to continue using the traditional 'accruals basis' which we examined in Sections 3.8 and 4.1 and which it is assumed you are using throughout the rest of this guide.

Joint owners other than spouses may each decide separately whether to elect out of the cash basis or not. Spouses who jointly own any UK rental property must both use the same basis of accounting for all their UK rental properties. Similarly, spouses who jointly own any overseas rental property must both use the same basis of accounting for all their overseas rental properties.

The new cash basis closely reflects what many landlords actually do in practice and generally means that all rent is taxable when received and allowable expenses may be claimed when paid. Subject to the points below, it does not generally alter the question of which expenses are allowable, only the timing of when they may be claimed. There are some important exceptions to this however.

Disadvantages of the Cash Basis

The cash basis is certainly simpler to operate than the normal accruals basis of accounting, but there are a number of reasons why it will not always be beneficial, including:

i)   Rent becomes fully taxable on receipt, even if it relates to a period which extends beyond the end of the tax year
ii)   Expenses which have been incurred but not yet paid at the end of the tax year cannot be claimed
iii)   There is a potential further restriction on interest relief (in addition to the measures set out in Section 4.5) – see further below

iv)   Abortive expenditure relating to potential purchases of new
        property which are abandoned will not be allowable
v)   Writing down allowances may not be claimed on previous capital
        expenditure (except for cars) (the treatment of capital
        expenditure under the cash basis is explained further below)
vi)   Costs of raising loan finance incurred in earlier years and which
        were being claimed over the useful life of the loan (see Sections
        4.4 and 4.6) cannot be claimed
vii)   No deductions will be allowed in respect of lease premiums paid
        (see Section 4.14)

Further Restriction on Interest Relief

The further restriction on interest relief applies where:

- The total amount borrowed for the purposes of the property
  letting business (which would otherwise all qualify under the
  principles set out in Section 4.4), is greater than
- The total value of all the rental properties in the business when
  first rented out plus other 'capital introduced' (see Section 4.4)

When this restriction applies, the allowable interest under the cash basis
is reduced by the appropriate proportion.

Example

*Joseph bought a rental property for £100,000 a few years ago. He also paid
purchase costs of £2,500 and spent £4,500 on furnishing the property. There
were a further £3,000 of initial 'set up' costs which he was able to claim for
Income Tax purposes.*

*He financed his total costs of £110,000 with a buy-to-let mortgage of £85,000
and a further £25,000 obtained by re-mortgaging his own home.*

*A few years later, he carried out some urgent roof repairs on his rental property
at a cost of £5,000. He financed this with a personal loan.*

*By 2017/18, his total qualifying borrowings (under the principles set out in
Section 4.4), are as follows:*

Buy-to-let mortgage	*£85,000*
Additional mortgage on home	*£25,000*
Personal loan	*£5,000*
Total	*£115,000*

*These give rise to total allowable interest costs of £4,600 which he would be
able to claim under the accruals basis (subject to the restrictions in Section 4.5).*

*However, his total 'capital introduced' (derived on the basis explained in Section
4.4) is as follows:*

Value of property when first rented	*£100,000**
Purchase costs	*£2,500*
Furnishings	*£4,500*
Total	*£107,000*

* - as in many cases, where a property is purchased specifically for rental purposes, the value equates to the purchase price

His other 'set up' costs of £3,000 do not count for this purpose as they qualified for Income Tax relief.

If Joseph adopts the cash basis in 2017/18, his allowable interest will be reduced as follows:

$$£107,000/£115,000 \times £4,600 = £4,280$$

He will therefore lose out on £320 of allowable interest. The £4,280 which is allowed will also continue to be restricted as set out in Section 4.5. He will therefore be able to claim a deduction of £3,210 (75%) and basic rate tax relief on the remaining £1,070 (25%).

An important point to note is that it is only 'capital expenditure' (see Section 3.8) which can count as 'capital introduced' for the purposes of calculating allowable interest. This seldom matters under the accruals basis, as all borrowings used to fund business expenditure qualify for relief. Under the cash basis, however, this distinction is critical.

In the example, I have included the initial cost of furnishing the property as 'capital introduced' (as this is not allowed for Income Tax purposes – see Section 4.10). However, even this is perhaps debatable since the draft legislation refers to expenditure 'in respect of the property' and one legal interpretation might be that furnishings (see Section 4.10) are not part of the property. Such an interpretation would further reduce Joseph's allowable interest cost under the cash basis to £4,100 – although I would argue that my own interpretation is correct.

Further complications will arise where the landlord is claiming interest on other borrowings which are not directly related to any individual rental property.

Example Revisited
Let us now assume that, under the accruals basis, Joseph would also be able to claim part of the hire purchase interest on his car and an element of the original mortgage on his home (before the additional £25,000 remortgaging referred to above) within his 'use of home' claim (see Section 3.9).

The balance on his hire purchase agreement is £20,000, he uses the car 25% for business purposes and the interest payable during 2017/18 is £4,000.

The balance on his original mortgage (excluding the £25,000 of additional remortgaging) is £200,000, the interest payable on this balance during 2017/18 is £6,000 and the proportion of fixed costs claimed within his 'use of home' claim is 1.5%. Hence, his total allowable interest claim under the accruals basis is:

Loans and mortgages (as before)	£4,600
Hire purchase (£4,000 x 25%)	£1,000
Use of home (£6,000 x 1.5%)	£90
Total	£5,690

His total qualifying borrowings are now as follows:

Buy-to-let mortgage	£85,000
Additional mortgage on home	£25,000
Personal loan	£5,000
Hire purchase (£20,000 x 25%)	£5,000
Original mortgage (£200,000 x 1.5%)	£3,000
Total	£123,000

His total 'capital introduced' remains £107,000 as before, so his interest claim under the cash basis would now be restricted to:

$$£5,690 \times £107,000/£123,000 = £4,950$$

Joseph is now losing £740 of allowable interest by using the cash basis and can only claim £3,713 (75%) as a deduction with basic rate relief on the remaining £1,237 (25%).

(Interestingly, if Joseph did not include his domestic mortgage interest within his 'use of home' claim, his total allowable claim under the cash basis would increase to £4,993. Landlords using the cash basis facing this interest relief restriction might therefore do better to exclude claims for any balances with lower rates of interest.)

As usual, these restrictions apply equally to other finance costs paid during the year. (But see point (vi) above regarding finance costs paid in earlier years.)

Further Illustration

Let's now look at another example which brings together some of the other disadvantages of using the cash basis.

Example
During 2017/18, Safiya receives rent totalling £120,000, pays interest of £70,000 and incurs other expenses of £20,000, including £1,000 for some

surveys on properties she later decided not to buy and £5,000 for some roof repairs carried out in March 2018 which she pays in late April.

For interest relief purposes, Safiya has total qualifying borrowings of £1.75m and total 'capital introduced' of £1.65m. £12,000 of Safiya's income was received in the first five days of April 2018 and relates to the rent due for the whole of that month.

Safiya's accountant works out her profit under normal accruals basis principles as follows:

Income due for the year	£110,000
(£120,000 - £12,000 x 25/30)	
Less expenses:	
Interest	£70,000
Other expenses incurred	£20,000
Accrued accountancy fees	£2,000
Rental profit	£18,000

(£17,500, or 25%, of Safiya's interest expense will be added back to profit for tax purposes and will instead give rise to a tax deduction at basic rate)

If Safiya does not elect to use normal accruals basis accounting, she will fall into the cash basis by default and her profit will then be calculated as follows:

Income received in the year	£120,000
Less expenses paid in the year:	
Interest (£70,000 x £1.65m/£1.75m)	£66,000
Other	£14,000
(£15,000 paid less survey costs not allowed £1,000)	
Net rental income	£40,000

(£16,500, or 25%, of Safiya's allowable interest will be added to her income for tax purposes and will instead give rise to a tax deduction at basic rate)

As we can see, the cash basis would cause a considerable increase in Safiya's tax liability!

It must be admitted that much of the difference arising in Safiya's case is only a question of timing. Nonetheless, she has also permanently lost out on £5,000 worth of allowable expenses (due to the further restriction in interest relief and the denial of relief for her abortive capital expenditure).

And timing is nothing to be sniffed at. Apart from the permanent loss of £5,000 of allowable expenses, a further £17,000 of taxable income has arisen at least a year earlier. For a higher rate taxpayer that means paying £6,800 in tax at least a year earlier, so it's not exactly unimportant.

Advantages of the Cash Basis

In addition to the fact that it is simpler to operate, the cash basis does have some other potential advantages. Many of these again relate to timing. In this context, it is particularly important to note that many landlords who are currently basic rate taxpayers will become higher rate taxpayers in the near future as a result of the restrictions to interest relief covered in Section 4.5. Some will suffer even higher effective tax rates as a result of those restrictions: due to the High Income Child Benefit Charge, the loss of their personal allowance, or being pushed over the additional rate tax threshold.

Hence, the cash basis might sometimes help in the following ways:

i)   The cash basis may sometimes accelerate income into an earlier tax year when the landlord has a lower tax rate

ii)   Expenses incurred during the year but paid after the year end may attract relief in a later tax year when the landlord has a higher tax rate

iii)   Costs of raising loan finance (see Sections 4.4 and 4.6) can be claimed when paid and will not need to be spread over the useful life of the loan. This will not only accelerate relief but will also reduce the impact of the restrictions set out in Section 4.5

As far as point (iii) is concerned, what is not clear is how a loan arrangement fee which is not paid 'up front', but is added to the balance of the loan, should be treated under the cash basis. Arguably, adding the fee to the loan balance might be regarded as paying it, but another view would be that it is only paid as that loan itself is repaid. This would diminish the potential advantage described above.

Capital Expenditure under the Cash Basis

Landlords operating the cash basis may claim capital expenditure as it is paid, but only if it would otherwise have qualified for either capital allowances (see Section 4.9) or replacement furniture relief (see Section 4.10).

This does not apply to cars, however. Landlords using the cash basis should continue to claim capital allowances on cars under the usual principles (see Section 3.10).

Apart from cars, landlords using the cash basis may not claim capital allowances. This means that they cannot claim writing down allowances on any balances brought forward on the main pool, special rate pool, or any 'puddles' (see Section 3.10). Those balances are effectively 'frozen' until such time (if any) that the landlord reverts to the accruals basis: when they may then resume claiming writing down allowances.

Entering or Leaving the Cash Basis

Transitional rules apply in the year that a landlord enters or leaves the cash basis. In effect, these rules ensure that:

- No income escapes tax
- No income is taxed twice
- Expenses cannot be claimed twice

Generally, the transitional rules should also ensure that allowable expenses are not omitted but this is subject to the points listed under 'Disadvantages of the Cash Basis' above.

Example Resumed
Safiya opted out of the cash basis in 2017/18, but she decides to use it in 2018/19. This means she will be taxed on the rent she actually receives, with deductions for the allowable expenses she actually pays, but she will also have to make the following adjustments:

i)   *The £10,000 (£12,000 x 25/30) of rent received in the first five days of April 2018 which was excluded from her income in 2017/18 will need to be added to her income for 2018/19*

ii) *The £5,000 which she paid for roof repairs in late April 2018 cannot be claimed in 2018/19 as she has already claimed this expense*

iii) *The £2,000 accrued for accountancy fees in 2017/18 will have to be deducted from any accountancy fees which she actually pays during 2018/19 (if this results in a negative figure, she must report a negative expense)*

Let us also now assume that Safiya had paid an insurance premium of £1,500 in September 2017 but only claimed half of it in her 2017/18 accounts (under the accruals basis) as it covered the period from October 2017 to September 2018. This would lead to a fourth adjustment under the transitional rules in her 2018/19 accounts, as she would then be able to claim the remaining half of that premium, together with any insurance premiums she actually paid during 2018/19.

Previous Concessionary Cash Basis

Prior to 2017/18, HMRC sometimes allowed individual landlords with total annual rental receipts not exceeding £15,000 to use a concessionary cash basis. They only allowed this method to be used if it was applied consistently and produced a reasonable result.

This earlier cash basis simply meant that income and expenditure were recognised when received or paid. Capital expenditure continued to be subject to the normal rules and the restrictions listed under points (iii), (iv) and (v) under 'Disadvantages of the Cash Basis' above did not apply.

Summary

In general, my view is that the cash basis will not usually be beneficial for most landlords for the simple reason that rent is usually received in advance and many expenses are paid in arrears.

Hence, even where the other disadvantages listed above do not apply, the cash basis will generally have the effect of accelerating taxable income into an earlier year. Accelerating taxable income will naturally have the direct consequence of accelerating tax liabilities – usually, at least.

Furthermore, due to the operation of inflation alone, accelerating taxable income into an earlier year will often lead to higher rates of Income Tax. (For example, £45,000 of income in 2016/17 would have made you a higher rate taxpayer; £45,000 of income in 2017/18 will not.) This effect is further exacerbated where the landlord's business is growing.

Apart from timing issues, those significantly affected by the other disadvantages listed above are unlikely to benefit from the cash basis.

On the other hand, there will be some landlords whose tax rate is set to increase and for whom the advantages listed above may therefore be beneficial. The ability to accelerate tax relief for part of your finance costs could also lead to savings over the next few years.

Lastly there is the appeal of simplicity. Frankly, however, my view is that most of the complications in property taxation relate to ***what*** expenditure is allowable rather than ***when*** – and the cash basis won't help there!

In conclusion, my view is that most landlords will be better off sticking with the accruals basis – BUT it will always be worth considering whether the cash basis might be beneficial when the landlord is eligible to use it.

Chapter 5

How to Save Tax on a Property Trade

5.1 THE TAXATION OF PROPERTY TRADING INCOME

Where your property business is deemed to be a trade, such as property development or property dealing, you will be taxed under a different set of principles to those outlined in Chapter 4. The major points to note are:

i) Properties held for development or sale are treated as trading stock rather than capital assets

ii) Taxpayers with property trades may choose any calendar date as their accounting year end

iii) Profits on property disposals are subject to both Income Tax and Class 4 NI. Property traders must also pay Class 2 NI until 5th April 2018

iv) There are no restrictions on the rate of tax relief for interest and finance costs incurred in the course of a property trade

v) Most 'abortive' legal and professional fees should be allowed as incurred, as an Income Tax deduction

vi) A broader range of administrative expenditure will be claimable

vii) Capital allowances will usually only be available on your own business's long-term assets

viii) Trading losses may be set off against all of your other income and capital gains for the same tax year and the previous one (subject to the restrictions explained in Sections 3.11 and 5.12)

ix) The same trade may involve both UK and overseas properties

x) Non-resident individuals are taxed on trading profits derived from UK land and property and on any trade which is managed in the UK. (For a UK resident but non-domiciled individual, a foreign-based property trade deriving profits from overseas properties may be taxed on the remittance basis, with the usual potential drawbacks – see Section 8.25)

xi) Individuals with small trading businesses may elect to use the cash basis outlined in Section 5.13 (which is different to the cash basis for landlords covered in Section 4.18)

5.2 PROPERTIES AS TRADING STOCK

The properties which you hold in the business for development and/or sale are not regarded as long-term capital assets. They are, instead, regarded as trading stock.

For tax purposes, all of your expenditure in acquiring, furnishing, improving, repairing or converting the properties becomes part of the cost of that trading stock.

Many of the issues we examined in Chapter 4 regarding the question of whether expenditure is revenue or capital therefore become completely academic. Most professional fees and repairs or improvement expenditure are treated as part of the cost of the trading stock in a property trade. (As explained in Section 3.8, 'revenue expenditure' means expenditure deductible from income; capital expenditure is subject to different rules.)

The way in which trading stock works for tax purposes can be illustrated by way of an example.

Example
In November 2017, Camilla buys a property in Windsor for £265,000. She pays SDLT of £11,200 and legal fees of £1,450. Previously, in October, she also paid a survey fee of £350.

Camilla is a property developer and draws up accounts to 31st December each year. In her accounts to 31st December 2017, the Windsor property will be included as trading stock with a value of £278,000 made up as follows:

	£
Property purchase	*265,000*
SDLT	*11,200*
Legal fees	*1,450*
Survey fee	*350*

	278,000
	======

Points to Note
The important point to note here is that, whilst all of Camilla's expenditure is regarded as revenue expenditure, because she is a property developer, she cannot yet claim any deduction for any of it, because she still holds the property.

Example Continued
Early in 2018, Camilla incurs further professional fees of £10,000 obtaining planning permission to divide the property into two separate residences. Permission is granted in July and by the end of the year, Camilla has spent a

further £40,000 on conversion work. In her accounts to 31st December 2018 the property will still be shown in trading stock, as follows:

	£
Costs brought forward	*278,000*
Additional professional fees	*10,000*
Building work	*40,000*

	328,000
	======

Camilla still doesn't get any tax relief for any of this expenditure.

By March 2019, Camilla has spent another £5,000 on the property and is ready to sell the two new houses she has created. One sells quickly for £190,000. Camilla incurs a further £3,500 in estate agent's and legal fees in the process. Camilla's taxable profit on this sale is thus calculated as follows:

	£	£
Sale proceeds		*190,000*
Less Cost:		
Total cost brought forward:	*328,000*	
Additional building costs:	*5,000*	

Trading Stock prior to sale of		
first property	*333,000*	

Allocated to property sold (50%):	*166,500*	
Add additional costs:	*3,500*	

		170,000

Profit on sale		*20,000*
		=======

This profit will form part of Camilla's trading profit for the year ending 31st December 2019.

Points to Note
The additional building spend of £5,000 was allocated to trading stock as this still related to the whole property. The legal and estate agent's fees incurred on the sale were specific to the part which was sold and may thus be deducted in full against those sale proceeds.

In the example I have split the cost of trading stock equally between the two new houses. If the two new houses are, indeed, identical then this will be correct. Otherwise, the costs should be split between the two properties on a reasonable basis – e.g. by total floor area, or in proportion to the market value of the finished properties.

The latter approach would be the required statutory basis if these were capital disposals subject to CGT. Although it is not mandatory here, it might still be a useful yardstick.

The most important point, however, is that, even if Camilla fails to sell the second new house before 31st December 2019, her profit on the first new house will still be taxable in full.

There is one exception to this, as we shall now examine.

Net Realisable Value

Trading stock is generally shown in the accounts at its cumulative cost to date. On this basis, Camilla's second house, if still unsold at 31st December 2019, would have a carrying value of £166,500 in her accounts.

If, however, for whatever reason, the market value of the property is less than its cumulative cost then, as trading stock, its carrying value in the accounts may be reduced appropriately.

Furthermore, since the act of selling the property itself will lead to further expenses, these may also be deducted from the property's reduced value in this situation. This gives us a value known in accounting terminology as the property's 'net realisable value'.

> **Practical Pointer**
> Trading stock should always be shown in the accounts at the lower of cost or net realisable value.

Example
The second new house in Windsor doesn't sell so quickly, so, in September Camilla decides to take it back off the market and build an extension on the back to make it a more attractive proposition to potential buyers. Unfortunately, however, there are some problems with the foundations for the extension and the costs are more than double what Camilla had expected.

By 31st December, Camilla has spent £30,000 on the extension work and it still isn't finished. Her total costs to date on the second house are now £196,500. Camilla's builder estimates that there will be further costs of £12,000 before the extension is complete and the property is ready to sell.

The estate agent reckons that the completed property will sell for around £205,000. The agent's own fees will amount to £3,000 and there will also be legal costs of around £750.

The net realisable value of the property at 31st December 2019 is thus:

	£	£
Market value of completed property		*205,000*
Less:		
Costs to complete	*12,000*	
Professional costs to sell	*3,750*	

		15,750

Net Realisable Value at 31/12/2019		*189,250*
		======

Since this is less than Camilla's costs to date on the property, this is the value to be shown as trading stock in her accounts. The result of this is that Camilla will show a loss of £7,250 (£196,500 less £189,250) on the second house in her 2019 accounts. This loss will automatically be set off against her £20,000 profit on the first house.

By March 2020, the second house is ready for sale. Fortunately, there is an upturn in the market and Camilla manages to sell the property for £220,000. Her actual additional expenditure on the extension work amounted to £11,800 and the professional fees incurred on the sale were actually £3,900.

Camilla's taxable profit on this property in 2020 is thus:

	£	£
Sale proceeds		*220,000*
Less:		
Value of trading stock brought		
forward, as per accounts:	*189,250*	
Additional building cost	*11,800*	
Professional fees on sale	*3,900*	

		204,950

Taxable profit in year to 31/12/2020		*15,050*
		======

Points to Note

When Camilla calculates her profit for 2020, she uses actual figures for everything which took place after 31st December 2019, her last accounting date (i.e. the sale price, the final part of the building work and the professional fees on the sale).

However, the property's net realisable value in the accounts at 31st December 2019 is substituted for all of the costs which Camilla incurred up until that date. Hence, the apparent loss which Camilla was able to claim in 2019 effectively reverses and becomes part of her profits in 2020.

In this example, some of the actual figures turned out to be different to the estimates previously available. Taxpayers would generally be expected to use the most accurate figures available at the time that they are preparing their accounts.

In the case of sale price, however, this should be taken to mean an accurate estimate of the completed property's market value at the accounting date (i.e. 31st December 2019 in this example), rather than its actual eventual sale price.

Potential Changes to Accounting for Trading Stock

As discussed in Section 3.12, the Government may consider allowing businesses to opt out of some accounting adjustments in the future and this could include accounting for trading stock. At present, however, it is not clear whether this proposal will actually come to fruition and, even if it does, this will not be until at least April 2020.

5.3   WORK-IN-PROGRESS & SALES CONTRACTS

Generally, for speculative property developers, their trading stock, as we have seen, is valued at the lower of its cumulative cost to date or its net realisable value. However, if a contract for the sale of the property exists, the developer has to follow a different set of rules.

This is a complex area of accounting but, broadly speaking, the developer is required to value properties under development, for which a sale contract already exists, at an appropriate percentage of their contractual sale value. This is done by treating the completed proportion of the property as if it had already been sold.

The same proportion of the expected final costs of the development can be deducted from this notional sale. Any remaining balance of development costs is included in the accounts as 'work-in-progress', which is simply a term for trading stock which is only partly completed.

Example

Aayan is building a new house on a plot of land and has already contracted to sell it for £525,000. Aayan draws up accounts to 31st March each year and, at 31st March 2018, the new house is 75% complete. His total costs to date are £320,000, but he expects to incur another £80,000 to complete the house.

Aayan will need to show a sale of £393,750 (75% of £525,000) in his accounts to 31st March 2018. He will, however, be able to deduct costs of £300,000, which equates to 75% of his anticipated final total costs of £400,000 (£320,000 + £80,000). In other words, Aayan will show a profit of £93,750 in his accounts to 31st March 2018, which is equal to 75% of his expected final profit of £125,000. The remaining £20,000 of Aayan's costs to date will be shown in his accounts at 31st March 2018 as work-in-progress.

During the following year, he completes the property at an actual cost of £77,000. His accounts for the year ending 31st March 2019 will show a sale of £131,250, i.e. the remaining 25% of his total sale proceeds of £525,000. From this, Aayan can deduct total costs of £97,000, which is made up of his £20,000 of work-in-progress brought forward and his actual costs in the year of £77,000.

This gives Aayan a development profit of £34,250 for the year ending 31st March 2019.

The effect of this accounting treatment is to accelerate part of the profit on the development. As there is no specific rule to the contrary, the tax position will follow the accounting treatment, so that the developer is taxed on part of their property sale in advance.

It follows that the whole profit on a property for which a sales contract exists will need to be included in the developer's accounts once the property is fully completed.

Where this accounting treatment applies, the developer may nevertheless claim deductions to reflect:

- Any doubt over the purchaser's ability, or willingness, to pay
- Rectification work which is still to be carried out
- Administration and other costs relating to completion of the sale

Practical Pointer

In Section 5.5 we will see that individuals with trading income between £100,000 and £123,000 are subject to an overall effective marginal tax rate of 62% and those with trading income over £150,000 are subject to an overall rate of 47%. The fact that general accounting principles may require developers to account for part of their profit in an earlier accounting period may not always, therefore, be an entirely bad thing.

Example, continued

Let us assume that Aayan has no other sources of income apart from his property development business and that he has only one development project in hand during the two year period ending 31st March 2019.

As things stand, his taxable profit of £93,750 for the year ending 31st March 2018 will give rise to an overall combined Income Tax and NI liability of £30,638. His profit of £34,250 for the year ending 31st March 2019 will give rise to a liability of £6,819: a total of £37,457.

If Aayan had not been required to spread his profit and it had all fallen into the year ending 31st March 2019, his total liability would have been £49,309. Hence, the fact that Aayan is required to account for part of his profit in an earlier year has actually saved him almost £12,000.

(The tax rates for 2018/19 used in this example have been estimated as set out in Appendix A)

The outcome will not always be as beneficial as in Aayan's case: especially where the developer has several projects in hand at the same time. However, the example does show that there is a potential benefit to the accounting treatment which some developers are required to follow.

Furthermore, whilst accounting standards must be adhered to in principle, there is often some leeway regarding the exact amounts to be taken into account in practice. The more profit that falls into an accounting period where the developer has an overall marginal tax rate of 29% or 42%, the less there may be to be taxed in a later period at 47% or 62%. (See Section 5.5 for an explanation of the overall marginal tax rates applying to trading income.)

Note that the proposals outlined in Section 3.12 regarding the relaxation of the accounting treatment required for trading stock did not extend to the situations where a sales contract exists which we have considered in this section.

5.4   ACCOUNTING DATE

As a property developer or dealer, you may choose any accounting date you like and do not have to stick with a 5th April year end. This provides some useful tax-planning opportunities.

For example, if you feel that you are likely to make more sales in the late Spring and Summer, a 30th April accounting date may be very useful.

Profits made on sales in May or June 2017 would then form part of your accounting profit for the year ending 30th April 2018. For tax purposes, this accounting period falls into the 2018/19 tax year, as it is generally the accounts year end date which determines when profits are taxable.

Under self-assessment, the Income Tax and NI due on these profits would not therefore be payable until 31st January 2020, almost *three years* after you made the sales!

Early Years

There are special rules which apply in the first two or three years of a trading business which would lead to a different effect: sometimes more beneficial and sometimes less so. Generally, in these early years, if your profit is static, or increasing, you will benefit from an accounting date early in the tax year, such as 30th April.

This usually results in some of your early profits being taxed twice (in two different tax years), but the tax on your later profits is effectively deferred by a year. You will ultimately get a deduction, known as 'overlap relief', for the profits which have been taxed twice, when you cease trading, or sometimes earlier if you change your accounting date.

Tax Tip
It is worth noting that transferring a trading business to a company counts as ceasing to trade for this purpose and hence will trigger any overlap relief which is due (see Section 5.12 for further benefits if this creates a loss).

If you are starting on high profits and expect them to fall thereafter, then a 31st March or 5th April accounting date will generally be preferable.

At present, accounting periods ending during your first three tax years of trading can generally be of almost any duration. Thereafter, you are generally expected to prepare accounts for twelve month periods, unless you change your accounting date.

Under the current rules, you can change your accounting date at any time, although, for the change to be recognised for tax purposes, you cannot generally make a second change within five tax years of a previous change.

Future Rules on Accounting Dates

As part of the proposals for MTD (see Section 3.12), the Government is considering some changes to the rules for accounting periods. The proposals, in brief, are:

- It will be possible to have accounting periods of any length up to twelve months (but never longer)
- The taxable profit for each tax year will be the sum of the taxable profits for all accounting periods ending during that year
- The current 'early years' rules (see above) will be abolished
- Those with an existing entitlement to overlap relief will only be able to claim relief on the cessation of their trade

As with the other MTD proposals, these changes are not certain and will not apply before April 2020 at the earliest.

Tax Tip
Those with an existing entitlement to overlap relief may wish to consider a change of accounting date before April 2020 in order to obtain relief earlier rather than wait until they cease trading. See the Taxcafe.co.uk guide *'Small Business Tax Saving Tactics'* for further details.

5.5   NATIONAL INSURANCE

Unlike a property investment business, the profits of a property trade are regarded as 'earnings' for NI purposes. This means that property dealers or developers operating on their own as sole traders, jointly with one or more other people, or in a more formal partnership structure, will be liable for Class 2 and Class 4 NI.

Class 2

Class 2 NI is to be abolished from 6th April 2018. For its final year of operation, it is being charged at the rate of £2.85 per week. Taxpayers with profits below the 'small earnings exception' limit (£6,025 for 2017/18) are exempt. Since 2015/16, Class 2 has been collected through self-assessment, although it is not included within the instalments due under that system.

Class 4

The abolition of Class 2 had been expected to be linked to a reform of Class 4. Indeed increases in the main rate of Class 4 were announced in the March 2017 Budget. However, in the fastest U-turn I have ever seen from a Chancellor, Philip Hammond quickly backed down and scrapped the planned increases. Nonetheless, future increases do still remain likely, albeit probably not until 2021.

For the time being then, Class 4 NI remains payable on trading profits at the rates set out in Appendix A. The profits on which it is based are generally the same trading profits as those calculated for Income Tax purposes.

For profits falling to be taxed in 2017/18, this has the result of giving most property traders with no other sources of income the following overall effective tax rates, combining Income Tax and Class 4 NI:

Profits up to £8,164:	Nil
Profits between £8,164 and £11,500:	9%
Profits between £11,500 and £45,000:	29%
Profits between £45,000 and £100,000:	42%
Profits between £100,000 and £123,000:	62%
Profits between £123,000 and £150,000:	42%
Profits over £150,000:	47%

Taxpayers are exempt from both Class 2 and Class 4 NI if they:

i)   Have reached state pension age (see below) on or before the first day of the relevant tax year, or
ii) Are aged under 16 on the last day of the tax year

National Insurance for Property Traders in Practice

To see the impact of NI, let's revisit an earlier example.

Example
In Section 3.4, we saw that Meera was paying a total of £3,800 in Income Tax under self-assessment for 2017/18. Let us now assume that Meera is a property developer and her £12,000 of property income is a property trading profit. In addition to her Income Tax bill, therefore, Meera will also be liable for Class 4 NI of £345 (9% of £12,000 less £8,164) and Class 2 NI of £148, bringing her total self-assessment tax liability up to £4,293.

Taxpayers like Meera with both employment and self-employed trading income may end up paying more NI than the law demands. This can arise where there is more than one source of earned income and the total income from all such sources exceeds the sum of:

i)   The upper threshold (currently £45,000), and
ii) The primary threshold (currently £8,164)

For the 2017/18 tax year, the relevant sum is £53,164.

In such cases, taxpayers may apply for a refund of the excess NI paid or, if they are able to foresee that this situation is likely to arise, apply for a deferment of their Class 2 or Class 4 contributions.

Tax Tip
If you are already in receipt of other earnings and anticipate that your property trading profits will result in your total earnings for the tax year exceeding £53,164 you may wish to consider applying for deferment of NI.

Remember that 'earnings' is generally restricted to employment income and self-employed or partnership trading income. It does not include pensions, rental income or other investment income.

State Pension Age

Taxpayers over state pension age on the first day of the relevant tax year are exempt from both Class 2 and Class 4 NI. This includes taxpayers reaching state pension age on 6th April. The current state pension age is 65 for men and somewhere between 64 and 65 for women. The state pension age for women will continue to increase until it reaches 65 towards the end of 2018. The state pension age for both genders will then increase from December 2018 onwards.

5.6   COMMENCING A PROPERTY TRADE

When you commence a new property trade, you will generally need to register with HMRC as a self-employed trader within three months from the end of the calendar month in which you commence your trade.

> **Wealth Warning**
> Failure to register as a self-employed trader within three months of the commencement of trading is subject to a penalty of £100.

In the case of a partnership or joint owners, each individual must register. If any person is already registered due to some other existing source of self-employment trading income, there is no need to register again.

5.7   TRADING DEDUCTIONS: GENERAL

Some individuals or partnerships with small property trades may be able to elect to use the cash basis which we will look at in Section 5.13. Apart from that, the basic principles outlined in Sections 3.8 and 3.9 apply to the deduction of business expenditure from trading profits. Many of the points discussed in Chapter 4 will also remain relevant.

As we already know, under general principles, expenditure must usually be 'revenue expenditure' if it is to be claimed for Income Tax purposes. As we have seen, however, this rule operates quite differently in the context of a property trade. Expenditure on long-term assets for use in the trade will nevertheless continue to be capital in nature, including:

- Office premises from which to run the trade
- Motor vehicles for use in the trade
- Computers
- Building tools and equipment

Capital allowances will be available on much of this expenditure as we shall see in Section 5.10.

Expenses incurred which are ancillary to the purchase of capital assets continue to be treated as capital expenditure also. Hence, whilst the legal fees incurred on the purchase of trading stock are a revenue expense, similar fees incurred on the purchase of the business's own trading premises will be capital in nature.

5.8   MILEAGE RATES

As an alternative to claiming a proportion of actual running costs for any vehicle used in the business, individuals or partnerships carrying on trading businesses may claim business mileage at the approved rates.

For cars and vans, the rate is 45p per mile for the first 10,000 business miles travelled in each tax year, and 25p per mile thereafter. For motorcycles, a single flat rate of 24p per business mile may be claimed.

If claiming fixed mileage rate deductions, it is essential to keep a mileage log (although a mileage log is advisable in any case).

This method has the advantage of simplicity but does have some drawbacks. If claiming business mileage rates you cannot also claim any running costs or capital allowances (see Section 3.10) for the vehicle; although you can claim a proportion of any finance costs, where relevant.

Once you have chosen one method or the other (i.e. either fixed mileage rates, or a proportion of actual running costs and capital allowances), you must stick to that method throughout your ownership of the vehicle.

5.9   TRADING DEDUCTIONS: SPECIFIC AREAS

Most forms of business expenditure which meet the criteria outlined in Section 3.8 should be allowable as deductions from trading income. These will include the items which we covered in Section 3.9.

There are a few exceptions which are specifically disallowed, such as business entertaining and gifts. (Even here there can be exceptions to the exceptions.)

In this section, we will quickly look at some of the other main trading deductions to be considered in the specific context of a property trade. As in Chapter 4, however, this is certainly not meant to be an exhaustive list of potential trading expenses.

Interest and Finance Costs

Interest is allowable if it is incurred on funds used for the purposes of the trade. The question of where the borrowings are secured is generally irrelevant (although borrowings secured on the business's own trading premises will follow the same principles as set out in Section 4.4).

The treatment of other finance costs, such as loan arrangement fees, will generally follow the same principles. However, where accounting principles dictate that a cost should be spread over the useful life of the loan, the tax relief will have to be spread over the same period (again following the principles discussed in Section 4.4).

The restrictions on tax relief for interest and finance costs discussed in Section 4.5 do not apply to property trades. Restrictions may, however, apply where properties are temporarily rented out and thus give rise to incidental letting income, as discussed in Sections 2.4 and 2.5.

Legal and Professional Fees

Legal fees and other professional costs incurred on the successful purchase or sale of properties classed as trading stock will be allowed as part of the cost of those properties in the computation of the profits arising on sale. However, costs relating to the purchase or sale of the business's long-term assets remain capital expenses. Other professional costs incurred year in, year out, in earning trading profits may include items such as debt collection expenses and accountancy fees. These costs are deductible as overheads of the business.

Abortive Expenditure

In a property development or dealing trade, abortive costs such as survey fees, advertising or legal fees relating to unsuccessful transactions should be allowed as a trading expense. This should also extend to the costs of any unsuccessful planning applications attempted in the course of the trade. Costs relating to your own business premises are an exception and should be dealt with as discussed in Section 4.6.

Training

The rule here is that expenses incurred in updating or expanding existing areas of knowledge may be claimed, but any costs relating to entirely new areas of knowledge are a personal capital expense. Hence, if you are already a competent plumber but go on a plumbing course to learn the latest techniques in the industry then the cost of this course should be allowable. The cost of the same course would, however, not be allowable if you knew nothing about plumbing.

Health & Safety

Notwithstanding the general rules given in Section 3.8, any expenditure on safety boots, hard hats and other protective clothing or equipment will be allowable. This may sometimes extend to 'all-weather' clothing if the taxpayer spends all or part of their working life outdoors and does not use that clothing for any non-business purposes.

5.10 CAPITAL ALLOWANCES FOR PROPERTY TRADES

The basic principles of capital allowances were explained in Section 3.10. Items typically qualifying as 'plant and machinery' include the following:

- Building equipment and tools
- Computers
- Office furniture, fixtures and fittings
- Vans

Property developers are likely to have greater scope to claim capital allowances than residential property investors but possibly less scope than those with commercial properties. Property dealers and those with property management businesses will not usually be able to claim quite as many allowances, although the same principles continue to apply.

Capital allowances cannot generally be claimed on any expenditure which is included within trading stock.

Capital allowances are available on motor cars used in a property trade, as again detailed in Section 3.10.

5.11 PROPERTY MANAGEMENT TRADES

Most of the principles outlined in this chapter apply equally to property management trades. The biggest difference is the fact that these trades are unlikely to hold properties as trading stock. Other than their own office premises, any properties held are likely to be investment properties and dealt with in accordance with Chapter 4.

Staff costs are often a significant issue in a property management trade. The NI consequences are examined in Section 7.17.

5.12   TRADING LOSSES

The general rule is that you may claim to set trading losses off against your total income for the same tax year and/or the previous one. Where you have claimed to set your losses off against income in one of these years (or you have no such income), you may also claim to set any further losses remaining against capital gains arising in the same year. This gives rise to a number of possible choices (I count eight!)

Any surplus loss remaining is automatically carried forward for set off against future profits from the same trade. This effectively gives rise to a ninth choice: make no claim under the above provisions and carry all of your losses forward.

Under a separate provision, losses arising in any of the first four tax years of a new trade may also be carried back against your total income in the three tax years prior to the loss-making year. The loss is relieved against earlier years first.

Under yet another provision, known as 'terminal loss relief', losses arising in the last twelve months of a trade (including 'overlap relief' – see Section 5.4) may be carried back against profits from the same trade arising in the final tax year of the trade and the previous three tax years. In this case, the loss is relieved against the most recent years first.

As we can see, there are many possible ways in which to relieve trading losses, especially in the early years of a new business. The best choice will depend on the effective tax rates applying in each year and the likelihood of you making profits from the same trade in the future. You generally have until one year after the 31st January following the tax year to decide (the deadline for making claims under most of the above provisions). For example, a claim in respect of a loss arising during 2017/18 must generally be made by 31st January 2020. Whatever choice you make, it is important to remember that the same loss can only ever be relieved once.

For the purpose of the above rules, partners are treated as commencing a trade when they join a trading partnership and as ceasing to trade when they leave the partnership.

Sole traders or partnerships transferring a trade to a company (often known as 'incorporation') are treated as ceasing to trade on the date of the transfer. Note, however, that any losses which cannot be relieved under any of the above provisions will effectively be lost: they cannot be transferred to the company.

Loss Relief Restrictions

Where trading losses are being set off against income (not capital gains), the relief is subject to the tax relief 'cap' discussed in Section 3.11. This does not apply where the losses are being set off against profits from the same trade, or to the extent that the losses include 'overlap relief' (see Section 5.4).

In addition, a 'non-active sole trader' may only claim tax relief against his or her other income and gains for a maximum of just £25,000 of trading losses each year.

Personally, I find the term 'non-active sole trader' to be as much of a contradiction in terms as an 'honest politician', but it is taken to mean someone who spends less than ten hours per week engaged in trading activities. Sadly, this restriction may hit many part-time property developers and other property traders. For those whose business activities average only just over the ten hours per week threshold, it will make sense to keep diaries or other time records to demonstrate hours spent.

Loss relief is also barred for trading losses of a 'non-active sole trader' arising as a result of arrangements made for tax avoidance purposes.

Similar restrictions apply to 'non-active partners' (see Section 8.32).

5.13 THE CASH BASIS FOR TRADING BUSINESSES

Individuals and partnerships with small trading businesses may elect to be taxed under the 'cash basis'. Currently, this is generally available to businesses with an annual turnover (i.e. total sales) not exceeding £150,000. Prior to 2017/18, it was generally only available where the annual turnover of the business did not exceed the VAT registration threshold (£83,000 for 2016/17).

Those already using the cash basis may continue to do so provided their turnover does not exceed the 'exit threshold'. This threshold is currently £300,000. Prior to 2017/18, it was set at an amount equal to twice the VAT threshold (e.g. £166,000 for 2016/17).

Businesses electing to use the cash basis are taxed simply on the difference between business income received during the year and business expenses paid during the year, instead of under normal accounting principles (the 'accruals basis' – see Section 3.8).

Where the cash basis is being used, there is no distinction between 'revenue expenditure' and 'capital expenditure' (see Section 3.8) and capital expenditure may simply be claimed as it is paid, except that:

- Expenditure on the purchase of cars is not allowed on a cash basis. Motor expenses must continue to be claimed under one of the two alternative methods described in Sections 3.9 and 5.8.

- The cost of vans or motor cycles may be claimed on a cash basis, but if the purchase cost is claimed in this way, the mileage allowances described in Section 5.8 will not be available.

- Capital expenditure may only be claimed under the cash basis where it would otherwise normally be eligible for capital allowances as 'plant and machinery' (see Section 5.10).

In addition to these restrictions, businesses using the cash basis are limited to a maximum claim of £500 per year in respect of interest on cash borrowings. Losses arising under the cash basis can only be carried forward for set off against future profits from the same trade and will not be eligible for the other reliefs described in Section 5.12.

In view of these restrictions, and the turnover limits described above, it seems unlikely that the cash basis will benefit many property developers or dealers. A few property management businesses might perhaps benefit but, again, the restrictions on loss relief and interest relief will often make the cash basis unattractive.

5.14 THE TRADING INCOME ALLOWANCE

The Government is proposing to introduce a new allowance of £1,000 to exempt small amounts of trading income from 2017/18 onwards. Where the taxpayer's total gross trading income for the tax year exceeds the £1,000 allowance, they will be able to either deduct expenses as normal, or deduct the allowance from the total income.

The allowance is not available against income from the trader's own partnership or company (the same rules apply as for the property income allowance – see Section 4.17).

Chapter 6

How to Save Capital Gains Tax

6.1 THE IMPORTANCE OF CAPITAL GAINS TAX

Although its impact is not as immediate as Income Tax, CGT is perhaps the most significant tax from a property investor's perspective (though not those who are classed as property developers or property dealers, as we have already seen).

Most property investments will eventually lead to a disposal and every property disposal presents the risk of a CGT liability arising and reducing the investor's after-tax return drastically. Paradoxically, however, CGT is also the tax which presents the greatest number and variety of tax-planning opportunities. We will be examining some of these further in Chapter 8.

In this chapter, we will be examining the current CGT regime and taking a detailed look at how it affects property investors and other people disposing of property. Before we look at the current regime, however, it is worth recalling how CGT developed.

6.2 THE DEVELOPMENT OF CAPITAL GAINS TAX

CGT was introduced by Harold Wilson's first Labour Government in 1965 to combat a growing trend for avoiding Income Tax by realising capital gains, which at that time were mostly tax free.

The high inflation of the 1970s and early 1980s brought about a significant change after March 1982, with the introduction of indexation relief. This was designed to exempt gains which arose purely through the effects of inflation.

In 1987, CGT moved from a flat rate of 30% to a system which was to last for 21 years, where gains were taxed at the taxpayer's top rate of Income Tax. The next major change came in 1988, when 're-basing' exempted all pre-March 1982 gains.

In 1997, Gordon Brown took over as Chancellor and a new CGT regime soon began. Over the next few years he introduced, and then refined, his brainchild: taper relief. This was designed to reward long-term investment by progressively reducing the effective rate of CGT as investments were held over a longer period. Eventually, we reached the point where the effective CGT rate on most commercial property was just 10%.

Then, suddenly, the golden days were over and, in 2008, Alistair Darling abolished both taper relief and indexation relief and, after 21 years, took us back to a flat rate system: this time at 18%.

Two years later, the Coalition Government took us into a 'two tier' CGT system by introducing a 'higher rate' of 28%. Then, in April 2016, this expanded to a 'four tier' system with the introduction of new, lower, rates of 10% and 20% for capital gains on most assets; but not on residential property.

Finally then, now that every major political party has 'stuck their oar in', we find ourselves lumbered with a CGT system where there is no protection against the effects of inflation, no reward for long-term investment and an effective penalty for investing in residential property!

In fact, what the current system actually means is that, when you do hold property as a long-term investment, inflation alone is likely to push you into a higher tax rate. And this makes understanding the tax system, the reliefs available, and the planning opportunities they give rise to, more important than ever!

6.3   WHO PAYS CAPITAL GAINS TAX?

CGT is currently payable in the UK by:

i)   UK resident individuals
ii)   UK resident trusts
iii)   Non-UK resident persons disposing of UK residential property
iv)   Non-UK resident persons trading in the UK through a branch, agency or other permanent establishment
v)   Companies and other 'non-natural' persons disposing of UK residential dwellings worth more than £500,000

The UK CGT regime applying to non-UK resident persons disposing of UK residential property is covered in detail in the Taxcafe.co.uk guide *'Tax Free Capital Gains'*. This regime applies to gains arising after 5th April 2015 on disposals made by non-UK resident individuals and trusts, as well as many non-UK resident companies.

The regime for companies and other 'non-natural' persons under (v) above does not apply where properties are used entirely for business purposes. This regime is also covered in detail in the Taxcafe.co.uk guide *'Tax Free Capital Gains'* since, although it applies equally to both UK resident and non-UK resident entities, the majority of the entities which are caught will be non-UK resident.

For the rest of this guide, I will be concentrating mainly on category (i) above: UK resident individuals investing in property.

Individuals who are UK resident and UK domiciled are liable for CGT on their worldwide capital gains. Individuals who are UK resident but not UK domiciled remain liable for CGT on capital gains arising from the disposal of UK property but may opt to only be liable for CGT on 'foreign' capital gains if and when they remit their disposal proceeds back to the UK (see Section 8.25).

The tax concepts of residence and domicile were examined in Section 3.7. For a detailed look at the rules on residence, see the Taxcafe.co.uk guide *'Tax Free Capital Gains'*.

6.4   CAPITAL GAINS TAX RATES

CGT is currently paid at five rates:

- 10% where entrepreneurs' relief is available
- 18% on gains on residential property made by basic rate taxpayers
- 28% on gains on residential property made by higher rate taxpayers
- 10% on most other gains made by basic rate taxpayers
- 20% on most other gains made by higher rate taxpayers

The 18% and 28% rates apply to:

- Any interest in land or property that has ever included a residential dwelling at any time during the taxpayer's ownership
- Contracts for off-plan purchases of residential property
- Companies and other 'non-natural' persons disposing of UK residential dwellings worth more than £500,000 (these gains are taxed at 28%)
- A few other, very limited, cases

Entrepreneurs' relief is seldom available to property investors, except in the case of furnished holiday lets (see Section 8.17). The relief may, however, be highly valuable to property developers, property dealers and those with property management businesses and we will therefore look at it in detail in Section 6.28.

The 'Higher Rates' of CGT

The higher rates of 20% or 28% apply to capital gains made by an individual to the extent that:

i)   Their total taxable income for the tax year (after deducting their personal allowance), plus
ii)   Their total taxable capital gains arising during the tax year,

Exceeds the basic rate band (see Appendix A).

The basic rate band for 2017/18 is normally £33,500, although this can be increased by making pension contributions or gift aid donations. Individuals who have sufficient income to fully utilise their basic rate band pay CGT at the higher rates on all their taxable capital gains.

Basic rate taxpayers pay CGT at 10% or 18% on the first part of their capital gains until their basic rate band is exhausted. Thereafter, any further gains are taxed at the higher rates.

In all cases, the rate applying is reduced to 10% where entrepreneurs' relief is available (see Section 6.28).

> **Tax Tip**
> The rate of CGT you pay is linked to the amount of income you have in the tax year. This means that you may be able to reduce your CGT bill by ensuring that your gains fall into a tax year in which you have a lower level of income. We will take a closer look at the potential savings arising in Section 8.30.

Example
Boudicca is a property investor with several 'buy-to-let' investments. In December 2017, she sells a residential property and realises a gain of £49,300.

Boudicca's taxable income for 2017/18 is £30,000. Deducting her personal allowance of £11,500 (see Appendix A) means that £18,500 of her basic rate band has been utilised, leaving £15,000 (£33,500 – £18,500) available for CGT purposes.

Boudicca deducts her annual exemption of £11,300 (see Section 6.29) from the £49,300 gain, leaving a taxable gain of £38,000. The first £15,000 is taxed at 18% and the remainder at 28%, giving her a CGT bill of:

£15,000 x 18% =   £2,700
£23,000 x 28% =   £6,440
Total   £9,140

As explained above, the basic rate band can be extended through the payment of pension contributions or gift aid donations. This simple way to save CGT is explored further in Section 8.30.

Allocating the Annual Exemption and Capital Losses

Taxpayers are generally free to allocate their annual exemption (see Section 6.29), their basic rate band, and any capital losses which they have available (see Section 6.33), between their capital gains in the most beneficial manner.

This will be useful for anyone who has both gains on residential property and other gains arising during the same tax year. In general, it will be preferable to allocate the annual exemption and any available capital losses to the gains on residential property, although the allocation of the basic rate band will usually have no overall effect (there is usually a 10% differential in the tax rate applying in either case).

It will also make sense to allocate the annual exemption and any available capital losses to gains which are *not* eligible for entrepreneurs' relief: although any available basic rate band *must* be utilised against these gains in priority to any others.

Effective Capital Gains Tax Rates

The CGT rates described above apply to the taxable capital gain, not the total gain. The *effective* rates of CGT can vary tremendously, depending on the circumstances.

6.5   WHAT IS A CAPITAL GAIN?

A capital gain is the profit arising on the disposal, in whole or in part, of an asset, or an interest in an asset. Put simply, the gain is the excess obtained on the sale of the asset over the price paid to buy it. (However, as we will see, matters rarely remain that simple.)

Sometimes, however, assets are held in such a way that their disposal gives rise to an Income Tax charge instead. The same amount of gain cannot be subject to both Income Tax and CGT.

Where both taxes might apply, Income Tax takes precedence, so that no CGT arises. (There is little comfort in this, as Income Tax will generally be charged at a higher rate than CGT and is not subject to any of the various CGT reliefs.)

The most common type of asset sale which gives rise to an Income Tax charge, rather than CGT, is a sale in the course of a trade. In other words, where the asset is, or is deemed to be, trading stock.

If a person buys sweets to sell in their sweet shop, those sweets are quite clearly trading stock and the profits on their sale must be subject to Income Tax and not CGT. This is pretty obvious because there are usually only two things you can do with sweets: eat them or sell them.

Properties, however, have a number of possible uses. A property purchaser may intend one or more of several objectives:

a) To keep for personal use, either as a main residence or otherwise
b) To provide a home for the use of family or friends
c) To use the property in a business
d) To let the property out for profit
e) To hold the property as an investment
f) To develop the property for profit
g) To sell the property on at a profit

Objectives (a) to (e) make the property a capital investment subject to CGT.

It has always been the case that, where objectives (f) and/or (g) are the sole or main purpose behind the purchase of the property, then this will render the ultimate gain on the property's sale a trading profit subject to Income Tax. As discussed in Section 2.9, from 5th July 2016, the ultimate gain may now be treated as a trading profit where these objectives are merely **one of the main purposes** behind the purchase of the property.

In the majority of cases, objective (g) is present to some degree. This does not necessarily render the gain on the property's sale a trading profit subject to Income Tax. This point is discussed further in Section 2.9.

In practice, there is often more than one objective present when a property is purchased and objectives (f) and (g) may exist to a lesser or greater extent. In many cases, the correct position is obvious but, in borderline situations, each case has to be decided on its own merits.

Some of the key factors to consider are described in Section 2.9. Here though, it is perhaps worth looking at a few more detailed examples.

Example 1
James bought a house in 1990 which he used as his main residence throughout his ownership. In 2005 he built an extension, which substantially increased the value. He continued to live in the house until eventually selling it in 2017.

This is clearly a capital gain because James carried on using the house as his private residence for several years after building the extension. Furthermore, the house will be exempt from CGT, as it was James's main residence throughout his ownership.

Example 2

Charles bought a house in 1990 and used it as his main residence for five years. In 1995, he moved into a new house and converted the first one into a number of flats. Following the conversion, Charles let the flats out until he eventually sold the whole property in 2017.

Charles has also realised a capital gain as the property was initially acquired as his own home, he occupied it for five years, and the conversion work was clearly intended as a long-term investment. (Charles would have a partial exemption under the main residence rules.)

Example 3

William, a wealthy man with three other properties, bought a derelict barn in 2016. He developed it into a luxury home. Immediately after the development work was complete, he put the property on the market and sold it in early 2018.

This would appear to be a trading profit subject to Income Tax. William simply developed the property for profit and never put it to any other use. (But see Section 2.9 regarding the importance of the investor's original intentions.)

Example 4

Anne bought an old farmhouse in 2017. She lived in the property for three months and then moved out while substantial renovation work took place. After the work was completed, she let it out for six months. Halfway through the period of the lease she put the property on the market and sold it with completion taking place the day the lease expired.

This is what one would call 'borderline'. Anne has had some personal use of the property, and has let it out, but she has also developed it and sold it after only a short period of ownership. This case would warrant a much closer look at all of the circumstances. It <u>should</u> be decided on the basis of Anne's intentions but who, apart from Anne herself, would ever know what these truly were?

Such a case could go either way. The more Anne can do to demonstrate that her intention had been to hold the property as a long-term investment, the better her chances of success will be. Her personal and financial circumstances will be crucial. For example, if she had got married around the time of the sale, or had got into unexpected financial difficulties, which had forced her to make the sale, then she might successfully argue for CGT treatment.

Note that, just because the profit arising on the sale is a capital gain, this does not necessarily mean that it is subject to CGT. A number of assets may be exempt from CGT, including motor cars, medals and Government securities.

Most importantly for property investors, the taxpayer's only or main residence is also exempt and we will return to this in Section 6.13.

The bad news is that no relief is allowed for capital losses derived from exempt assets.

6.6   WHEN DOES A CAPITAL GAIN ARISE?

For CGT purposes, a disposal is treated as taking place as soon as there is an unconditional contract for the sale of an asset. The effective disposal date may therefore often be somewhat earlier than the date of completion of the sale. This is an absolutely vital point to remember when undertaking any CGT planning.

Example
Aidan completes the sale of an investment property on 8th April 2018. However, the unconditional sale contract was signed on 1st April 2018. Aidan's sale therefore falls into the tax year ending on 5th April 2018 and any CGT due will be payable by 31st January 2019. The effective acceleration of Aidan's CGT bill is bad enough, but what if he had also emigrated on 3rd April 2018?

Where the contract remains conditional on some event beyond the control of the parties to it, then the sale is not yet deemed to have taken place for CGT purposes. The most common scenarios here are for the sale to be conditional on:

- The granting of planning permission
- Completion of a satisfactory survey
- Approval of finance arrangements

Many English investors who have travelled north of the border get caught out by the Scottish system where the conclusion of missives generally creates an unconditional binding contract.

What if there is no sale?

The conclusion of an unconditional contract only determines the **date** of the disposal for CGT purposes. If the sale subsequently falls through, then no sale will have taken place and there will be no disposal for CGT purposes.

6.7 SPOUSES AND CIVIL PARTNERS

There are a number of cases where, although an asset is held as a capital investment, there is deemed to be no gain and no loss arising on a disposal.

The most important instance of this is that of transfers between spouses or registered civil partners. The effect of this is that these transfers are **totally exempt** from CGT.

The exemption comes into force on the date of marriage or registration and continues to apply for the whole of any tax year during any part of which the couple are living together as spouses or civil partners.

Separated couples remain 'connected persons' (see Section 6.9) even after the exemption has been lost. Divorced couples only become unconnected persons for tax purposes once more after the grant of a decree absolute.

Wealth Warning
If the couple separate, the exemption ceases to apply at the end of the tax year of separation.

6.8 THE AMOUNT OF THE GAIN

Having established that a gain is subject to CGT, we now need to work out how much the gain is.

The essence of this is that the gain should be the excess obtained on the sale of the asset over the price paid to buy it. However, in practice, thanks to the many complexities introduced by tax legislation over more than 50 years, there are a large number of other factors to be taken into account.

Hence, one has to slightly amend the definition to the following:

'A capital gain is the excess of the actual or deemed proceeds arising on the disposal of an asset over that same asset's base cost.'

A shorter version of this is: Gain = Proceeds Less Base Cost

The derivation of 'Proceeds' is examined in Section 6.9 below. 'Base Cost' is covered in Sections 6.10 and 6.11.

6.9 PROCEEDS

In most cases, the amount of 'Proceeds' to be used in the calculation of a capital gain will be the actual sum received on the disposal of the asset. However, from this, the taxpayer may deduct incidental disposal costs in order to arrive at 'net proceeds', which is the relevant sum for the purposes of calculating the capital gain.

Incidental disposal costs which may be deducted from sales proceeds include any expenditure incurred wholly and exclusively for the purpose of making the sale, such as legal fees, estate agents' commission, advertising costs and the cost of producing a 'Seller's Pack'.

Professional fees incurred for the preparation of valuations required for CGT purposes may also be included in disposal costs.

Example
In July 2017, George sells a house for £375,000. In order to make this sale, he spent £1,500 advertising the property, paid £3,750 in estate agents' fees and paid £800 in legal fees. His net proceeds are therefore £368,950 (£375,000 LESS £1,500, £3,750 and £800).

Now this sounds very simple, but it is not always this easy.

Exceptions

There are a number of cases where the proceeds we must use in the calculation of a capital gain are not simply the actual cash sum received. Three of the most common exceptions are set out below.

Exception 1 – Connected persons

Where the person disposing of the asset is 'connected' to the person acquiring it, the open market value at the time of the transfer must be used in place of the actual price paid (if any). Connected persons include:

- Husband, wife or registered civil partner (but note that no gain usually arises in such transfers)
- Mother, father or remoter ancestor
- Son, daughter or remoter descendant
- Brother or sister
- Mother-in-law, father-in-law, son-in-law, daughter-in-law, brother-in-law or sister-in-law
- Business partners
- Companies under the control of the other party to the transaction or of any of his/her relatives as above
- A trust where the other party to the transaction, or any of his/her relatives as above, is a beneficiary

Example
Mary sells a property to her son Philip for £500,000, at a time when its market value is £800,000. She pays legal fees of £475. Mary will be deemed to have

received net sale proceeds of £800,000 (the market value). The legal fees she has borne are irrelevant, as this was not an 'arm's-length' transaction.

Exception 2 – Transactions not at 'arms-length'

Where a transaction takes place between 'connected persons' as above, there is an automatic assumption that the transaction is not at 'arm's-length' and market value must be substituted for the actual proceeds.

There are, however, other instances where the transaction may not be at 'arm's-length', such as:

- The transfer of an asset from one partner in an unmarried couple to the other
- A sale of an asset to an employee
- A transaction which is part of a larger transaction
- A transaction which is part of a series of transactions

The effect of these is much the same as before – the asset's market value must be used in place of the actual proceeds, if any.

The key difference from Exception 1 is that it's the circumstances involved in the transaction which determine whether or not it's at 'arm's-length', rather than there being an automatic assumption that it is not at 'arm's-length' simply because of the relationship between the parties.

Example
John has a house worth £200,000. If he sold it for this amount, he would have a capital gain of £80,000. Not wishing to incur a CGT liability, John decides instead to sell the house to his friend Richard for £120,000. However, John only does this on condition that Richard also gives him an interest-free loan of £80,000 for an indefinite period.

The condition imposed by John means that this transaction is not at 'arm's-length'. The correct position is that John should be deemed to have sold the house for £200,000 and still have a capital gain of £80,000.

Wealth Warning
Where a person has disposed of an asset at less than an 'arm's length' value, whether to a connected person or not, there is a danger of Income Tax charges arising if the original owner later makes any use of, or derives any benefit from, the transferred asset. IHT charges may also arise if the original owner dies within seven years of making the transfer.

These charges do not apply to transfers between spouses however.

Exception 3 – Non-cash proceeds

Sometimes all or part of the sale consideration will take a form other than cash. The sale proceeds to be taken into account in these cases will be the market value of the assets or rights received in exchange for the asset sold.

Example

Matilda is an elderly widow with a large house. She no longer needs such a large house, so she offers it to Stephen, who lives nearby with his wife and young children. Rather than pay the whole amount in cash, Stephen offers £150,000 plus his own much smaller house, which is worth £200,000.

Matilda incurs legal fees of £2,400 on the transaction and also pays SDLT of £1,500 to acquire Stephen's house. 75% of the legal fees are for the sale of her old house and the rest for the purchase of Stephen's house.

Matilda's total sale proceeds are £350,000. This is made up of the cash received plus the market value of the non-cash consideration received, i.e. Stephen's house. Matilda may deduct her incidental costs of disposal from her proceeds in her CGT calculation. This is unaltered by the existence of non-cash consideration: the transaction has still taken place on 'arm's-length' terms.

However, as far as her legal fees are concerned, it is only the element which relates to the disposal of her old house (£1,800) which may be deducted.

The element relating to the purchase of Stephen's house will be treated as an acquisition cost of that house, as will the SDLT Matilda paid.

Hence, the net sale proceeds to be used in Matilda's CGT calculation are £348,200 (£350,000 LESS £1,800).

6.10 BASE COST

The 'Base Cost' is the amount which may be deducted in the CGT calculation in respect of the cost of the asset being disposed of. The higher the base cost, the less CGT payable!

In most cases, the basic starting point will be the actual amount paid. To this may be added:

- Incidental acquisition costs (e.g. legal fees, SDLT)
- Enhancement expenditure (e.g. the cost of building an extension)
- Expenditure incurred in establishing, preserving or defending title to, or rights over, the asset (e.g. legal fees incurred as a result of a boundary dispute)

Interest payable and any other costs associated with raising finance, i.e. mortgaging or re-mortgaging the property, cannot be included in the base cost. For rental property, these are dealt with as set out in Sections 4.4 and 4.5.

Survey fees will often be part of the cost of raising finance, especially if the survey was only carried out at the lender's request. However, a survey carried out at the purchaser's own instigation prior to their making, or finalising, any offer for the property may be claimed as an acquisition cost for CGT purposes.

Any costs claimed for Income Tax purposes cannot also be claimed for CGT purposes. As explained in Section 4.7 however, any expenditure on newly acquired rental properties which is not allowed for Income Tax purposes on the grounds that it is capital in nature should be allowed for CGT purposes on the disposal of that property.

Example
George (remember him from Section 6.9?) bought a house in July 1984 for £60,000. He paid Stamp Duty of £600, legal fees of £400 and removal expenses of £800.

Shortly after moving into the house, George spent £3,000 on redecorating it. £1,800 of this related to one of the bedrooms, which was in such a bad state of repair that it was unusable. The remainder of the redecorating expenditure merely covered repainting and wallpapering the other rooms in the house.

In March 1985, George's neighbour erected a new fence a foot inside George's back garden, claiming this was the correct boundary. George had to take legal advice to resolve this problem, which cost him £250, but managed eventually to get the fence moved back to its original position.

In October 1987, the house's roof was badly damaged by hurricane-force winds. The repairs cost £20,000, which, unfortunately, George's insurance company refused to pay, claiming he was not covered for an 'Act of God'.

In May 1995, George did a loft conversion at a cost of £15,000, putting in new windows and creating an extra bedroom. Unfortunately, however, he had not obtained planning permission and, when his neighbour filed a complaint with the council, George was forced to restore the loft to its original condition at a further cost of £8,000.

In August 1998, George had the property extended at a cost of £80,000. He also incurred professional fees of £2,000 obtaining planning permission, etc.

When George eventually sold the property in July 2017 for £375,000, his base cost for the house for CGT purposes was made up as follows:

- *Original cost - £60,000*
- *Incidental costs of acquisition - £1,000 (legal fees and Stamp Duty, but not the removal expenses, which were a personal cost and not part of the capital cost of the property)*
- *Enhancement expenditure - £1,800 (restoration of the 'unusable' bedroom; the remaining redecoration costs are not allowable, however, as the other rooms were already in a fit state for habitation and George's expenditure was merely due to personal taste, rather than being a capital improvement)*
- *Expenditure incurred in defending title to the property - £250 (the legal fees relating to his neighbour's new fence)*
- *Further enhancement expenditure - £82,000 (the cost of the new extension, including the professional fees incurred to obtain planning permission)*

Total base cost: £145,050

Notes to the Example

i. If the house were George's only or main residence throughout his ownership, his gain would, in any case, be exempt from CGT. However, we are assuming that this is not the case here for the purposes of illustration.

ii. The cost of George's roof repairs do not form part of his base cost. This is not a capital improvement, but repairs and maintenance expenditure of a revenue nature.

iii. Neither the cost of George's loft conversion, nor the cost of returning the loft to its original condition, form part of his base cost. This is because enhancement or improvement expenditure can only be allowed in the capital gains calculation if the relevant 'improvements' are reflected in the state of the property at the time of the sale.

iv. Based on net proceeds of £368,950 (Section 6.9), George has a capital gain of £223,900 (£368,950 - £145,050) before any applicable reliefs.

Wealth Warning

An additional point to note under (iii) above is that enhancement or improvement expenditure is only deductible if still reflected in the state of the property at the date of <u>completion</u> of the sale.

Practical Pointer

In practice, George might perhaps be able to argue that part of the cost of the loft conversion was still reflected in the state of the property at the date of sale. It is always worth looking at these things in detail!

6.11   BASE COST – SPECIAL SITUATIONS

As with 'Proceeds', there are a number of special situations where base cost is determined by reference to something other than the amount paid for the asset. The major exceptions fall into two main categories:

- The asset was not acquired by way of a 'bargain at arm's length'
- The asset was acquired before 1st April 1982

Inherited Assets

All assets are 'rebased' for CGT purposes on death. Hence, the base cost of any inherited asset is determined by reference to its market value at the date of the previous owner's death.

Note that, whilst transfers on death are exempt from CGT, they are, of course, subject to IHT. See the Taxcafe.co.uk guide *'How to Save Inheritance Tax'* for further details.

Example 1
Albert died on 20th January 2001, leaving his holiday home, a cottage on the Isle of Wight, to his son Edward. The property was valued at £150,000 for probate purposes. In August 2002, Edward had a swimming pool built at the cottage at a cost of £40,000. He sold the cottage for £297,000 in March 2018.

Edward's base cost is £190,000. His own improvement expenditure (£40,000) is added to the market value of the property when he inherited it. Any expenditure incurred by Albert is, however, completely irrelevant.

Assets acquired from spouses

As explained in Section 6.7, when an asset is transferred between spouses, that transfer is treated as taking place on a no gain/no loss basis. In the case of a subsequent disposal, the transferee spouse effectively takes over the transferor spouse's base cost.

Example 2
Henry bought a house for £350,000 in 1999. He spent £100,000 on capital improvements and then gave the house to his wife Katherine in 2001. Katherine had the house extended in 2003 at a cost of £115,000 and eventually sold it in 2017 for £750,000. Katherine's base cost for the house is £565,000. This includes both her own expenditure and her husband's.

The 'no gain/no loss' rule does not apply in the case of a transfer on death, when the inheritance rules explained above take precedence.

Note that, where the transferor spouse originally acquired the property before April 1998 and transferred it to the transferee spouse before 6th April 2008 (but not on death), the indexation relief which the transferor would have been entitled to at that time (if they had actually sold the property) is added to the transferee spouse's base cost.

Example 3
Andrew bought a house for £100,000 in March 1985. In March 2008, he transferred the house to his wife Sarah. If Andrew had actually sold his house before 6th April 2008, he would have been entitled to indexation relief at 75.2%, i.e. £75,200. Sarah's base cost for the house is therefore £175,200.

Details of indexation relief rates which apply to a transfer between spouses at any time between 1st April 1998 and 5th April 2008 (inclusive) can be found in earlier editions of this guide.

Where a part share in a property has been transferred between spouses, the same principles continue to apply to the part which was transferred.

Assets acquired from connected persons or by way of a transaction not at 'arm's length'

As explained in Section 6.9 above, the transfer of an asset to a connected person is deemed to take place at market value. The market value rule also applies in other circumstances where an asset has not been acquired by way of a transaction at 'arm's length' ('Exception 2' in Section 6.9 provides further guidance).

In both cases, for the person acquiring an asset by way of such a transfer, the market value at that date becomes their base cost.

Assets with 'held-over gains'

From 6th April 1980 to 13th March 1989, it was possible to hold over the gain arising on the transfer of any asset by way of gift. Since then, it has only been possible to hold over gains arising on transfers by way of gift which are:

- Transfers of qualifying business assets, or
- Chargeable transfers for IHT purposes

Gains may not be held over on transfers into a 'settlor-interested trust' after 9th December 2003. This is a trust which includes the transferor, their spouse or, from 6th April 2006, a dependent minor child of the transferor, as one of its beneficiaries.

The base cost of an asset which was subject to a hold-over election when it was acquired is reduced by the amount of the held over gain.

Example 4
In January 1989, Arthur gave Camelot to his son Lancelot. Camelot's market value at that date was £100,000 and Arthur and Lancelot jointly elected to hold over Arthur's gain of £70,000. In 1990 Lancelot had the property extended for £55,000. Lancelot's base cost is £85,000 (£100,000 LESS £70,000 PLUS £55,000 – his own enhancement expenditure is still added on, as normal).

Where the held over gain arose before 6th April 2008, the amount held over will be the gain arising after any indexation relief. Hence, as with transfers between spouses (see above), where the transferor originally acquired the property before April 1998, the transferee's base cost will effectively include the indexation relief which the transferor would have been entitled to if they had actually sold the property.

Note that, whilst gains held over before 6th April 2008 were calculated after indexation relief, any taper relief which the transferor would have been entitled to is simply ignored. In other words, a held over gain preserved the transferor's indexation relief but their taper relief was lost.

Assets acquired for non-cash consideration

Where an asset was acquired for non-cash consideration, its base cost will be determined by reference to the market value of the consideration given.

Example 5
Julius bought a house in Chester from his friend Brutus. Instead of paying Brutus in cash, Julius gave him his ancient sword collection, which he had recently had valued at £125,000. Julius's base cost in the Chester house will therefore be £125,000.

Assets acquired before 1st April 1982

Where an asset was acquired before 1st April 1982, its market value at 31st March 1982 must be substituted for its original cost.

Example 6
Alfred bought a house for £20,000 in December 1981. He also incurred legal fees and other incidental costs of £1,000. The house's market value on 31st March 1982 was £19,750. Alfred's base cost is therefore £19,750. His original purchase cost and all other costs incurred prior to 1st April 1982 are ignored.

Where a property was originally acquired before 1st April 1982, any enhancement or improvement expenditure may only be included where it was incurred after 31st March 1982.

6.12 CAPITAL GAINS TAX RELIEFS

It is at this point in the CGT calculation, after deducting the base cost, that most reliefs and exemptions may be claimed, where appropriate. These include:

- Principal private residence relief (for taxpayers selling their current or former only or main residence). This is covered in detail from Section 6.13 onwards
- Private letting relief (where a property which is eligible for principal private residence relief has also been let out as private residential accommodation). See Section 6.14
- Relief for reinvestment of gains in Enterprise Investment Scheme shares or Seed Enterprise Investment Scheme shares (see Sections 8.21 and 8.23 for further details)
- Holdover relief on gifts of business assets
- Holdover relief in respect of chargeable transfers for IHT purposes
- Holdover relief on transfer of a business to a limited company
- Rollover relief on replacement of business assets (Section 8.29)

All these reliefs are claimed before entrepreneurs' relief, capital losses and the annual exemption. We shall look at these last three items later, but first we must look at the most important relief for the residential property investor: principal private residence relief.

6.13   THE PRINCIPAL PRIVATE RESIDENCE EXEMPTION

Most people are well aware that the sale of their own home is exempt from CGT. In technical terms, this is known as the principal private residence ('PPR') exemption. What is less well known is just how far PPR relief can extend, especially when combined with other available exemptions and reliefs.

Each unmarried individual, and each legally married couple, is entitled to the PPR exemption in respect of their only or main residence. The PPR exemption covers the period during which the property was their main residence PLUS their last eighteen months of ownership.

Example
Elizabeth bought a flat for £160,000 in January 2010. In January 2016, she married Philip and moved out of her flat. In July 2017, she receives an offer to sell the flat for £190,000, but is concerned about her potential tax liability.

Elizabeth needn't worry. If she makes this sale, her gain on the flat will be exempt under PPR relief. The first six years of her ownership are exempt because it was then her main residence and the last eighteen months because it was a former main residence.

What if the property has been let out?

Because the PPR exemption always extends to the final eighteen months of ownership of a former main residence, letting the property out for up to eighteen months after you have moved out of it will make no difference to your CGT position if you then go ahead and sell the property. (Income Tax is, of course, due on the rental profits.)

If you retain the property for more than eighteen months after it ceased to be your main residence, you will no longer be fully covered by the PPR exemption alone. However, at this point, as long as the property is being let out as private residential accommodation, another relief will come into play: private letting relief. We will examine this in the next section.

Does The Property Have to Become Your Main Residence Immediately on Purchase to Qualify?

To be **fully** exempt from CGT under the PPR exemption alone, the property will generally need to become your only or main residence immediately on purchase; or perhaps shortly afterwards, under the circumstances outlined in Section 6.17.

Practical Pointer
Technically, a property which was your only or main residence at some point and which you then sold no more than eighteen months after purchase should also be fully covered by PPR relief. However, such a short period of ownership could lead to doubts over whether the property was genuinely purchased as a capital asset (see Sections 2.9 and 6.5 for further details). Similarly, a very short period of occupation of the property can lead to doubts over whether it is genuinely a private residence (see Section 8.10). Nonetheless, where there are good reasons for the short period of ownership and residential occupation, full relief may be available.

If you don't fit one of the situations above, you won't be fully covered by PPR relief alone. However, you will still get a proportional relief based on your period of occupation of the property as your main residence, plus last eighteen months of ownership.

When combined with other reliefs, this will often be enough to prevent any CGT from arising, although you may have to report the gain on your tax return.

Example

Alexander buys a house in June 2011 as an investment and lets it out for two years. In June 2013, he sells his own home and moves into the new house. Alexander then sells the new house in June 2017. Alexander has used the house as his own main residence for four years out of six and hence he will be exempt on four sixths of his capital gain by virtue of PPR relief.

Alexander cannot benefit from the additional 'last eighteen months of ownership' rule because he was living in the house at the time anyway. The extra eighteen month period is not given in addition to an exemption for actual occupation during the same period. (He will, however, still be eligible for private letting relief, as we shall see in the next section.)

This is why when people ask me "do you need to live in the house at the beginning to get PPR relief?" I always answer "no, but it works best that way".

> **Tax Tip**
> Occupying a property as your only or main residence will produce the best result if this is not within the last eighteen months of your ownership.

What If Part Of The Property Is Unused?

The PPR exemption is not restricted merely because part of the property is left vacant and unused. Restrictions will apply, however, where part of the property is used for some purpose other than the owner's own private residential occupation.

6.14   PRIVATE LETTING RELIEF

In the previous section, we saw how the PPR exemption often extends to cover the capital gain on a former only or main residence for a further eighteen months after it ceases to be your own home.

Additionally, any property which qualifies as your only or main residence at any time during your period of ownership, and which you have, at some time, let out as private residential accommodation, will also qualify for private letting relief. This relief will also apply where you let out a part of your home.

Private letting relief is given as the lowest of:

i)   The amount of gain already exempted under PPR relief,
ii)   The gain arising as a consequence of the letting, and
iii) £40,000

Usually, it is the lower of (i) and (iii), especially if the property has been let out ever since the owner ceased to reside in it.

Example
Since marrying Philip in January 2016, Elizabeth has been renting her flat out. She turned down the July 2017 offer, but in January 2025 she receives an offer of £240,000. Again, she is concerned about her potential tax liability.

Elizabeth still has nothing to worry about. As before, a total of seven and a half years of her ownership is exempt under PPR relief. Her total gain over 15 years is £80,000. Half of this (7½ out of 15) is covered by PPR relief, leaving £40,000, which is covered by private letting relief.

Hence, Elizabeth still has no CGT liability on her flat!

Bayley's Principal Private Residence Relief Law

The general rule here is that a gain of up to £80,000 is covered until at least 2N + 3 years after you first bought the property. 'N' is the number of years that it was your own main residence, not counting the last eighteen months of ownership.

In Elizabeth's case 'N' was 6, so 2N + 3 is 2 x 6 + 3 = 15 years of exemption!

Multiple Sales of Former Homes

The £40,000 private letting relief limit described above applies to every property which has been your only or main residence at any time during your ownership. Hence, even if you were to sell two or more former homes during the same tax year, you would still be entitled to up to £40,000 of private letting relief on each property.

What if the property was let out <u>before</u> becoming your main residence?

Any property which qualifies for partial exemption under PPR relief, and which has also been let out as private residential accommodation at <u>any time</u> during the taxpayer's ownership, is also eligible for private letting relief. Hence, although in our example we have been looking at a <u>former</u> main residence, which is subsequently let out, private letting relief will apply equally where a property is let out first and then subsequently becomes the owner's main residence.

If, in the latest example, Elizabeth had instead rented her flat out from 2010 to 2012, then lived in it as her main residence for six years before continuing to rent it out again, the result would be exactly the same.

(Elizabeth's flat would have had to be Philip's main residence too after they got married, as a married couple are only allowed one main residence for PPR relief purposes.)

As we have already seen though, there is no additional benefit to be derived from the extension to the PPR exemption for a former main residence's last eighteen months of ownership if, in fact, it is still your main residence throughout that time in any case.

We left Alexander in just this sort of situation in Section 6.13. How will private letting relief operate in his case?

Example
Alexander, as we know, had a rented property from 2011 to 2013 which he then lived in as his own main residence from 2013 to 2017. His total capital gain was £180,000 and four sixths of this was covered by the PPR exemption. This leaves him with a gain of £60,000. He will be able to claim private letting relief of £40,000, leaving a taxable gain of just £20,000.

Even this may not be the end of the story for Alexander, as he will probably still have his annual exemption to reduce his taxable gain still further (see Section 6.29). This would reduce his taxable gain to just £8,700 (£20,000 - £11,300), giving him a CGT bill somewhere between £1,566 (18%) and £2,436 (28%). Even at the most, this is still just 1.35% of his total gain of £180,000.

6.15   PLANNING WITH PPR RELIEF

In our first example in Section 6.14, Elizabeth managed to make a tax-free capital gain of £80,000 despite living in her flat for only six years out of a total of fifteen and she didn't even need to use her annual exemption. This remarkable result arose due to the powerful combination of reliefs available for a former main residence.

These reliefs are invaluable to both those with a former home they now wish to sell and those who wish to plan for future tax-free capital growth.

Things were not quite so rosy for Alexander and he did end up with a tax bill after only six years of ownership, despite living in the property for four years.

To some extent, this shows how much better the PPR exemption works if you move into the property as your main residence immediately on purchase.

However, Alexander's effective tax rate of just 1.35% still shows how the combination of reliefs available on a property occupied as your main residence at any time during your ownership often operates to eliminate most, if not all, of any taxable capital gain.

In Chapter 8 we will look at more ways in which the PPR exemption and its associated reliefs can be used to allow a taxpayer to invest in property with little or no exposure to CGT.

6.16   GARDENS AND GROUNDS

There have been a large number of cases before the Courts over whether the 'grounds' of a house, including some of the subsidiary outbuildings, are covered by the PPR exemption.

In the usual situation, where a house has a reasonably normal sized garden and perhaps a shed, a garage or other small outbuildings, there is no doubt that the entire property is covered by the PPR exemption.

Naturally, we are talking here only of the situation where there is no use of any of the property other than private residential occupation.

Where the whole property is let out at some point, so that private letting relief also applies, the garden and 'modest' grounds continue to be covered by the relevant reliefs in the same way as already outlined in the previous sections.

The general rule for grounds is that these are deemed to form a normal part of the property where they do not exceed half a hectare (1.235 acres) in area (including the area on which the house itself stands). Beyond this, it is necessary to argue that the additional space is required 'for the reasonable enjoyment of the dwelling-house as a residence'.

What does this mean? Well, unfortunately, this is one of those rather enigmatic answers which judges love to give and which can only be decided on an individual case-by-case basis.

The whole situation changes once any part of the property is used for any other purpose. Here the position differs for buildings or gardens and grounds. For gardens and grounds, they will obtain the same exemptions that are due on the house itself as long as they are part of the 'private residence' at the time of sale.

For subsidiary buildings, it becomes necessary to apportion any gain arising between the periods of residential occupation and the periods of non-residential use.

Example
Lady Jane has a large house with grounds totalling half a hectare in area. For several years, she leased half her grounds to a neighbouring amusement park for use as a car park. Within this half of her grounds there is a small outbuilding which was used as the parking attendant's hut.

When the amusement park gave up its lease over Lady Jane's grounds, she hired a landscape gardener to restore them. The outbuilding reverted to its previous use as a storage shed for garden equipment.

In 2017, Lady Jane sold the entire property. Apart from the lease of the car park, the whole property had been used as her main residence throughout her ownership.

Lady Jane's main house and her entire grounds will be fully covered by the PPR exemption. However, the element of her gain relating to the outbuilding must be apportioned between the periods of private use and the period of non-residential use. The non-residential element of the gain will be chargeable to CGT.

Tax Tip
Lady Jane may have been better off demolishing the outbuilding prior to the sale of her house. No part of her gain would then have related to this building and her entire gain would have been covered by the PPR exemption. Naturally, it is only worth doing this if demolishing the building does not impact on the whole property's sale price by more than the amount of the potential tax saving.

Wealth Warning
Unlike the house itself, the PPR exemption does not extend to unused outbuildings or gardens and grounds and <u>actual use</u> for private residential purposes is required.

6.17   DELAYS IN OCCUPYING A NEW HOME

Many people buy a 'run-down' property and then embark on substantial renovation works before occupying it as their own main residence. In other circumstances, a planned move may be held up by unforeseen delays in selling the existing home.

The tax rules cater for this and the PPR exemption specifically extends to cover any period of up to one year in which the taxpayer cannot occupy a newly acquired property due to either:

i) An unavoidable delay in selling their old property, or
ii) The need to await the finalisation of renovation or construction work on the new property

During this period, it is possible for both the old and new properties to simultaneously be covered by the PPR exemption. Of course, the scope for claiming this exemption is lost if the new property is being used for some other purpose between purchase and initial occupation as the taxpayer's main residence (although private letting relief could apply to this period in appropriate circumstances).

Under exceptional circumstances, HMRC may allow this initial period to be extended to up to two years. This extension is not granted lightly and is reserved for genuine cases of delay caused by factors beyond the taxpayer's control. You would also be expected to have done everything in your power to facilitate the property being ready for your occupation within the original one year period.

If the delay in occupation extends beyond the first year or beyond any additional period which HMRC permits, then the PPR exemption is lost for the whole of the period prior to occupation of the property.

The initial period allowed for the renovation of property also applies to a new property which you have built on a vacant plot of land.

In both cases the property or land must be bought with the intention of adopting it as your main residence and must not be used for any other purpose prior to occupation.

6.18   TEMPORARY ABSENCES

The PPR exemption remains available in full for certain temporary periods of absence, as follows:

i)   Any single period of up to three years, or shorter periods totalling no more than three years, regardless of the reason,

ii) A period of up to four years when the taxpayer or their spouse is required to work elsewhere by reason of their employment or their place of work, and

iii) A period of any length when the taxpayer or their spouse is working in an office or employment whose duties are all performed outside the UK.

These temporary absences are only covered by the PPR exemption if:

a) PPR relief has not been claimed on any other property in respect of the same period

b) The taxpayer occupies the property as their main residence for a period before the absence period, and

c) Either:

  • The taxpayer occupies the property as their main residence for a period after the absence period, or

  • In the case of absences under (ii) or (iii) above, the taxpayer or their spouse is prevented from resuming occupation of the property following their absence by reason of their place of work or a condition imposed by their contract of employment which requires them to reside elsewhere.

A condition imposed on an employee under (c) above needs to be a reasonable condition required to secure the effective performance of the employee's duties.

Benefits and Pitfalls

It is worth noting that it is only any period for which the owner actually **claims** PPR relief on another property which must be excluded. This opens up a whole area of tax planning, especially for individuals who spend a period working overseas. The tax-saving opportunities for these individuals are examined in the Taxcafe.co.uk guide *'Tax Free Capital Gains'*.

In other cases, however, the absence rules may be disadvantageous. In Section 8.16 we will look at the potential pitfalls and how to avoid them.

6.19   PROPERTIES HELD IN TRUST

A trust is a separate legal entity in its own right for tax purposes. The PPR exemption extends to a property held by a trust when the property is the only or main residence of one or more of the trust's beneficiaries.

However, the PPR exemption is not available on a property held by a trust if a hold-over relief claim was made on the transfer of that property into the trust. In some cases this may lead to a difficult decision:

- Decline to make a hold-over relief claim at the outset and pay some CGT immediately, or

- Make the hold-over relief claim and risk paying a great deal more CGT on the eventual sale of the property

In essence, one has to weigh up the prospective current tax bill against the ultimate tax potentially arising in the future.

Properties with held over gains already held in trust before 10th December 2003 are still eligible for PPR relief in respect of periods of occupation by a beneficiary as their main residence prior to that date. The additional eighteen month period of relief at the end of the trust's ownership does not, however, apply.

Similar restrictions apply where a hold over relief claim has been made when a property was transferred out of a trust. Once again, PPR relief cannot be claimed on a subsequent disposal of that property by the transferee.

Despite these restrictions, trusts can still be used as a means to obtain PPR relief on properties occupied by adult children or other friends and relatives. We will return to this subject in Section 8.14.

Trusts also have their own annual exemption. This is generally half the amount of an individual's annual exemption (see Section 6.29), but must be further reduced where the same person has transferred assets into more than one trust.

Subject to any available reliefs (including entrepreneurs' relief), trusts pay CGT at the higher rates of 20% and 28%.

6.20   WHAT IS A RESIDENCE?

Before we go any further, it is worth pausing to consider what we mean when we refer to a property as a taxpayer's residence.

As we will see in Section 6.22, we are sometimes concerned with situations where a taxpayer has more than one residence. One of these will be their main residence and will qualify for PPR relief.

But no property can be a **_main_** residence until it is **_a_** private residence of that individual taxpayer or married couple.

The question of whether a property qualifies as the owner's private residence at any given time is generally decided purely as a question of fact: based on the principles which I shall outline throughout the rest of this section. In some cases, however, those principles are subject to the additional rules set out in Section 6.21.

Having said that, it is worth pointing out that the additional rules in Section 6.21 can never apply to a disposal of UK property by an individual who has been UK resident throughout their ownership of that property. Hence, most UK residents selling UK property will only need to be concerned with the basic principles covered below.

Residence Principles

A residence is a dwelling in which the owner habitually lives. Whilst it needs to be habitual, however, their occupation of the property might still be occasional and short.

Example
Constantine owns a small cottage in Pembrokeshire but lives and works in London. Constantine bought the Pembrokeshire cottage as a holiday home, but he only manages to visit it about two or three times each year, when he will

typically stay for the weekend. Despite the rarity of Constantine's visits to his cottage, it nevertheless qualifies as his private residence.

Some actual physical occupation of the property (including overnight stays) is necessary before it can be a residence. Constantine's situation is probably just about the minimum level of occupation which will qualify.

'Dwelling' means a property suitable for occupation as your home and can include a caravan or a houseboat. It will not, however, include a plainly unsuitable property such as an office, shop or factory. (Although there are flats over shops and offices which are dwellings!)

To 'live' in a property means to adopt it as the place where you are based and where you sleep, shelter and have your home. In principle, these guidelines apply equally to both UK and overseas property, so a foreign property could also be classed as the owner's residence: although this is now subject to the additional rules set out in Section 6.21.

Some other use of a property at other times, when not occupied as the taxpayer's private residence, does not necessarily prevent it from qualifying as a residence. If such a property were to be treated as your main residence though, there would be a proportionate reduction in the amount of PPR relief available.

Example
On 1st April 2008, Bonnie bought a small cottage on Skye for £100,000. For the next ten years, she rented the cottage out as furnished holiday accommodation for 48 weeks each year and occupied it herself for the remaining four weeks. Bonnie's regular occupation of the cottage is enough to make it a residence. In this example we are also going to assume that it is her main residence throughout her ownership.

On 1st April 2018, Bonnie sells the cottage for £204,000, realising a total capital gain of £104,000. For the eight and a half year period from 1st April 2008 to 1st October 2016, Bonnie is only entitled to PPR relief on 4/52nds of her capital gain, reflecting her own private use of the property. As usual, Bonnie is entitled to full relief for the last eighteen months of her ownership.

Bonnie's capital gain amounts to £10,400 per year (£104,000/10), so her total PPR relief is therefore as follows:

£10,400 x 8½ x 4/52 =	*£6,800*
£10,400 x 1½ =	*£15,600*

Total relief:	*£22,400*

In addition to this, Bonnie will also be entitled to private letting relief of £22,400 and possibly also her annual exemption of £11,300.

Assuming that the latter exemption is available in full, her taxable capital gain would be reduced to £47,900.

(Bonnie might also be entitled to other reliefs and we will therefore return to this example in Section 8.17.)

Bonnie is still able to treat the cottage as her private residence, even though she is renting it out as holiday accommodation. However, where a property is rented out for longer periods under a lease, it cannot be regarded as the owner's residence during the period of the let.

A residence for CGT purposes must also be a property in which the taxpayer has a legal or equitable interest. A legal interest means any form of ownership, sole or joint, including freehold, leasehold, commonhold, or the tenancy of a property rented under a lease.

An equitable interest in a property is less easy to define. Generally it must mean some sort of right over the property itself and not merely an ability to reside in it. Hence, for example, if an individual stays rent free with family or friends, they are occupying the property under a gratuitous licence and they clearly have no equitable interest.

Occupation of property may also be under contractual licence, such as staying in a hotel, hostel, guest house or private club. This also does not give the guest any equitable interest in the property.

An unmarried partner in a co-habiting couple may perhaps have an 'equitable interest' in the couple's home when it is owned wholly by the other partner, although this particular point has not yet been tested in the courts in connection with CGT.

For married couples, all of the principles regarding residences and main residences must be applied to the couple as a single unit. Hence, for example, if William owns a property in Brixham which he has never visited, but his wife Mary stays there regularly, then that property must be counted as a private residence of the couple.

If an individual or married couple has only one property which qualifies as a private residence, then that property must be their main residence for CGT purposes. Indeed, HMRC's own Capital Gains manual sets out the principle that where an individual's main home is occupied under licence, but they also own another residence, the residence which that individual owns must be regarded as their main residence for CGT purposes.

Once an individual or married couple has more than one eligible private residence, we need to work out which is their main residence.

6.21 PRIVATE RESIDENCE RESTRICTIONS

In some cases, the basic principles set out in Section 6.20, which determine whether a property qualifies as the owner's private residence, are subject to an additional rule.

For taxpayers who are non-UK resident at the time of the disposal, the additional rule applies to any period throughout their ownership of the property. The implications of this are covered in detail in the Taxcafe.co.uk guide *'Tax Free Capital Gains'*.

For taxpayers who are UK resident at the time of the disposal, the additional rule only applies to determine whether a property qualifies as their private residence during periods of ownership after 5th April 2015.

The Rule for UK Residents

For taxpayers who are UK resident at the time of the disposal, a property cannot be their private residence for any tax year from 2015/16 onwards unless the owner is either:

a)   Resident for tax purposes (for at least half of that tax year) in the country in which the property is located, or
b)   Physically present in the property at midnight on at least 90 days during that tax year

For the second test, 'days' spent in the property by the owner's spouse may also be counted, as well as 'days' spent (by either of them) in another residential property which the taxpayer owns in the same country (but the same 'day' cannot be counted twice).

For the years in which the property is purchased or sold, the 90 day requirement is proportionately reduced, as appropriate. For example, where a property was purchased on 1st May 2017, the test under (b) above becomes 84 days (90 x 340/365 – rounded up).

The Cinderella Syndrome

It is worth noting that, for the purposes of the '90 day test' you need to be present in your home at midnight in order for a day to be counted. This could mean that, like Cinderella, you may need to leave the ball (or the party, dinner, friend's house, bar, restaurant, etc) early in order to get back home by midnight.

This may seem like a really petty point (indeed it is), but I would not put it past HMRC to make use of it when your day count is exactly 90 or only just over.

Who Is Affected?

The additional restrictions on private residence status affect three types of taxpayer:

i)   Non-UK residents disposing of UK property (see the Taxcafe guide *'Tax Free Capital Gains'*),

ii)   UK residents disposing of overseas property, and

iii)   UK residents disposing of UK property after having been non-UK resident at some earlier point in their ownership of the property after 5th April 2015

I will take a closer look at the impact of the new rules on UK residents disposing of overseas property in Section 6.23.

Those falling in the third category will often benefit from the 'periods of absence' rules in Section 6.18. This issue is also explored in the Taxcafe.co.uk guide *'Tax Free Capital Gains'*.

6.22   SECOND HOMES

The detailed rules on what constitutes a private residence are set out in Sections 6.20 and 6.21. Any reference to a 'residence' or 'private residence' in this section is based on the assumption that the property in question qualifies as a private residence under those rules.

For CGT purposes, each unmarried individual and each legally married couple can generally only have one main residence at any given time. Many people, however, have more than one private residence.

When someone acquires a second (or subsequent) private residence they may, at any time within two years of the date that they first occupy the new property as a private residence, elect which of their properties is to be regarded as their main residence for the purpose of the PPR exemption.

The election must be made in writing, addressed to 'Her Majesty's Inspector of Taxes' and sent to the taxpayer's tax office. An unmarried individual must sign the election personally in order for it to be effective. A married couple must both sign the election.

There is no particular prescribed form for the election, although the following example wording would be suitable for inclusion:

'In accordance with section 222(5) Taxation of Chargeable Gains Act 1992, [I/We] hereby nominate [Property] as [my/our] main residence with effect from [Date*].'

* - The first such election which an individual or a married couple makes in respect of any new combination of private residences will automatically be treated as coming into effect from the beginning of the period to which it relates – i.e. from the date on which they first occupied that new combination of residences. It is this first election for the new combination of residences to which the two-year time limit applies.

Tax Tip

If the two year period for making an election has expired, a new one can be opened up in a number of ways, such as:

- Acquiring an additional private residence
- Selling the main home and moving elsewhere
- Renting out one of the properties for a short period and then re-occupying it as a private residence thereafter

Once an election is in place, it may be changed, by a further written notice given to the Inspector under the same procedure, at any time. A new election may be given retrospective effect, if desired, by up to two years. We will take a closer look at the benefits of this in Chapter 8.

Example

Alfred lives in a small flat in Southampton where he works. In September 2012 he also bought a house on the Isle of Wight and started spending his weekends there. In August 2014, Alfred realised that his island house had appreciated in value significantly since he bought it. His small mainland flat had not increased in value quite so significantly. He therefore elected, before the expiry of the two-year time limit, that his island house was his main residence.

In 2017 Alfred sells the Isle of Wight house at a substantial gain, which is fully exempted by PPR relief. Alfred's flat will not be counted as his main residence from September 2012 until the time of sale of his island house. However, should he sell the flat, his final eighteen months of ownership will be covered by the PPR exemption.

Tax Tip

As soon as Alfred sold his Isle of Wight house, he should have submitted a new main residence election nominating the Southampton flat as his main residence once more: with effect from a date eighteen months previously. This would give an extra eighteen months of PPR relief on the flat, whilst still leaving the Isle of Wight house fully exempt. In fact, where the annual exemption or other reliefs are available, it might be worth backdating the new main residence election a little further (up to two years).

Regardless of any election, a property may only be a main residence for PPR relief purposes if it is, in fact, the taxpayer's own private residence. Hence, a property being let out cannot be covered by the PPR exemption whilst it is being let. (It could nevertheless still attract private letting relief if it were the taxpayer's main residence at some other time.)

Furthermore, if one of a taxpayer's residences ceases to be occupied by them as a private residence (e.g. because it is let out or sold), any main residence election which has been made will cease to apply, even an election in favour of a different property!

Wealth Warning
A new election is required every time the taxpayer, or married couple, has a new combination of two or more private residences. Where a third residence is acquired, for example, a new election must be made. Remember that a property may qualify as a residence whenever the taxpayer or their spouse has *any* legal or equitable interest in it, no matter how small.

Where the number of private residences reduces to one, no election is required as the sole remaining residence must now be the main residence.

In the absence of a valid election, the question of which property is the taxpayer's main residence has to be determined on the facts of the case. Often the answer to this will be obvious but, in borderline cases, HMRC may determine the position to the taxpayer's detriment. Clearly then, it is always wise to make the election!

The factors to be considered when determining which property was a taxpayer's main residence for any given period not covered by an election, include:

- The address given on the taxpayer's tax return
- The address shown on other correspondence, utility bills, bank statements, etc.
- Where a mortgage was obtained over a property before April 2000, whether mortgage interest relief (MIRAS) was claimed
- Whether the mortgage over a property was obtained on the basis that it was the taxpayer's main home
- The security of tenure (leasehold, freehold, etc) held over each residence
- How each residence is furnished
- Where the taxpayer's family spend the majority of their time
- Where the taxpayer is registered to vote
- The location of the taxpayer's place of work
- The location of the medical practices with which the taxpayer is registered (doctor, dentist, etc)
- The registered address for the taxpayer's car

As always, a married couple have to be considered as a single unit.

Each factor above is not conclusive in its own right but will contribute to the overall picture of which property may be regarded as the main residence.

In Section 6.20 we considered the issue of whether a property was occupied under licence or whether an equitable interest existed. Where a taxpayer has only one residence in which they have a legal or equitable interest, a main residence election will not be valid.

My advice, however, is that whenever there is any possibility that a taxpayer may have two or more eligible private residences they should make a main residence election. If this election proves to be invalid, no harm is done and the property in which the taxpayer has a legal or equitable interest will automatically be treated as their main residence.

6.23 HOMES ABROAD

It is important to remember that the PPR exemption applies to a taxpayer's main residence, not, as some people have mistakenly thought to their cost, their main UK residence.

Subject to the rules set out in Section 6.21, it is possible for a UK resident individual or married couple to have a private residence overseas. For periods prior to 6th April 2015, this will continue to be determined purely under the principles set out in Section 6.20, even when the property concerned is disposed of after that date.

Where this means that the individual or married couple had two or more private residences at some time in the past, and there was no main residence election in place at the time, the position will have to be determined under the principles set out in Section 6.22. Generally, one would expect this to lead to the conclusion that the UK home was the main residence, although there will be exceptions. Naturally, where there was a main residence election in place, this will determine the position.

Where an overseas property was an individual or married couple's main residence for any period of time (whether by way of a main residence election or otherwise), the PPR exemption will apply in the same way as for a main residence in the UK. Private letting relief will also be available in exactly the same way, where applicable. As we have already seen, these reliefs are extremely valuable!

It is fairly unusual for an overseas property to qualify as a UK resident's main residence as a question of fact: although it can happen (perhaps where the overseas property is the only property in which the owner has any legal or equitable interest, as discussed in Section 6.22). Furthermore, some overseas properties will have been a UK resident owner's main residence at some time in the past when they were resident overseas.

But, apart from these exceptions, in the vast majority of cases, the only way for a UK resident to achieve main residence status on an overseas property is to make a main residence election in favour of that property. As we shall see in Chapter 8, such an election will almost always be beneficial, even if it is only for a short period.

Sadly, it is no longer possible to make a main residence election in favour of an overseas property unless it qualifies as a private residence under the rules set out in Section 6.21. For a UK resident, this will generally mean needing to spend at least 90 days during one or more UK tax years in the foreign holiday home: and that could have foreign tax consequences.

Example
Abdul and Vicky, a UK resident married couple, own a holiday home in Spain. In June 2017, Vicky spends 25 nights in the Spanish property. Abdul spends 25 nights there in August. In January 2018, Vicky returns and spends another 23 nights in the property and Abdul makes a return visit of 20 nights in March.

Between them, the couple have spent 93 nights in the property during 2017/18. They therefore pass the '90 day test', the property qualifies as their private residence and they can make a main residence election in favour of it covering all or part of the 2017/18 UK tax year.

Furthermore, as (like most countries) Spain uses a calendar year for its tax year, neither of them has spent more than 25 days in Spain in any Spanish tax year (assuming that the nights in their holiday home were the only nights they each spent in Spain). Hence, although it always remains essential to take local advice on such matters, neither Abdul nor Vicky are likely to be treated as being resident in Spain for tax purposes.

Assuming that the Spanish property did not qualify as Abdul and Vicky's private residence in 2016/17, the time limit for their main residence election will be 6th April 2019. This would appear to remain the case even if the property qualified as their private residence at some earlier time.

Tax Tip
Failing to meet the '90 day test' in one year and then meeting it in the next would appear to be another way to create a new combination of private residences and thus open up a new two year period for making a main residence election – even one in favour of an entirely different property.

Wealth Warning 1
Where an overseas property qualifies as a private residence in one year, having not qualified in the previous year, this will have exactly the same implications for any existing main residence elections as detailed in the previous section.

Wealth Warning 2
Disposals of overseas property may also have foreign tax implications: even when the owner remains UK resident.

It is worth remembering that the '90 day test' is proportionately reduced in the year of acquisition or disposal of the property. Hence, for example, where a foreign holiday home were purchased on 1st February, it would only be necessary to occupy it for 16 nights between then and 5th April for it to qualify as a private residence and thus be eligible for a main residence election covering that period.

Where an overseas property has qualified as a private residence for more than two years, it remains possible to make a main residence election in favour of that property where there is an earlier existing election in favour of another property within the same combination of two or more residences (see Section 6.22).

6.24   JOB-RELATED ACCOMMODATION

In many occupations, it is sometimes necessary, or desirable, for the taxpayer to live in accommodation specifically provided for the purpose. Examples include:

- Caretakers
- Police officers (in some rural areas)
- Pub landlords
- Members of the clergy
- Members of the armed services
- Teachers at boarding schools
- The Prime Minister and the Chancellor of the Exchequer

For people in this type of situation, the PPR exemption may be extended to a property which they own and which they eventually intend to adopt as their main residence.

In these circumstances, the PPR exemption will thus cover their own property during the period that they are living in 'job-related accommodation', despite the fact that their own property is not their residence at that time and even whilst they are letting it out.

This provides an exception to the general rule that there must be some actual physical occupation of a property for it to be eligible for PPR relief.

This treatment can also be extended to a property owned by the spouse of a person living in job-related accommodation, which the couple eventually intend to adopt as their main residence.

If a taxpayer in job-related accommodation has a property which might qualify as a main residence under these rules but also has another residence, such as a holiday home, they can use a main residence election to determine which property is given the PPR exemption.

The election will also be appropriate where the taxpayer has some legal or equitable interest in the job-related accommodation itself.

6.25 WHAT IF PART OF YOUR HOME IS NOT PRIVATE?

Whenever any part of your home is put to some use other than your own private residential occupation, you are inevitably putting your PPR exemption at risk. In the next two sections, we will look at the most common types of 'other use' and their tax implications.

One fundamental principle to note is that if any part of your home is used exclusively for purposes other than your own private residential occupation throughout the period when that property qualifies as your main residence, then that part will not be eligible for any PPR relief at all.

Hence, in order to maximise your PPR relief, I would always recommend making some private use of every part of the property at some time whilst it is your main residence.

Private letting relief does extend to a part of a main residence which has never been used privately by the owner, where appropriate; provided that it remains part of the same 'dwelling' (e.g. bedrooms within a flat which the owner shares with other flatmates). There is sometimes some resistance on this point from HMRC in the case of guest houses and hotels with live-in owners, however.

6.26 LETTING OUT PART OF YOUR HOME

Taking a Lodger

HMRC generally accepts that taking in one individual lodger does not necessitate any restriction to the PPR exemption. In this context, a 'lodger' is someone who, whilst having their own bedroom, will otherwise live as a member of the taxpayer's household.

Other lettings within the same 'dwelling'

Where a part of the property is let out under other circumstances, the PPR exemption will be restricted. However, private letting relief is available to cover this restriction in very much the same way as it applies to the letting out of the whole property (subject to the points raised in the previous section).

Example

Robert, a higher rate taxpayer, bought his five-storey house for £300,000 in September 2001. From September 2011 to December 2016 he let the top two floors out as a flat. He then resumed occupation of the whole house, before selling it in September 2017 for £750,000. Robert's total gain of £450,000 is covered by the PPR exemption as follows:

Lower three floors: The gain of £270,000 (three fifths) is fully covered by the PPR exemption.

Upper two floors: The gain of £180,000 is covered by the PPR exemption from 2001 to 2011 AND for the last eighteen months of Robert's ownership, a total of 11½ years out of 16. Hence, £129,375 of this gain is exempt, leaving £50,625 chargeable.

Robert can then claim private letting relief equal to the lowest of:

i)   *The amount of PPR exemption on the <u>whole</u> property: £399,375 (£270,000 + £129,375),*
ii)   *The gain arising by reason of the letting: £50,625, or*
iii) *£40,000*

The relief is thus £40,000, leaving Robert with a gain of only £10,625. Assuming he has not used his 2017/18 annual exemption of £11,300 elsewhere, this will exempt the remaining part of his gain, leaving him with no CGT to pay at all!

Now, all that Robert probably did was to fit a few locks in order to separate the flat from his own home. As a result, re-occupying the whole property was a simple matter and when he came to sell it, it remained a single 'dwelling' for tax purposes.

The situation would have been quite different, however, if he had carried out extensive conversion work in order to create a number of separate dwellings and we will examine the position arising in those circumstances in Section 8.12.

Adult Placement Carers

Any occupation of part of your home by another person under an adult placement scheme is disregarded for PPR relief purposes.

6.27   USING PART OF YOUR HOME FOR BUSINESS PURPOSES

Where any part of the property is used **exclusively** for business purposes, the PPR exemption is not available for that part of the property for the relevant period.

Where the exclusive business use covers the entire period that the property is the taxpayer's main residence, the exemption for the final eighteen months of ownership will also be withdrawn for this part of the property.

The effect on the PPR exemption is the same whether part of the property is being used exclusively in the taxpayer's own business or is being rented out for use in someone else's. However, where it is the taxpayer's own trading business which is concerned, then this part of the property becomes 'business property' for the purposes of a number of tax reliefs, including entrepreneurs' relief (see Section 6.28), rollover relief and holdover relief for gifts.

Where the 'business use' of part of the property requires extensive conversion work, that part will no longer be part of the original 'dwelling' and hence the PPR exemption will not be available for the last eighteen months of ownership.

Non-Exclusive Business Use (The 'Home Office')

Where part of the home is used non-exclusively for business purposes, there is no restriction on the PPR exemption. This is a fairly common situation amongst self-employed people who work from an office or study within their home.

To safeguard the PPR exemption, it is wise to restrict your Income Tax claim in respect of the office's running costs to a maximum of, say, 99%, in order to reflect the room's occasional private use. Hence, for example, if the office is one of four rooms in the house (excluding hallways, kitchen and bathrooms), one would claim 99% of one quarter of the household running costs.

Just about any kind of private use will suffice, such as:

- A guest bedroom
- Additional storage space for personal belongings
- A music room
- A library

Naturally, it makes sense to adopt some form of private use which will only lead to a small reduction in the Income Tax claim.

Tax Tip
Whilst restricting one room to, say, 99% business use, you may also be able to argue for 1% business use in another room, thus effectively reversing the effect of the restriction without affecting your CGT position on the house.

Section 3.9 provides further details of how to claim an expense deduction for Income Tax purposes when using part of your home as an office from which to run your business. Claiming the flat rate allowances available should not affect your home's CGT exemption, although it remains important to avoid exclusive business use of any part of the property.

6.28 ENTREPRENEURS' RELIEF

Entrepreneurs' relief operates by simply applying a reduced CGT rate of 10%.

Gains on which entrepreneurs' relief are claimed are taken to use up the individual's basic rate tax band first, in priority to any other gains.

Sadly, entrepreneurs' relief is not generally available to property investors, except in the case of qualifying furnished holiday lets (see Section 8.17).

Nevertheless, entrepreneurs' relief will sometimes be available to property developers and other taxpayers with property trades (see Chapter 2) on the disposal of their own trading premises and other business assets.

Broadly speaking, entrepreneurs' relief is available on the disposal of:

i)   The whole or part of a qualifying business
ii)   Assets previously used in a qualifying business which has ceased
iii)   Shares or securities in a 'personal company'

A qualifying business for this purpose is generally a trade, although, as already stated, furnished holiday letting businesses also qualify. We will return to look in more detail at the application of entrepreneurs' relief to qualifying furnished holiday lets in Section 8.17.

A 'part' of a business can only be counted for these purposes if it is capable of operating as a going concern in its own right, but an 'interest' in a business, such as a partnership share, may qualify.

A disposal of assets previously used in a qualifying business must take place within three years after the business ceases.

The individual making the disposal must have owned the qualifying business for at least a year prior to its disposal or cessation.

Entrepreneurs' relief may sometimes also extend to property owned personally but used in the trade of a 'personal company', or a partnership in which the owner is a partner. A number of restrictions apply, however.

184

The relief is only available where the owner is also disposing of shares in the company, or an interest in the partnership. The stake being disposed of must be either:

a) At least a 5% stake, or
b) Their entire remaining stake out of an earlier stake of at least 5%

Entrepreneurs' relief is also restricted where any payment has been received for the use of the property after 5th April 2008.

Where the property was acquired after 5th April 2008 and a full market rent was received throughout the period of its use in the company or partnership's trade, no entrepreneurs' relief will be available. Where the property was acquired earlier, or rent was charged at a lower rate, there will be a partial restriction in entrepreneurs' relief.

The definition of a 'personal company' for the purposes of entrepreneurs' relief is broadly as follows:

i)   The individual holds at least 5% of the ordinary share capital
ii)   The holding under (i) provides at least 5% of the voting rights
iii) The company is a trading company
iv)   The individual is an officer or employee of the company (an 'officer' includes a non-executive director or company secretary)

Each of these rules must be satisfied for the period of at least one year prior to the disposal in question or, where the company has ceased trading, for at least one year prior to the cessation. In the latter case, the disposal must again take place within three years after cessation.

A disposal of property or other assets used in a trade carried on by the owner's 'personal company', or a partnership in which the owner is a partner, is referred to as an 'associated disposal'. The entrepreneurs' relief available on an associated disposal is also restricted to reflect any periods when the asset was not being used in a qualifying business carried on by the company or partnership.

There is no similar restriction on other entrepreneurs' relief claims and a property used in the owner's own qualifying business will be eligible for full relief as long as it was used in that business immediately prior to the disposal or cessation of the business.

Each individual may only claim entrepreneurs' relief on a maximum cumulative lifetime total of £10m of capital gains. This maximum applies to all claims made on gains arising after 5th April 2008. Thereafter, the CGT rate on all further business asset disposals will revert to the normal rates set out in Section 6.4.

Example

Arkwright began trading as a property developer in the late 1980s. After almost 30 years he decides to retire and ceases trading in September 2017. For just over a year before cessation, Arkwright ran the business from Granville House: a building which he initially purchased as an investment property for £5m and rented out for over 25 years.

In July 2016, Arkwright adopted Granville House as his trading premises and remained there until ceasing trading in September 2017. After his property development business ceased, Arkwright put Granville House up for sale and sold it for £15.1m in March 2018, realising a capital gain of £10.1m.

As Arkwright owned his business for more than a year and sold Granville House within three years of cessation, he is eligible for entrepreneurs' relief. The fact that Granville House was an investment property for over 25 years makes absolutely no difference!

His £10.1m gain does exceed the £10m lifetime limit, however, so Arkwright's CGT bill is calculated as follows:

	£
Total gain	10,100,000
Less:	
Annual exemption	(11,300)
Taxable gain	10,088,700
CGT due:	
£10m @ 10%	1,000,000
£88,700 @ 20%	17,740
Total	1,017,740

If Arkwright had not adopted Granville House as his trading premises, his CGT bill (assuming he is a higher rate taxpayer) would have been £2,017,740. That's £1m more!

As we can see from the example, adopting an investment property as your own trading premises prior to sale could save you up to £1m.

Not everyone already has a handy trading business like Arkwright, but we will look at how other property investors might benefit from entrepreneurs' relief in Section 8.20.

Note that entrepreneurs' relief is not mandatory and taxpayers may choose whether to claim it. This avoids the need to waste any of the cumulative lifetime maximum on claims which would be covered by the annual exemption or capital losses (see Section 6.33).

Wealth Warning

To qualify for entrepreneurs' relief, the individual making the disposal must have owned the qualifying business for at least a year prior to cessation. A pre-sale transfer of property to a spouse might therefore result in the loss of entrepreneurs' relief if the spouse did not also own a share of the business for at least a year prior to cessation.

Tax Tip

On the other hand, it is also worth noting that the £10m cumulative lifetime maximum applies on a 'per person' basis. Hence, if a share in the business were transferred to a spouse for at least a year prior to cessation, entrepreneurs' relief would then be available on total gains of up to £20m.

Another Tax Tip

From a tax point of view, it will almost always be worth transferring a property to a spouse when they are using it in their own trading business. In addition to the possibility of obtaining entrepreneurs' relief on the property, the spouse using the asset in their trade would be eligible for several other reliefs, including rollover relief on replacement of business assets (see Section 8.29). The asset would also generally be exempt from IHT if held by the partner using it in their own trade.

Against this, however, one must bear the commercial risks in mind. If the trade fails, a property held by the trader's spouse may be safe from the trade's creditors, but a property held by the trader themselves could be lost.

6.29 THE ANNUAL EXEMPTION

Each individual is entitled to an annual exemption. It is available to exempt from CGT an amount of capital gains after all other reliefs have been claimed, including the compulsory set-off of capital losses arising in the same tax year.

Where capital losses are brought forward from a previous tax year, the set-off is limited to an amount which reduces the taxpayer's capital gains in the current year to the level of the annual exemption.

Individuals with more than one capital gain arising in the same tax year may allocate their annual exemption in the most beneficial way.

Any unused annual exemption is simply lost; it cannot be carried forward.

Tax Tip
To make the most of your available annual exemptions, try to time your capital gains so that each disposal falls into a different tax year whenever possible.

The current annual exemption, for capital gains arising during the year ending 5th April 2018, is £11,300.

Example
Harry has a capital gain of £12,500 in 2017/18, after claiming all relevant reliefs. After setting off his annual exemption of £11,300, he will be left with a taxable gain of just £1,200.

In this example, as well as many others in this guide, I have assumed that the annual exemption is fully available. This will not always be the case and it should be remembered that only one annual exemption is available each tax year.

6.30 WHEN IS CAPITAL GAINS TAX PAYABLE?

At present, the total CGT payable for each tax year is due by 31st January following the end of the tax year. For example, any CGT liability for 2017/18 is due by 31st January 2019.

CGT liabilities are excluded from the instalment system applying to Income Tax liabilities under self assessment (see Section 3.4).

The Government is proposing to make the CGT due on property disposals taking place after 5th April 2019 payable within 30 days after the date of disposal. This rule already applies to non-UK residents who are not in the self-assessment system (see the Taxcafe.co.uk guide *'Tax Free Capital Gains'* for further details).

6.31 WHAT MUST I REPORT TO HMRC?

The general rule is that where all of a taxpayer's disposals in a tax year, taken together, give rise to total proceeds exceeding four times the annual exemption, or where any of them give rise to an actual CGT liability, then they will all need to be reported.

It is also wise to report all disposals in any tax year where an overall net capital loss arises: so that the loss can be recorded and carried forward for relief in the future.

Disposals which are fully covered by PPR relief and private letting relief are exempted from reporting requirements. This does not include cases where the taxpayer is additionally relying on the annual exemption or any other relief to ensure full relief from CGT.

If you have a reportable property disposal, you will need to complete a tax return, including the capital gains supplement, and attach a copy of your capital gains computation. The return is due for submission by 31st January following the end of the relevant tax year if filed online (i.e. by the same date that any CGT liability is due), or by 31st October if a paper return is used.

If you are not yet in the self-assessment system, it is sensible to advise HMRC that you have a reportable capital gain as soon as possible after the end of the relevant tax year and definitely by 5th October at the latest. This is so that HMRC can issue you with a Unique Taxpayer Reference ('UTR') to enable you to submit your tax return on time. It is almost impossible to submit a tax return without a UTR and, if you have not advised HMRC that you need to do so by 5th October after the end of the tax year, the fact that you do not receive it in time will not be a valid excuse for filing late.

6.32   JOINTLY HELD ASSETS

Where two or more taxpayers hold assets jointly, they must each calculate their own CGT based on their own share of the net proceeds received less their own base cost.

Example
George and Charlotte are equal joint owners of a residential buy-to-let property which they bought together for £100,000. In November 2017 they sell the property for £200,000. Each person's taxable capital gain is calculated as follows:

	£
Net proceeds (£200,000 x ½)	*100,000*
Less:	
Base cost (£100,000 x ½)	*(50,000)*
	50,000
Less:	
Annual exemption	*(11,300)*
Taxable capital gain	*38,700*

George is a higher rate taxpayer, so his CGT bill, at 28%, amounts to £10,836.

Charlotte's total income for 2017/18 is less than her personal allowance, so she pays CGT at 18% on the first £33,500 of her gain (the basic rate band) and 28% on the remainder:

£33,500 @ 18% =	*£6,030*
£5,200 @ 28% =	*£1,456*
Total	*£7,486*

The couple's total CGT bill therefore amounts to £18,322 (£10,836 + £7,486).

Had the property been owned by George alone, his CGT liability would have been £24,836 (£100,000 - £11,300 = £88,700 x 28%). The couple have therefore saved £6,514 (£24,836 - £18,322) by owning the property jointly. This is the value of an additional annual exemption (£11,300 x 28%) plus the saving generated by using Charlotte's basic rate band (£33,500 x 10%: the difference between 18% and 28%).

Hence, it can readily be seen that there will often be significant CGT savings to be had by owning investment property jointly.

There may also be other good reasons for holding property jointly, including significant Income Tax savings, as we shall see in Section 8.2.

Another important point to note when looking at jointly held property is that the £40,000 limit for private letting relief (see Section 6.14) applies to each individual. Hence, a total of up to £80,000 can be exempted when a property is held jointly. We will examine the potential effect of this in more detail in Chapter 8.

6.33   CAPITAL LOSSES

Capital losses are generally computed in the same way as capital gains.

In the first instance, capital losses are automatically set off against any capital gains arising in the same tax year.

Where a taxpayer has an overall net capital loss for the year, it is carried forward and set off against gains in later years BUT only to the extent necessary to reduce future gains down to the annual exemption applying for that later year.

As explained in Section 6.4, individual taxpayers with more than one capital gain arising in the same tax year may generally allocate any available capital losses in the most beneficial way.

Where a taxpayer is claiming entrepreneurs' relief on business assets, however, any capital losses arising on those disposals must be set off against capital gains on assets which were used in the same business. Entrepreneurs' relief is then claimed on the overall net gain.

Any other capital losses set off against gains subject to entrepreneurs' relief are set off after entrepreneurs' relief has been claimed, meaning that the relief for those losses is given at an effective rate of only 10% and more of the taxpayer's lifetime maximum will have been used up.

Capital losses arising on any transactions with 'connected persons' (see Section 6.9) may only be set off against gains arising on transactions between the same parties.

Furthermore, relief is denied for 'artificial' capital losses arising as a result of transactions which were carried out with a main purpose of creating a tax advantage.

6.34   LEASES

Granting a long lease of more than 50 years' duration

This is a capital disposal, fully chargeable to CGT (subject to applicable reliefs). The base cost to be used has to be restricted under the 'part disposal' rules. In essence, what this means is that the base cost is divided between the part disposed of (i.e. the lease) and the part retained (the 'reversionary interest') in proportion to their relative values.

Example
Llewellyn owns the freehold of a commercial property in Cardiff. He grants a 60-year lease to Brian, a businessman from Belfast moving into the area. Brian pays a premium of £90,000 for the lease. The value of Llewellyn's reversionary interest is established as £10,000. The base cost to be used in calculating Llewellyn's capital gain on the grant of the lease is therefore 90% of his base cost for the property as a whole.

Granting a short lease of no more than 50 years' duration

As we saw in Section 4.14, part of any lease premium obtained will be taxable as income. The rest is a capital disposal and is dealt with in the same way as the grant of a long lease, as outlined above.

Assigning a lease

This is treated entirely as a capital disposal and any applicable reliefs may be claimed in the usual way.

However, leases with less than 50 years remaining at the time of disposal are treated as 'wasting assets'. The taxpayer is therefore required to reduce their base cost in accordance with the schedule set out in Appendix B.

For example, for a lease with 20 years remaining, and which had more than 50 years remaining when first acquired, the base cost must be reduced to 72.77% of the original amount.

Where the lease had less than 50 years remaining when originally acquired, the necessary reduction in base cost is achieved by multiplying the original cost by the factor applying at the time of sale and dividing by the factor applying at the time of purchase.

Example
John acquires a ten year lease over a building and pays a premium of £10,000. Five years later, John assigns his lease to Asha at a premium of £6,000. When calculating his capital gain, the amount which John may claim as his base cost is £10,000 x 26.722/46.695 = £5,723.

Any part of a lease premium which was treated as income in the hands of the grantor under the rules outlined in Section 4.14 will not form part of the grantee's base cost for the lease. The grantee may, instead, be able to claim an Income Tax deduction for this part of the premium, spread over the period of the lease (if the grantee is using the property for business purposes).

In the example above, I have assumed for the sake of illustration that this did not apply in John's case.

Chapter 7

Other Taxes to Watch Out For

7.1 STAMP DUTY LAND TAX – INTRODUCTION

Stamp Duty is the oldest tax on the statute books. It was more than a century old already when Pitt the Younger introduced Income Tax in 1799. In 2003, however, for transfers of real property (i.e. land and buildings, or any form of legal interest in them), Stamp Duty was replaced by SDLT.

From 1st April 2015, SDLT no longer applies to property in Scotland and, from 1st April 2018, it will also cease to apply to property in Wales (see Sections 7.20 and 7.23 for details of its replacements).

The rates applying to transfers of property are generally the same regardless of what type of property business the purchaser has. The rates are also mostly unaffected by whether the purchaser is an individual, a trust, a partnership or a company. The rates are, however, different for residential property and non-residential property: as we shall see over the next few sections.

7.2 STAMP DUTY LAND TAX ON RESIDENTIAL PROPERTY

The basic underlying rates of SDLT on residential property are:

Up to £125,000	Nil
£125,000 to £250,000	2%
£250,000 to £925,000	5%
£925,000 to £1.5m	10%
Over £1.5m	12%

Since December 2014, these rates have been applied on a 'progressive' basis, which represents a major reform compared to the old 'slab' system which applied previously.

It is, however, important to note that these rates will now seldom actually apply to purchases of property by landlords and other property business owners. Generally speaking, these basic underlying rates will only apply in the case of a purchase made by:

- An unmarried individual or married couple who have no other interest in any residential property, or
- An unmarried individual or married couple buying a new main residence to replace a former main residence sold within the previous three years

In most other cases, an additional 3% charge will apply to all residential property purchases taking place after 31st March 2016. We will look at this dreadful new charge and the pitiful few exemptions available, in the next section.

Before that, let us look at a brief example of the SDLT arising where the higher charges do not apply.

Example
The SDLT arising on a purchase price of £400,000 where an individual is buying their first, or only, residential property, or replacing a main residence sold within the previous three years, is:

First £125,000 @ 0%:	*£0*
Next £125,000 @ 2%:	*£2,500*
Next £150,000 @ 5%:	*£7,500*
Total:	*£10,000*

7.3 HIGHER CHARGES ON RESIDENTIAL PROPERTY

From 1st April 2016, higher SDLT charges apply to most purchases of residential property by landlords, other property business owners and companies.

The basic rule is that the higher charges apply to any purchase:

- By an individual who has any interest in more than one residential property at the end of the day of purchase
- By two or more persons jointly where any of them has any interest in more than one residential property at the end of the day of purchase, or
- By a company or other 'non-natural' person

The higher charges are as follows:

Up to £125,000	3%
£125,000 to £250,000	5%
£250,000 to £925,000	8%
£925,000 to £1.5m	13%
Over £1.5m	15%

Purchases for under £40,000 are exempt from SDLT but, apart from this, the charges apply on a progressive basis, as illustrated in the following examples:

Example 1
The SDLT arising on a residential property purchased for £100,000 where the higher charges apply is £100,000 @ 3% = £3,000

Example 2
The SDLT arising on a residential property purchased for £400,000 where the higher charges apply is:

First £125,000 @ 3%:	£3,750
Next £125,000 @ 5%:	£6,250
Next £150,000 @ 8%:	£12,000
Total:	£22,000

Example 3
The SDLT arising on a residential property purchased for £1.6m where the higher charges apply is:

First £125,000 @ 3%:	£3,750
Next £125,000 @ 5%:	£6,250
Next £675,000 @ 8%:	£54,000
Next £575,000 @ 13%:	£74,750
Next £100,000 @ 15%:	£15,000
Total:	£153,750

Replacement of Main Residence

There is an exemption from the higher charges where the purchaser is buying a property which they intend to adopt as their main residence and is replacing a previous main residence sold within the previous three years. (The three year time limit does not apply where the new purchase is made before 26th November 2018.)

The exemption also applies where the purchaser's former main residence is sold within three years **after** the new main residence is purchased. However, in this case, the higher charges will apply in the first place and a refund will have to be claimed later, on the sale of the former main residence.

Where all of two or more joint purchasers are either eligible for this exemption, or will not have any interest in any other residential property at the end of the day of purchase, then the higher charges will not apply (or can be refunded later, as the case may be).

In any other cases involving joint purchasers, the higher charges will apply. This includes cases where one of the joint purchasers lived in the former main residence but did not own any share of it (and has an interest in another residential property).

Example
Prior to their marriage in 2010, Jack and Rose each had their own main residence. After the wedding, Jack moved in with Rose and rented out his old flat. Rose kept her flat in her own name until selling it in January 2018. The couple then bought a new property jointly together for £600,000 and adopted it as their new main residence.

The higher SDLT charges are payable on the new property because Jack is not replacing a former main residence which he owned and he still owns another residential property. This costs the couple an additional £18,000.

There are a few ways of avoiding this problem, but they all have other potential implications, especially where mortgages are involved:

- Rose could buy the new property in her name alone (this may lead to difficulties in obtaining a mortgage). She might also subsequently transfer the property into joint names with Jack (but see Section 7.7 for problems arising if there is a mortgage outstanding on it at that time)

- They could put their existing main residence into joint names before selling it. Again, this might cause problems if there is an outstanding mortgage (see Section 7.7)

- Jack could sell his old flat before they buy the new property (this may give rise to a CGT liability – see Chapter 6 for details)

If Jack and Rose were not married, the position might be even more difficult as any transfers of property into joint names could give rise to a CGT liability if the property concerned had not always been the existing owner's main residence.

See Chapter 6 for a detailed examination of what is a 'main residence'. Note, however, that it will not be possible to elect which property is, or was, your main residence for the purposes of the higher SDLT charges: it will need to be determined as a question of fact.

Interests in Residential Property

Subject to the exceptions outlined below, any interest in any residential property anywhere in the world is counted for the purpose of the higher charges. An 'interest' means any form of legal right to a share in the property for any period of time.

There are a few exceptions, as follows:

- Interests in property worth less than £40,000
- Caravans, mobile homes and houseboats
- Shares of 50% or less in property inherited within the last three years
- Leasehold interests for a period of less than seven years at commencement
- Superior interests where there is a leasehold interest in the property with more than 21 years left to run

Each individual must also include any interests in residential property held by their spouse, civil partner or minor children (e.g. property held in trust on their behalf).

Contrary to earlier expectations, there is no exemption from the higher charges for large scale investors, or for bulk purchases of multiple properties. The reliefs described in Section 7.8 remain available however.

7.4   RESIDENTIAL PROPERTY PURCHASES BY 'NON-NATURAL' PERSONS

A special SDLT rate of 15% applies to the entire purchase price on purchases of residential properties in excess of £500,000 by companies and other 'non-natural' persons, such as collective investment schemes, unit trusts, and partnerships in which any 'non-natural' person is a partner.

The rate only applies where a single dwelling is purchased for a price in excess of £500,000, or where one or more separate dwellings included in the purchase of a larger portfolio are worth more than £500,000 each.

Properties are exempt from this special rate when acquired for use in a business. This exemption covers both trading businesses and property investment businesses, so property investment companies should not generally have to pay this punitive rate.

The special 15% rate should not generally apply to most trusts or partnerships made up entirely of individuals as, from a technical standpoint, the purchase is usually still being made by one or more individuals. In case of doubt, however, legal advice is essential!

Where this special rate applies, neither multiple dwellings relief nor the alternative treatment outlined in Section 7.8 is available.

7.5 STAMP DUTY LAND TAX ON NON-RESIDENTIAL PROPERTY

The rates of SDLT on non-residential property are:

Up to £150,000	0%
£150,000 to £250,000	2%
Over £250,000	5%

From 17th March 2016 onwards, these rates also apply on a 'progressive' basis. For example, the SDLT payable on the purchase of a non-residential property for £300,000 is:

First £150,000 @ 0%:	£0
Next £100,000 @ 2%:	£2,000
Next £50,000 @ 5%:	£2,500
Total:	£4,500

7.6 APPLICATION OF STAMP DUTY LAND TAX

The thresholds given in the tables in Sections 7.2, 7.3 and 7.5 generally refer to the actual consideration paid for the purchase, whether in cash or by any other means (but see Section 7.7 for potential exceptions).

SDLT is currently payable on all transfers of property located in England, Wales or Northern Ireland; regardless of where the vendor and purchaser are resident, and regardless of where the transfer documentation is drawn up. SDLT has now ceased to apply to property in Scotland. See Section 7.20 for further details.

SDLT is the legal responsibility of the purchaser or transferee, though the vendor/transferor will sometimes arrange to pay it.

Substantial Performance

The liability for SDLT is triggered when a purchase is 'substantially performed'. Generally, this occurs on the earliest of:

a) Completion of the purchase contract,
b) Payment of at least 90% of the purchase consideration,
c) Occupation of the property (including occupation under licence after the date of the contract or lease agreement),
d) Payment of the first rent (in the case of a lease), or
e) Subletting of the property (in the case of a lease).

In most cases, it is the completion of the purchase contract which triggers the liability.

7.7　MARKET VALUE AND MORTGAGES

Generally speaking, there is no 'market value' rule for SDLT and the tax is only payable on actual consideration.

Where property is transferred to a connected company, however, SDLT is payable on the market value. The implications of this are examined in the Taxcafe.co.uk guide *'Using a Property Company to Save Tax'*.

There is no SDLT exemption for transfers between spouses or civil partners, although many of these are gifts with no consideration.

Note that where property is transferred subject to a mortgage, the balance outstanding on the mortgage will be treated as consideration for SDLT purposes. Hence if a woman transfers a house to her husband with an outstanding mortgage of £200,000, he will have a SDLT liability of £1,500 (see Section 7.2), or £7,500 where the higher charges apply (Section 7.3).

In such a case, where possible, it might be worth repaying the mortgage prior to the transfer, or at least reducing it to less than £40,000: thus avoiding any SDLT charge. Where the higher charges do not apply, a mortgage balance not exceeding £125,000 would avoid any SDLT.

Where property is being put into joint names, SDLT is payable on whatever share of the mortgage the transferee is taking on. Hence, where putting a property into equal joint names, a mortgage of less than £80,000 should not give rise to any SDLT (or £250,000 where the higher charges do not apply).

7.8　LINKED TRANSACTIONS

SDLT is calculated after taking account of any 'linked transactions'. 'Linked transactions' can arise in a number of ways, including a simultaneous purchase of several properties from the same vendor.

The effect of the 'linked transactions' depends on whether 'multiple dwellings relief' is claimed. This relief is only available for multiple purchases of residential property.

Basic Rule without Multiple Dwellings Relief

The basic rule which applies where multiple dwellings relief is not claimed is that the 'linked transactions' are treated as if they were a single purchase for SDLT purposes. In practice, this will mainly apply to multiple purchases of non-residential property, although it will also apply to any other 'linked transactions' where multiple dwellings relief is not available.

For example, if a property investor were to buy three commercial properties from the same developer at the same time for £250,000 each, this would be treated for SDLT purposes as if it were one single purchase for £750,000. The SDLT charge would therefore be:

£100,000 @ 2%:	£2,000
£500,000 @ 5%:	£25,000
Total:	£27,000

Multiple Dwellings Relief

Multiple dwellings relief is available where multiple *residential* properties are purchased from the same vendor at the same time.

Where multiple dwellings relief is claimed, the rate of SDLT is based on the *average* consideration paid for each 'dwelling'. The relief is not automatic and must be claimed by the purchaser.

The higher charges detailed in Section 7.3 continue to apply to the average price, where applicable. It is, in fact, hard to envisage a scenario where they will not apply, so I am going to assume that they do apply in the examples which follow.

A minimum charge of 1% applies under multiple dwellings relief, although this will now seldom arise in practice.

Example 1
Jat buys five houses from a developer for a total consideration of £1.2m. Without multiple dwellings relief, his SDLT bill would be:

First £125,000 @ 3%:	*£3,750*
Next £125,000 @ 5%:	*£6,250*
Next £675,000 @ 8%:	*£54,000*
Next £275,000 @ 13%:	*£35,750*
Total:	*£99,750*

However, as the average price for each property is just £240,000, Jat claims multiple dwellings relief. The SDLT calculation is then as follows:

First £125,000 @ 3%:	*£3,750*
Next £115,000 @ 5%:	*£5,750*
Total per property:	*£9,500*
x 5 =	*£47,500*

Multiple dwellings relief could potentially also be used to reduce the SDLT charge on a single large property.

Example 2

Pippa is planning to buy a house in Middleton at a cost of £750,000. Her SDLT bill will currently amount to:

First £125,000 @ 3%:	*£3,750*
Next £125,000 @ 5%:	*£6,250*
Next £500,000 @ 8%:	*£40,000*
Total:	*£50,000*

In order to reduce her SDLT cost, Pippa arranges to buy two small flats from the same developer at the same time as the house.

The flats cost £51,000 each, bringing her total consideration to £852,000, but the average consideration is now just £284,000. Pippa can claim multiple dwellings relief to give her a reduction in her SDLT charge as follows:

First £125,000 @ 3%:	*£3,750*
Next £125,000 @ 5%:	*£6,250*
Next £34,000 @ 8%:	*£2,720*
Total per property:	*£12,720*
x 3 =	*£38,160*

Hence, by buying the flats at the same time as the house, Pippa has saved £11,840. That's equivalent to getting a discount of almost 12% on the flats!

I assumed here that the higher charges in Section 7.3 would have applied to Pippa's original planned purchase of the house alone. If that were not the case, this strategy would not be worthwhile.

A Benefit for Property Investors

Self-contained flats within a single property each constitute a separate 'dwelling' for the purposes of multiple dwellings relief. This provides a major benefit for property investors buying larger properties. If, for example, an investor buys a property which has been divided into four flats, this would constitute four dwellings, so that multiple dwellings relief can be claimed and thus significantly reduce the SDLT due.

Alternative Treatment

A simultaneous purchase of six or more residential dwellings (from the same vendor) can alternatively be treated as a non-residential property purchase for SDLT purposes. This may sometimes produce a better outcome than claiming multiple dwellings relief. For example, a purchase of six dwellings for a total of £1.8m would attract SDLT of £84,000: even with multiple dwellings relief. The charge at non-residential rates would be £79,500.

7.9   STAMP DUTY LAND TAX ON LEASES

On the granting of a lease, SDLT is payable on the 'Net Present Value' of all the rent payable under the lease over its entire term.

Where the net present value does not exceed £125,000 (for residential property), or £150,000 (for non-residential property), no SDLT will be payable.

For new leases with a net present value exceeding these limits, SDLT is payable at a rate of 1% on the excess. The rate increases to 2% on any amounts in excess of £5m.

VAT is excluded from the rent payable under the lease for the purposes of SDLT calculations <u>unless</u> the landlord has already exercised the option to tax (this applies to commercial property only).

Example
In January 2018, Clive takes on a ten year lease over a house in Kent at an annual rent of £18,000.

The SDLT legislation provides that the net present value of a sum of money due within the next 12 months is equal to the sum due divided by a 'discount factor'. The applicable discount factor is currently 103.5%. Hence, the 'Present Value' of Clive's first year's rent of £18,000 is £17,391 (i.e. £18,000 divided by 103.5%).

Similarly, the second year's rent, which is due a further 12 months later, must be 'discounted' again by the same amount, i.e. £17,391/103.5% = £16,803.

This process is continued for the entire ten year life of the lease and the net present values of all the rental payments are added together to give the total net present value for the lease. In this case, this works out at £149,699. The SDLT payable by Clive is therefore just £247 (£149,699 less £125,000 = £24,699 x 1% = £247).

Note that it does not matter whether the rent is payable monthly, quarterly or annually, or whether it is payable in advance or in arrears. Net present value is, in each case, always calculated by reference to the total annual rental payable for each year of the lease.

The current 'discount factor' (103.5%) may be changed in the future, depending on a number of factors, including the prevailing rates of inflation and interest.

Lease Premiums

Lease **premiums** also attract SDLT, usually at the same rates as shown in Sections 7.2 to 7.5 for outright purchases.

However, where the lease of a commercial property is also subject to an annual rent of more than £1,000, the 0% rate for the first £150,000 does not apply and SDLT is payable at the rate of 2% on the first £250,000 of any premium.

The restriction of this rule to commercial property only means that it may sometimes be possible to grant a lease over a residential property with a premium of up to £125,000 **and** annual rental with a net present value of up to £125,000 with no SDLT cost whatsoever. (But not where the higher charges shown in Section 7.3 apply to the premium.)

7.10   FIXTURES AND FITTINGS

There is a great deal of misunderstanding over the issue of SDLT on fixtures and fittings.

Firstly, it must be understood that 'fixtures' are part of the fabric of the building and are therefore subject to SDLT. This includes items such as fitted kitchens, baths, toilets, sinks, etc, and is unaffected by whether these items qualify for capital allowances (see Section 4.9).

Moveable fittings, however, are **not** part of the fabric of the building and therefore not subject to SDLT. This includes furniture, carpets, curtains and free-standing 'white goods' such as fridges, freezers and washing machines.

It is therefore often possible to allocate a small part of a property's purchase price to the moveable fittings in the property and thus reduce the SDLT cost. For residential property purchases by landlords and other property business owners this will generally save 3%, 5% or 8% of the amount allocated to the fittings and will therefore often be worthwhile. For non-residential property purchases over £250,000, the saving will be 5%. Remember, however, that it is only the moveable fittings which escape SDLT and there will often be very few of these in a non-residential property.

Generally, it is sensible to purchase moveable fittings by way of a side agreement (which may be no more than a handshake). The informality of such an agreement does not, however, prevent it from having to be included as part of the property's purchase price if the price allocated to the fittings is excessive.

In summary, a small allocation of the purchase price to moveable fittings is a sensible way to reduce your SDLT bill; but be reasonable!

7.11 STAMP DUTY ON SHARES

Before we leave the subject of Stamp Taxes, it is just worth briefly mentioning that the rate of Stamp Duty on purchases of shares and securities in excess of £1,000 is just 0.5%.

Purchases not exceeding £1,000 are exempt (although where quoted shares are purchased through a broker, they will usually pass on the Stamp Duty which arises owing to the fact that they have purchased a larger block of shares in a single transaction).

This lower rate of Duty has led to many tax planning strategies, designed to avoid the excessive rates applied to property transactions by making use of this more palatable rate. However, anti-avoidance legislation introduced over the last few years has effectively blocked most of the more popular methods.

Nevertheless, for those investing in property through a company, there remains the possibility of selling shares in that company at a much lower rate of Duty than would apply to the sale of individual properties within the company. (But see Sections 7.4 and 7.18 regarding additional or higher tax charges on companies owning any individual residential property worth over £500,000 which is not used for business purposes.)

7.12 VAT – INTRODUCTION

VAT, or Value Added Tax, to give it its proper name, arrived on our shores from Europe in 1973. Despite its comparative youth, VAT is one of the UK's most hated taxes and there are some nasty pitfalls for the unwary property investor.

VAT is currently charged at three different rates in the UK: a standard rate of 20%, a reduced rate of 5% and a zero rate. All of these rates may be encountered by property businesses.

For VAT purposes, a sale of a property is a supply of 'goods' and rent on a property is a supply of 'services'. Not all supplies of 'goods and services' are subject to VAT, some are exempt.

The VAT treatment of 'goods and services' in a property business depends on a number of things, including the type of property. Where a supply of 'goods or services' is subject to VAT at any of the three rates given above (including the 'zero rate') it is referred to as a 'taxable supply'.

Goods and services subject to VAT at the standard rate of 20% are often referred to as 'standard-rated'.

VAT Registration

VAT is charged by VAT registered businesses. Sadly, they do not keep it, but must pay it over to HMRC. They are, however, able to claim back the VAT on their purchases of the goods and services used to make their own taxable supplies.

Where a business is making annual taxable supplies of goods or services in excess of the VAT registration threshold, registration is compulsory.

The VAT registration threshold is currently £85,000. The threshold applying for the period from 1st April 2016 to 31st March 2017 was £83,000. (As explained in Sections 3.5 and 5.13, the VAT registration threshold is also relevant for certain other tax purposes.)

Businesses making taxable supplies of goods or services but whose annual sales are less than the VAT registration threshold may register for VAT voluntarily. This is particularly beneficial for those making 'zero rated' supplies, as we shall see later.

Making VAT Digital

Under current Government proposals, businesses which are registered for VAT **and** making annual sales in excess of the VAT registration threshold will be required to keep their records in digital format, using software which is compatible with HMRC's own systems, and submit their VAT returns using an online digital reporting system. This requirement is expected to apply from April 2019.

The Flat Rate Scheme

VAT registered businesses with annual sales not exceeding £150,000 may join the VAT flat rate scheme. This does not alter the amount of VAT they must charge customers or the amount of VAT they pay on their purchases. What it does alter is the amount of VAT paid over to HMRC.

Under the flat rate scheme, a special reduced rate is applied to calculate the VAT payable to HMRC on the business's sales. However, the downside is that the business is unable to recover the VAT paid on most of its purchases.

Wealth Warning
Any individual, partnership, company, or other entity, registering for the flat rate scheme must apply the reduced VAT rate to **all** of their business income, including any rental income which would normally be exempt from VAT.

The flat rate scheme is seldom beneficial to property businesses, with the potential exception of property management businesses and property investors renting out commercial property. Even in these cases, there are 'pros' and 'cons' to be considered.

Furthermore, the introduction of a new rate for 'Low Cost Traders' from April 2017 means that many of those who might have benefited in the past will no longer do so. Broadly speaking, this new rate applies where a business's VAT-inclusive expenditure on goods amounts to less than 2% of its VAT-inclusive sales income. Capital expenditure and certain other items are excluded for the purpose of this test.

At 16.5% of the business's gross VAT-inclusive sales income, the 'Low Cost Trader' rate provides little benefit. (The VAT within gross standard-rated sales income only amounts to 16.67% in any case!)

7.13   VAT ON RESIDENTIAL PROPERTY

Residential Property Letting

Generally speaking, a property investment business engaged primarily in residential property letting does not need to be VAT registered because the letting of residential property is an exempt supply for VAT purposes.

VAT is therefore not chargeable on rent, although, of course, VAT cannot be recovered on expenses and the landlord should therefore claim VAT-inclusive costs for Income Tax and CGT purposes.

The letting of holiday accommodation is, however, standard-rated for VAT purposes, whether or not it qualifies for the special treatment outlined in Section 8.17.

Beware also that the provision of ancillary services (e.g. cleaning or gardening) may sometimes be standard-rated, and hence subject to VAT at 20%, if the value of annual supplies of these services exceeds the VAT registration threshold.

Some landlords making ancillary supplies of this nature prefer to register for VAT, even if they have not reached the registration threshold, as this means that they are able to recover some of the VAT on their expenses.

Residential Property Development

Sales of newly constructed residential property are zero-rated for VAT purposes. This means that the developer can recover all of the VAT on their construction costs without having to charge VAT on the sale of the property. (In theory, VAT is charged, but at a rate of zero.)

This treatment is extended to the sale of a property which has just been converted from a non-residential property into a residential property (*e.g. converting a barn into a house*). It is also extended to 'substantially reconstructed protected buildings'. In essence, this means the sale of a listed building following the carrying out of major alterations. Such alterations do, of course, require approval from the authorities.

Property developers carrying out construction work under any of these headings are therefore able to register for VAT and then recover the VAT on the vast majority of their business expenses.

Other Residential Property Sales

Other sales of residential property are generally an exempt supply meaning, once again, that the taxpayer making the sale is unable to recover any of the VAT on his or her expenses. This means VAT cannot be recovered by most residential property investors and dealers.

Property developers who merely renovate or alter existing residential property prior to onward sale are also generally unable to recover VAT on their costs. But where the work qualifies as a 'conversion', as described below, they may at least be able to reduce the amount of VAT payable.

Conversions

A reduced VAT rate of 5% is available for building work carried out on a residential property where the work results in a change to the number of dwellings in the property. This would apply to the conversion of:

- One house into several flats
- Two or more flats into a single house
- Two semi-detached houses into a single detached house

The reduced rate also applies to conversions of commercial property into residential use.

Property investors or developers carrying out projects of this nature should try to ensure that they only pay the lower VAT rate from the outset, as it is difficult to recover any excess paid in error.

Renovations of Vacant Property

The 5% rate also applies to renovation work on residential property which had been vacant for two years or more before work commenced.

7.14   VAT ON COMMERCIAL PROPERTY

Commercial Property Letting

For commercial property, there is an 'option to tax'. In other words, the landlord may choose, for each property and on a property-by-property basis, whether or not the rent should be a VAT exempt supply.

If the 'option to tax' is exercised, the rent becomes standard-rated for VAT purposes. The landlord may then recover VAT on all of the expenses relating to that property. Ancillary services are again likely to be standard-rated, regardless of whether you have opted to tax the rent itself.

> **Tax Tip**
> If the potential tenants of a commercial property are all, or mostly, likely to be VAT-registered businesses themselves, it will generally make sense to exercise the 'option to tax' on the property in order to recover the VAT on expenses incurred.

If your tenants themselves have a VAT-registered and fully taxable business (for VAT purposes), then everyone's happy. The problem comes when your tenants cannot recover some or all of the VAT which you are charging them.

And remember that (after a short 'cooling off' period) you cannot change your option on a property for a minimum of 20 years once it has been exercised. Hence, if you opt to charge VAT to a fully taxable tenant, you will probably still need to charge VAT to the next tenant in the same property, even if they cannot recover it.

Sometimes, though, with non-taxable (for VAT) tenants, where you have not yet exercised your option to tax, you can refrain from doing so and negotiate a higher rent to compensate you for your loss of VAT recovery on your own costs.

Example
Norman owns an office building and hasn't yet opted to tax the rents. By early 2018, he has monthly costs of £500 plus VAT (i.e. £600 gross) and expects a monthly rent of £2,500. If Norman opts to tax he will recover £100 a month from HMRC and make a monthly profit of £2,000.

However, Lenny, the prospective tenant, is not registered for VAT. If Norman opts to tax the property, Lenny's rent will effectively be 20% higher, i.e. £3,000 per month. So, as a better alternative, Norman and Lenny agree that Norman will not opt to tax the building but will, instead, charge Lenny £2,750 a month rent. Now Norman is making a monthly profit of £2,150 (£2,750 minus £600) and Lenny's rent is effectively £250 less than it would have been. Norman and Lenny both win and HMRC loses.

Commercial Property Sales & Purchases

Where the 'option to tax' has been exercised by the owner of a commercial property, their sale of that property will be standard-rated and this has major implications for such transactions. Sales of new commercial property are also standard-rated.

Wealth Warning

Where VAT must be charged on a commercial property sale, the SDLT must be calculated on the basis of the gross, VAT-inclusive price. This can lead to combined tax rates of up to 26%! This represents a pretty hefty cost if the purchaser is not VAT registered, possibly enough to prevent the sale from taking place in some cases. Imagine a large insurance company buying a new office block in central London – the combined VAT and SDLT cost would be astronomical!

Furthermore, even when the purchaser is able to recover the VAT on their purchase, the extra SDLT paid on that VAT cannot be recovered.

Where a property investor incurs VAT on the purchase of a commercial property, the only way to recover that VAT will be for the investor to exercise the 'option to tax' on the property. In this way, the Government generally forces everyone to maintain the taxable status of the building.

If a VAT registered property developer incurs VAT on the purchase of a commercial property, they can recover the VAT in the same way as on any other purchase of goods or services for use in the business. This initial recovery is not dependent on exercising the 'option to tax', as the developer has a taxable business for VAT purposes, but ...

Wealth Warning

If VAT has been recovered on the purchase of a commercial property, a sale of that property without first exercising the option to tax would be an exempt supply. If that property were trading stock, this would result in the loss of all the VAT initially reclaimed on its purchase and on any development, renovation or conversion work carried out on it. Some of the VAT recovered on general overhead costs would probably also become repayable.

Furthermore, when more than £250,000 has been spent on the purchase or improvement of a property for use as the business's own trading premises, a sale of that property within ten years without first exercising the option to tax would also trigger VAT.

7.15   VAT ON PROPERTY MANAGEMENT

Property management services are standard-rated for VAT and hence a property management business will need to be registered if its annual turnover exceeds the £85,000 registration threshold. The taxpayer may still register voluntarily even if the level of sales is below the threshold.

Whether the properties under management are residential or commercial makes no difference for this purpose.

Naturally, a property management business which is registered for VAT can recover the VAT on most of its business expenses. There are, however, a few exceptions where VAT cannot be wholly recovered, as we shall see in the next section.

7.16   INTERACTION OF VAT WITH OTHER TAXES

Any business which is registered for VAT should generally include only the net (excluding VAT) amounts of income and expenditure in its accounts for Income Tax purposes. Where VAT recovery is barred or restricted, however, the additional cost arising should be treated as part of the relevant expense.

Expenses subject to restrictions on the recovery of VAT include:

- Business entertaining
- Purchases of motor cars
- Leasing/contract hire of motor cars
- Provision of private fuel for proprietors or staff

As you can see, many of the expenses subject to a VAT recovery restriction are also subject to some form of Income Tax restriction.

A non-registered business should always include the VAT in its business expenditure for Income Tax purposes. Similar principles apply for CGT and Corporation Tax purposes.

7.17   NATIONAL INSURANCE

See Section 5.5 and Appendix A for details of NI rates. The NI treatment of property trading income is also covered in Section 5.5.

Any incidental trading income arising as part of a property investment business may be subject to NI. Subject to this, property rental income is not classed as 'earnings' and hence NI should never be due. Despite this, some HMRC offices have sought to collect Class 2 NI from landlords. Part of the reason for this relates to the way in which landlords have registered for self-assessment (see Section 3.6). Landlords with income from furnished holiday lettings have also sometimes been charged Class 2 NI.

This is incorrect: property income is not 'business income' for NI purposes and the vast majority of landlords should not, therefore, be subject to Class 2 NI. Fortunately, as Class 2 NI is due to be abolished in April 2018, this issue will soon be consigned to history!

Non-trading taxpayers can pay voluntary Class 3 NI in order to secure state retirement benefits, etc, if they so wish. The rate of Class 3 contributions is, however, currently £14.25 per week, having been increased by 76% since 2009.

Naturally, if you should employ anyone to help you in your property business, their salary will be subject to both employee's and employer's Class 1 NI (at 12% and 13.8% respectively). However, employers are not required to pay employer's NI on earnings up to the upper earnings limit paid to any employee under the age of 21, or qualifying apprentices under the age of 25. Each employer is also eligible to claim exemption from the first £3,000 of employer's NI arising in the year.

If you provide an employee with any taxable benefits-in-kind, you will additionally be liable for Class 1A NI (again at 13.8%).

Capital Gains

NI is never payable on capital gains. However, if you are classed as a property developer or a property trader, your profit on property sales will be taxed as trading income and hence will be subject to NI.

7.18 THE ANNUAL TAX ON ENVELOPED DWELLINGS & RELATED CHARGES

A series of additional tax charges apply to UK residential property owned by 'non-natural persons'. The definition of 'non-natural persons' includes companies, partnerships where a company is a partner, and collective investment schemes. Most commonly, the charges apply to companies. They do not apply to property investors operating purely as individuals.

Three charges are involved:

- The Annual Tax on Enveloped Dwellings ('ATED')
- CGT at 28% on the disposal of the property
- The 15% rate of SDLT (see Section 7.4)

The charges only apply to single dwellings worth in excess of £500,000. They do not apply by reference to the total value of the property portfolio.

Business Exemption

The good news for most property investors operating through a company (or any other 'non-natural person') is that properties are exempt from these charges if they are being used in a business: including a property rental business.

Hence, in most cases, property investment companies should be exempt from these charges; although it will be essential to ensure that properties are being acquired for use in the business, and continue to be held for business purposes thereafter.

The bad news, however, is that any company or other 'non-natural person' which is eligible for this exemption will need to claim it – whenever they buy property worth more than £500,000 for SDLT purposes; and on an annual basis when they own any property worth more than £500,000 for the purposes of ATED. Hence, even if there is no extra tax, there will still be plenty of extra administration to deal with!

The annual charge under ATED currently ranges from £3,500 (for property worth more than £500,000 but not more than £1m) to £220,350 (for property worth more than £20m).

The charges described above apply regardless of where the 'non-natural person' is resident for tax purposes. For further information see the Taxcafe guide 'Tax Free Capital Gains'.

7.19   SCOTTISH TAXES

From 2017/18 onwards, the Scottish Parliament has powers to vary the rates of Income Tax paid by Scottish taxpayers. Whilst these powers are much wider than any previous devolved powers, they are still subject to certain limitations. I will look at these powers and their impact on Scottish property investors in Section 7.22.

Scotland also has two devolved taxes, including LBTT, which is covered in Sections 7.20 and 7.21.

7.20   LAND AND BUILDINGS TRANSACTION TAX

Since April 2015, SDLT has been abolished for property located in Scotland and has been replaced by LBTT. LBTT operates in a broadly similar way to SDLT, subject to a few variations, as noted below.

Residential Property
The basic underlying rates of LBTT on residential property are as follows:

Purchase Consideration	Rate Applying
Up to £145,000	Nil
£145,000 to £250,000	2%
£250,000 to £325,000	5%
£325,000 to £750,000	10%
Over £750,000	12%

Residential property purchases by landlords and other property business owners are, however, also subject to the Additional Dwelling Supplement ('ADS') which we will examine in Section 7.21.

Non-Residential Property
The rates of LBTT on non-residential property are as follows:

Purchase Consideration	Rate Applying
Up to £150,000	Nil
£150,000 to £350,000	3%
Over £350,000	4.5%

LBTT is applied on a 'progressive' basis for both residential and non-residential property.

Example
Isla buys a small shop in Aberdeen for £270,000. She pays LBTT at 3% on £120,000 (£270,000 - £150,000), which amounts to £3,600.

Key Differences

Apart from the rates applying, LBTT operates in broadly the same way as SDLT. Many of the principles examined in Sections 7.1 to 7.10 continue to apply. In particular, the LBTT rates on leases are the same as those for SDLT (see Section 7.9), except that the 2% rate on net present value in excess of £5m does not apply.

Multiple dwellings relief operates differently under LBTT. Instead of taking an average price, LBTT is calculated separately on each dwelling comprised in the purchase. The total LBTT due cannot be less than 25% of the amount due on the total consideration for the whole transaction.

Purchases of six or more dwellings may again alternatively be taxed at non-residential rates based on the total consideration for the whole transaction.

This is by no means an exhaustive list of all the differences between LBTT and SDLT, so it is essential to take legal advice when purchasing property in Scotland (just as it is when purchasing property anywhere else!)

7.21 THE ADDITIONAL DWELLING SUPPLEMENT

The ADS operates in a similar way to the higher SDLT charges examined in Section 7.3. It applies an additional 3% LBTT charge to purchases of residential property in Scotland from April 2016 onwards.

Purchases for under £40,000 are exempt but, otherwise, the basic rule is that ADS applies to any purchase:

i)   Made for the purposes of a property business, including property letting, etc.
ii) By an individual who has a relevant interest in more than one residential property at the end of the day of purchase,
iii) By two or more persons jointly where any of them has a relevant interest in more than one residential property at the end of the day of purchase, or
iv) By a company or other 'non-natural' person.

Heading (i) above means that **all** purchases of residential property in Scotland by landlords and other property business owners, for use in their business, will be subject to the additional 3% charge under ADS (except for any purchases for less than £40,000).

Replacement of Main Residence

There is an exemption from ADS where the purchaser is buying a property which they intend to adopt as their main residence and is replacing a previous main residence sold within the previous eighteen months.

The exemption also applies where the purchaser's former main residence is sold within eighteen months **after** the new main residence is purchased. However, in this case, ADS will apply in the first place and a refund will have to be claimed later, on the sale of the former main residence.

Where all of two or more joint purchasers are either eligible for this exemption, or will not have any relevant interest in any other residential property at the end of the day of purchase **and** are not buying the property for business purposes, then ADS will not apply (or can be refunded later, as the case may be). In any other cases involving joint purchasers, ADS will apply (including the scenario outlined in the example of 'Jack and Rose' in Section 7.3, where a couple are buying their new home jointly but did not both own a share of their old home).

Relevant Interests in Residential Property

Subject to the points below, any interest in any residential property anywhere in the world will be a relevant interest for the purpose of ADS. An 'interest' means any form of legal right to a share in the property for any period of time.

Leases of more than 20 years are regarded as a relevant interest. Where such a lease exists, the person holding the superior interest in the property (the landlord) is not treated as having a relevant interest in the property.

Where an individual is buying a property for use as their own home, any property to which ADS applied as a consequence of heading (i) above (or would have applied if the property had been in Scotland) can be disregarded.

Tax Tip
An individual who already owns rental property, none of which was purchased before April 2016, can avoid higher charges by buying a home in Scotland.

By buying a rental property in England* first and then a home in Scotland, you could avoid both sets of higher charges on both properties.

Wealth Warning
If you buy a rental property in Scotland first and then a home in England*, you will pay higher charges on both properties.

* - at present, the same goes for Wales or Northern Ireland, but see Section 7.23

The following interests may also be disregarded for the purposes of ADS:

- Interests in property worth less than £40,000
- Caravans, mobile homes and houseboats

Each individual must also include any relevant interests in residential property held by their spouse, civil partner, co-habitant (i.e. an unmarried partner), or minor children aged under 16 (e.g. property held in trust on their behalf).

7.22   SCOTTISH INCOME TAX RATES

From 2017/18 onwards, the Scottish Parliament has control over Scottish Income Tax rates and thresholds. It may not, however, alter:

- The personal allowance (although it could effectively extend it by introducing a zero-rate tax band – as noted below)
- The High Income Child Benefit Charge (see Section 3.3)
- The withdrawal of personal allowances where income exceeds £100,000
- UK tax rates on dividends, interest, savings income, etc. (see below)
- Capital allowances

Similarly, it has no power over other taxes, such as NI, VAT, CGT, Corporation Tax and IHT.

The amount of income on which a Scottish taxpayer is liable for tax continues to be computed in exactly the same way as for other UK resident taxpayers: it is only the rates of tax which may be different. Hence, the vast majority of the advice in this guide remains equally valid for Scottish taxpayers – it is only the amount of tax which can be saved (or may be suffered) which may vary.

Scottish Income Tax rates apply to all a Scottish taxpayer's income except:

- Dividends
- Interest and other savings income
- Income from Real Estate Investment Trusts or Property Authorised Investment Funds

Hence, Scottish Income Tax rates apply to all of a Scottish taxpayer's property rental or trading income, regardless of where their properties are located.

In other words, a Scottish taxpayer pays Scottish Income Tax rates on income derived from property both within and outwith Scotland. Other taxpayers continue to pay Income Tax at normal UK rates on all of their income, even if it is derived from property in Scotland.

Scottish Income Tax Rates

The Scottish Government has frozen the higher rate tax threshold for Scottish taxpayers at £43,000 for 2017/18. The basic rate band for Scottish taxpayers in 2017/18 is therefore £31,500. This will lead to additional Income Tax of £400 for Scottish higher rate taxpayers this year. We will look at some more practical impacts of the lower higher rate tax threshold for Scottish property investors later in this section.

It is also proposed that the higher rate tax threshold for Scottish taxpayers will only rise by inflation from 2018/19 until at least 2021/22 and will not be increased to at least £50,000 by 2020/21 (as has been proposed for other UK taxpayers).

Estimating annual inflation at 2.5% would produce a Scottish higher rate tax threshold of around £46,350 by 2020/21, costing Scottish higher rate taxpayers an additional £730 per year: including those forced into higher rate tax by the restrictions on interest relief examined in Section 4.5.

The tiny silver lining is that the Scottish Government proposes to introduce a small zero-rate band by 2021/22 to ensure that at least the first £12,750 of Scottish taxpayers' income is free from Income Tax.

No changes to the 45% additional rate have been announced for Scottish taxpayers so far; although we may see changes in a few years' time.

Practical Impacts

Every Scottish taxpayer effectively has two different basic rate bands for 2017/18:

- A Scottish basic rate band of £31,500 which applies to employment, self-employment, rental and pension income, and
- A UK basic rate band of £33,500 which applies to dividends, interest and savings income and also for CGT purposes

Example 1

For 2017/18, Wallace has total gross rental income of £50,000, allowable interest costs of £8,000 and other qualifying expenses of £500. This gives him a taxable rental 'profit' of £43,500 (his deductible interest is restricted to just £6,000 – see Section 4.5). Deducting his personal allowance of £11,500 leaves £32,000. As he is a Scottish taxpayer, he will pay Income Tax on this sum as follows:

£31,500 @ 20% = £6,300
£500 @ 40% =   £200
Less
£2,000 @ 20%   (£400) – basic rate tax relief on 25% of his allowable interest
Net total due: £6,100

Wallace also has a taxable capital gain (after deducting his annual exemption) of £10,000 on a residential property sale. His CGT bill will be:

£1,500 @ 18% = £270
£8,500 @ 28% = £2,380
Total   £2,650

*This is because he has £1,500 of his **UK** basic rate band available for CGT purposes.*

If Wallace had been living in a different part of the UK, his Income Tax bill would have been £100 less but his CGT bill would still have been the same.

Tax Tip
Scottish taxpayers have the same basic rate band for CGT purposes as other UK taxpayers. The CGT planning techniques explored in Sections 8.28 and 8.30 and throughout this guide will therefore produce the same savings for Scottish taxpayers.

Another important point to note is that the upper earnings limit for NI purposes remains at the UK level (£45,000 for 2017/18) for Scottish taxpayers.

Example 2
Gruoch is a property developer based in Dundee. Her taxable profits for 2017/18 are £43,800 and she also has interest income of £1,500. She pays Income Tax as follows:

Trading profits
£31,500 @ 20%= £6,300 (the Scottish basic rate band)
£800 @ 40% =   £320   (excess over Scottish higher rate tax threshold)
Interest income
£500 @ 0% =   £0   (the 'personal savings allowance' – see Appendix A)
£700 @ 20% =   £140   (amount still within the UK basic rate band)
£300 @ 40% =   £120   (excess over UK higher rate tax threshold)
Total   £6,880

She also has to pay Class 4 NI at 9% on £35,636 (£43,800 – £8,164). The NI rate does not drop to 2% until profits exceed £45,000. Her total tax bill is thus £10,087, which is £160 more than it would have been if she had been living in a different part of the UK.

It is worth noting that the overall effective tax rate on the top £800 of Gruoch's trading profits is 49%. This rate applies to any Scottish taxpayer's trading profits which fall into the 'gap' between the Scottish higher rate tax threshold and the UK higher rate tax threshold (i.e. between £43,000 and £45,000 in 2017/18).

Employment income falling into this 'gap' suffers an overall tax rate of 52%!

Who Is A Scottish Taxpayer?

You are classed as a Scottish taxpayer if you are UK resident and your main place of residence in the UK is in Scotland. Your main place of residence in the UK must be determined as a question of fact, and it is important to remember that, for *this* purpose:

- It is not possible to elect which property is to be treated as your main place of residence
- Only property in the UK is counted

- It is not necessary to have any legal or equitable interest in the property
- Any type of abode may be counted, including hotel rooms and berths on ships and oil rigs
- Each person must be considered individually (i.e. married couples are not treated as a single 'unit')

Hence, whilst your 'main place of residence' for this purpose will often be the same as your 'main residence' for CGT purposes, the rules are slightly different and may sometimes lead to a different result.

See Section 6.22 for further guidance on the factors to be considered in determining a main place of residence. Issues such as where your spouse lives or whether you have any legal title in the property are no longer critical for this purpose, but continue to be amongst those factors.

If you move to or from Scotland during the tax year, you will be classified according to where your main place of residence in the UK is for the majority of the year.

If it is not clear whether your main place of residence is located in Scotland for any given tax year then the question of whether you are a Scottish taxpayer for that year will be based on where you have spent the most days. For this purpose, a 'day' is based on where you are at midnight and you become a Scottish taxpayer if you are present in Scotland at midnight on at least as many days as you are present in any of: England, Wales or Northern Ireland (taking each country separately).

Non-UK residents cannot be Scottish taxpayers.

7.23   WALES AND NORTHERN IRELAND

From 1st April 2018, SDLT will cease to apply to property located in Wales and will be replaced by a new Welsh tax called 'Land Transaction Tax'. The rates and bands for Land Transaction Tax are to be announced by 1st October 2017. We can only hope that the authorities in Cardiff will be less eager to persecute landlords and other property businesses than their counterparts in London and Edinburgh (but I am not holding my breath!)

Further tax powers are expected to be given to Wales in the next few years and are expected to be similar to the powers devolved to Scotland.

Northern Ireland has been given the power to set its own Corporation Tax rate and seems likely to cut the rate to 12.5%, in line with the Irish Republic. The date for the introduction of this new rate is uncertain however. The Northern Irish rate will apply to most companies trading in the province. For more details see the Taxcafe.co.uk guide *'Using a Property Company to Save Tax'*.

Chapter 8

Advanced Tax Planning

8.1 INTRODUCTION TO TAX PLANNING

In previous chapters we have looked at the mechanics of the UK tax system as it applies to the individual property investor. In this chapter we will take a look at some more advanced aspects of UK property taxation and some further useful planning strategies. These strategies relate in the main to those investors who continue to hold their property investments personally.

In many cases, the best tax-planning results will be obtained through the use of a combination of different techniques, rather than merely following any single one.

Each situation is different and the optimum solution only comes through detailed analysis of all the relevant facts. Tax planning should never be undertaken without full knowledge of the facts of the case and the exact circumstances of the individuals and other legal entities involved.

For this reason, the techniques laid out in this chapter, which are by no means exhaustive, are intended only to give you some idea of the tax savings which can be achieved through careful planning. If and when you come to undertake any tax-planning of your own you should seek professional advice from someone fully acquainted with your situation.

Remember also that tax law is constantly changing and a technique which works well now may later be undermined by changes made in Parliament or decisions made in Court.

Bayley's Tax Planning Law

All tax planning should be based on these four guiding principles:

- Hope for the best,
- Plan for the worst,
- Review your position constantly, and
- Expect the unexpected!

The Budgets and Autumn Statements which we have seen over the last few years have provided some of the best arguments for these principles that I have ever seen. Especially the last one!

8.2   THE BENEFITS OF JOINT OWNERSHIP

Owning property jointly with one or more other people can be highly beneficial for tax purposes. In this section, we will look at joint ownership benefits which are available to anyone. In the next section, we will concentrate on married couples.

A number of important tax reliefs, bands and allowances are available on a 'per person' basis, these include:

- The personal allowance
- The annual CGT exemption
- Private letting relief
- Entrepreneurs' relief
- The basic rate tax band
- The £100,000 threshold for withdrawal of personal allowances
- The £150,000 additional rate threshold
- The small earnings exception for NI
- The NI earnings threshold
- The nil rate band for IHT

Furthermore, as discussed in Section 4.9, it is also possible to structure investments so that the AIA effectively operates on a 'per person' basis.

The value of these allowances, bands and reliefs can effectively be doubled in the case of properties held jointly by two people (or tripled for three joint owners, etc.).

How Much Is At Stake?

Sticking with two joint owners, the maximum tax savings which joint ownership can generate in 2017/18 alone are:

- £6,514 on most capital gains on residential property
- £17,714 on capital gains with private letting relief (but see the 'wealth warning' in Section 8.4)
- £1,803,164 on capital gains with entrepreneurs' relief (but see the 'wealth warning' in Section 6.28)
- £18,400 in Income Tax on rental income
- £15,688 in Income Tax and NI on trading profits
- £84,900 in additional Income Tax savings (or even repayments) when claiming the AIA on commercial property, qualifying furnished holiday accommodation, or assets within 'communal areas' (see Sections 4.9 and 8.17)
- £170,000 in Inheritance Tax

The maximum Income Tax savings described above are based on taxpayers with high levels of income such that joint ownership can be used to reduce their taxable income down to £100,000. Most higher-rate taxpayers can still achieve considerable savings, however.

Wealth Warning
Not every tax relief or band is given on a 'per person' basis. Exceptions to be wary of include:

- All SDLT and LBTT bands
- The VAT registration threshold
- Rent-a-room relief

Additionally, in the case of the upper earnings limit for NI, the fact that this works on a 'per person' basis will actually work against joint owners in a trading situation (although this is usually outweighed by Income Tax savings).

Non-Equal Splits

When considering the benefits of joint ownership, remember that it is possible to have any split of beneficial ownership which you desire, as long as the correct form of joint ownership is in place (see Section 2.14). In this context, it is worth mentioning that a joint tenancy can be changed fairly easily into a tenancy in common. This change is not treated as a disposal for CGT purposes unless at the same time there is also a change to a non-equal split of beneficial ownership.

Changing the Split

Where the joint owners are not married, it is difficult to transfer any share in the property to the other person without incurring CGT or other charges. In Section 8.8 we will look at a possible way around this. Nevertheless, for joint owners other than married couples, it is generally advisable to get your ownership structure right from the outset.

Optimising Rental Income Shares

Joint owners who are not a married couple may agree to share rental income in different proportions to their legal ownership of the property (perhaps because one of the investors is carrying out the management of the jointly held portfolio). The Income Tax treatment should follow the agreed profit-sharing arrangements. It is wise to document your profit-sharing agreement in order to avoid any dispute, however.

Sales by Former Joint Owners

For the purposes of calculating the PPR exemption, a former joint owner's period of ownership of the whole property is treated as commencing with the date on which they first acquired any beneficial ownership of any part of the property.

8.3 USING YOUR SPOUSE OR CIVIL PARTNER

Putting property into joint names with your spouse can generate considerable tax savings, just like any other joint owners, as we have seen in the previous section. In some cases, an outright transfer of the whole property may even be more beneficial.

The major difference between those who have legally 'tied the knot' and the rest of us, however, is the fact that the transfer itself is free from tax (subject to the points made in Section 7.7 regarding SDLT or LBTT).

Despite this, the transfer is not necessarily free of tax **consequences** and we will look at the impact of transfers to a spouse on PPR relief and private letting relief in Section 8.4.

The example of George and Charlotte in Section 6.32 demonstrated the potential CGT savings in a simple case where PPR relief did not apply. In such a case (and where the couple are married), it is normally immaterial whether the property was in joint ownership throughout, or was only transferred into joint ownership at a later date, prior to the ultimate sale (often known as a 'pre-sale transfer'). The effect on the couple's final tax liabilities usually remains exactly the same.

As we saw in Section 6.32, the potential CGT saving on a typical residential investment property is now up to £6,514. However, the position will differ from one couple to another, so investors need to weigh up the costs of any 'pre-sale transfer' against the saving available in their own particular case.

Two key provisos must be made regarding transfers of property to a spouse:

a) The transferee spouse must be beneficially entitled to his/her share of the sale proceeds. Any attempt to prevent this could make the transfer invalid for tax purposes.

b) An interim transfer of property into joint names prior to sale must take place early enough to ensure that the transferee spouse genuinely has beneficial title to their share. If it is left until the ultimate sale is a contractual certainty, it may be too late to be effective for tax purposes.

Timing

Where a transfer to a spouse prior to sale is planned, the following guidelines may assist in making it effective for tax purposes. Bear in mind always, though, that the transferee must have beneficial ownership for the transfer to work as intended.

- It is preferable to do the transfer as soon as possible
- Ideally, it should be before the property is put on the market
- A transfer at any time after there is a contract for sale to a third party is likely to be ineffective in providing the transferee with the requisite beneficial ownership

But Joint Ownership Is Not Always Beneficial

A transfer into joint names prior to sale is not always beneficial. Sometimes, it is preferable to have the property in the sole name of one spouse at the time of sale. This may arise, for example, if:

- One spouse's annual exemption will be used on other capital gains in the same year, whilst the other's annual exemption remains fully available,
- Some or all of one spouse's basic rate band is available but the other spouse is a higher rate taxpayer,
- Only one spouse is entitled to PPR relief or private letting relief on the property (see Section 8.4),
- Only one spouse is entitled to entrepreneurs' relief on the property (see Section 6.28), or
- One spouse has capital losses available to set off against the gain on the property

If the best spouse to hold the property at the time of the sale is not the one who already holds it, a pre-sale transfer could generate considerable savings. The same provisos as set out above apply equally here.

In summary, when a sale is in prospect, it is well worth assessing whether a transfer into joint ownership, or to the other spouse outright, might result in a significant CGT saving. Always remember, however, that whoever has title to the property at the time of the sale must be entitled to the proceeds!

Lastly, it is also worth remembering that joint ownership does not have to mean equal shares and any other allocation is also possible.

8.4   SAVING MORE TAX WITH TRANSFERS TO SPOUSES

Please note that the principles outlined in this section only apply to transfers between legally married spouses or registered civil partners.

A lifetime transfer of a property, or a share in a property, between spouses usually results in the transferee spouse taking over the transferor spouse's base cost (or an appropriate share of it). However, it does not necessarily follow that the transferee takes over the reliefs to which the transferor was entitled. Sometimes the reliefs will transfer; sometimes they will not: which could be utterly disastrous, but could also sometimes work in the couple's favour. It's all a question of getting your timing right!

Principal Private Residence Relief

For the purposes of PPR relief, the position depends entirely on whether the property is the couple's main residence at the time of the transfer. If it is their main residence at that time then, for the purposes of the relief, the transferee is treated as if they had owned the property since the transferor first acquired it. The transferee spouse is then also entitled to the PPR exemption for the same periods as the transferor spouse.

Example
In March 2006, Babur bought a house in London for £500,000 and adopted it as his main residence. In 2012, he married Zainab and she moved into the house with him. In 2013, Babur put the house into equal joint names with Zainab. In September 2014, the couple moved out of the house and began to rent it out. Later, in March 2018, the couple sold the house for £1.4m. As Babur put the property into joint names whilst it was their main residence, Zainab will be entitled to the same periods of PPR exemption as he is. Each of them will therefore have the same CGT calculation, as follows:

	£
Sale proceeds (half share)	*700,000*
Less: Cost (half share)	*(250,000)*
	450,000
PPR relief (10/12 x £450,000)*	*(375,000)*
Private letting relief	*(40,000)*
	35,000
Annual exemption	*(11,300)*
Taxable gain	*23,700*

* The property is exempt for the eight and a half years that it was Babur's main residence plus the last eighteen months of the couple's ownership.

If we assume that Babur is a higher rate taxpayer and Zainab has enough of her basic rate band available to cover her share of the capital gain then the couple's total CGT liability will be £10,902 (£23,700 x 28% for Babur plus £23,700 x 18% for Zainab). If Babur had still held the property in his sole name at the time of sale, his CGT calculation would have been:

	£
Sale proceeds	*1,400,000*
Less: Cost	*(500,000)*
	900,000
PPR relief (10/12 x £900,000)	*(750,000)*
Private letting relief	*(40,000)*
	110,000
Annual exemption	*(11,300)*
Taxable gain	*98,700*

Babur's CGT liability would then have been £27,636 (£98,700 x 28%).

Under these circumstances, transferring the property into joint names while it was the couple's main residence has resulted in a CGT saving of £16,734. This saving arises from a number of sources:

- A couple owning a property jointly are entitled to up to £40,000 of private letting relief **each**; meaning that up to £80,000 of relief may be available.
- Each joint owner has their own annual exemption.
- In this particular case, the transferee's basic rate band was available to reduce the rate of CGT that she paid from 28% to 18%.

The maximum savings arising from each of these sources in 2017/18 are £11,200, £3,164 and £3,350 respectively; making the maximum total saving of £17,714 referred to in Section 8.2.

Tax Tip
Where a property has a period of PPR relief built up already, it will generally be beneficial to put it into joint names whilst it is still the couple's main residence.

If the property is **not** the couple's main residence at the time of the transfer then, whilst the transferee spouse still effectively takes over an appropriate share of the transferor's base cost, they are **not** entitled to any historic periods of PPR exemption which the transferor has already built up and are treated as having acquired their share of the property on the date of the transfer.

Example Revisited

Let us assume that Babur did not put the house into equal joint names with Zainab until 2015: after the couple had moved out of the property. His CGT calculation remains the same, but Zainab's is now as follows:

	£
Sale proceeds (half share)	*700,000*
Less: Cost (half share)	*(250,000)*

	450,000
Annual exemption	*(11,300)*

Taxable gain	*438,700*
	=======

Zainab's CGT liability will now be at least £119,486 (£33,500 x 18% + £405,200 x 28%); bringing the couple's total tax bill up to at least £126,122 (£119,486 + £23,700 x 28%). The transfer of the property into joint ownership has therefore effectively cost the couple at least an extra £98,486 (£126,122 – £27,636).

Wealth Warning

As we can see, a transfer of a property with a prior period of PPR exemption which takes place whilst the property is **not** the couple's main residence can have disastrous consequences. The transferee is not entitled to the prior period of PPR exemption and, unless the property is re-adopted as their main residence at a later date, they will also not be entitled to the exemption for the last eighteen months of ownership and nor will they be entitled to any private letting relief.

Tax Tip

The easiest way to avoid the disastrous outcome outlined above would be to simply transfer the property back into the sole ownership of the original owner.

As explained in Section 8.2, a former joint owner is treated for the purposes of PPR relief as if they had owned the whole property since the date on which they first acquired any beneficial ownership of any part of it. Hence, in our example, if the property were put back into Babur's sole ownership prior to sale, he would be treated for the purposes of PPR relief as having a single uninterrupted period of ownership of the whole property from 2006 to 2018.

An alternative method for restoring some of the lost PPR exemption and private letting relief would be for the couple to re-adopt the property as their main residence. However, where the couple are willing to do this, there is actually a far better technique which they could use instead, as we will now examine.

Turning the Rules to Your Advantage

So far we have established that a transfer of a property, or a share in it, from one spouse to another results in the transferee effectively taking over the transferor's base cost, or a suitable proportion of it, but that the transferee is only entitled to earlier periods of PPR exemption on the property when it is the couple's main residence at the time of the transfer.

What we have not yet looked at is the situation where the property becomes the couple's main residence **after** the transfer. In these cases, a transfer of the property into the sole name of the transferee **before** it becomes their main residence could be highly advantageous.

Example
In September 2003, Caleb bought a property in Manchester for £40,000 and began renting it out. In June 2017 Caleb transfers the property to his civil partner, David. In September 2017, the couple move into the property and adopt it as their main residence. Two years later, in September 2019, David sells the property for £148,000. David's CGT calculation is as follows:

	£
Sale proceeds	*148,000*
Less: Cost	*(40,000)*

	108,000
PPR relief (24/27 x £108,000)*	*(96,000)*
Private letting relief	*(12,000)*

Taxable gain	*Nil*
	======

* - The property was the couple's main residence for 24 months out of David's total ownership period of 27 months. Caleb's ownership period is ignored because the property was not their main residence at the time of the transfer.
If Caleb had held on to the property himself until the date of sale, his CGT calculation would have been as follows:

	£
Sale proceeds	*148,000*
Less: Cost	*(40,000)*

	108,000
PPR relief (2/16 x £108,000)	*(13,500)*
Private letting relief	*(13,500)*

	81,000
Annual exemption	*(11,300)*

Taxable gain	*69,700*
	======

Transferring the property to David before it became the couple's main residence has therefore saved up to £19,516 (£69,700 x 28%) in CGT.

Tax Tip
Where a property has no previous period of PPR exemption, transferring it to your spouse **before** you adopt it as your main residence can lead to significant savings.

What If the Property Is Already Held Jointly?

The technique used by Caleb and David would not work if the couple already held the property jointly because, as explained in Section 8.2, PPR relief is always calculated on the basis that a former joint owner has held the property since the date that they first acquired any interest in any share of it. However, a variation on this technique is possible and can be best explained with another example.

Example
In February 2005, Mary and Philip, a married couple, bought a flat in Kensington together for £600,000 and began to rent it out. In 2015, Mary transferred her share to Philip, so that he became the sole owner.

In January 2018, Philip transferred the property back to Mary, making her the sole owner. In March 2018, the couple adopted the property as their main residence. They then lived there for nearly two years until selling the flat for £1.8m in February 2020.

Under the usual rule in Section 6.7, the transfers in 2015 and 2018 are each treated as having taken place on a 'no gain/no loss' basis, so that Mary is treated as having acquired the property for its original cost of £600,000.

*However, the 'former joint owner' rule explained in Section 8.2 does **not** apply in this case because Mary did not own **any** share in the property between 2015 and 2018. She is therefore treated as having acquired the property in January 2018 for PPR relief purposes and her CGT calculation is as follows:*

	£
Sale proceeds	*1,800,000*
Less: Cost	*(600,000)*

	1,200,000
PPR relief (23/25 x £1.2m)*	*(1,104,000)*
Private letting relief	*(40,000)*

	56,000
Annual exemption for 2019/20 (say)	*(12,000)*

Taxable gain	*44,000*
	=======

* - The property was the couple's main residence for 23 months out of Mary's final ownership period of 25 months from January 2018 to February 2020.

Mary's maximum CGT bill will therefore be just £12,320 (£44,000 x 28%). If Philip had retained the property until the date of sale, his CGT bill would have been up to £278,507. If the couple had kept the property in equal joint ownership throughout the whole time that they owned it, their combined CGT bill would have been up to £263,947.

This double transfer technique has therefore saved the couple a considerable amount of CGT.

Private Letting Relief

As we have seen in the examples throughout this section, where a spouse loses entitlement to any PPR relief, they will also lose entitlement to any private letting relief. In addition to this, private letting relief operates on a strictly **individual** basis. As a result, a transferee spouse may not be entitled to as much private letting relief as the transferor; or sometimes even none at all.

Example
In May 2010, Alex bought a house in Norfolk for £200,000 and began renting it out. In May 2016, she married Eddie and they moved into the house together so that it became their main residence. In July 2016, Alex put the house into equal joint names with Eddie. The couple sold the house for £400,000 in May 2018. Their CGT calculations are as follows:

	Alex *£*	*Eddie* *£*
Sale proceeds (half shares)	*200,000*	*200,000*
Less: Cost (half shares)	*(100,000)*	*(100,000)*
	100,000	*100,000*
PPR relief (2/8 x £100,000)	*(25,000)*	*(25,000)*
Private letting relief	*(25,000)*	*-*
	50,000	*75,000*
Annual exemption 2018/19 (say)	*(11,600)*	*(11,600)*
Taxable gain	*38,400*	*63,400*

*As we can see, Eddie is entitled to the same PPR relief as Alex because the property was the couple's main residence at the time that he acquired his share; but he is not entitled to any private letting relief because **he** never rented the property out!*

The result is that the couple have a total CGT liability of up to £28,504 (£38,400 x 28% + £63,400 x 28%).

If Alex had simply held on to the property herself, she would have had a maximum CGT bill of £27,552: so the transfer may have cost the couple up to £952 in extra tax (although this does depend on whether any of Eddie's basic rate band band is available to reduce his CGT liability).

*The best approach would have been to follow the same technique as Caleb in one of our earlier examples. If Alex had married Eddie and transferred the property to her new husband shortly **before** the couple adopted it as their main residence, they could have avoided any CGT altogether!*

8.5   MARRIAGE, DIVORCE AND CIVIL PARTNERSHIPS

Getting married alters your tax status dramatically. One major aspect of this for property owners is the fact that, from that date onwards, the couple can only have one main residence between them for PPR relief purposes.

When the 'happy day' comes, there are some important tax-planning points to bear in mind:

i)   If each of you still has your own private residence, you should elect which one is to be your main residence (see Section 6.22). In these circumstances, the election must be done within two years of the date of marriage.

ii)   You will normally have at least eighteen months during which the residence, no longer regarded as a main residence, continues to be exempt under the PPR exemption.

Maximising Your Reliefs

Where each person still has their own main residence immediately prior to the marriage, and those properties have not previously been put to any other use, the best way to maximise your overall tax reliefs would generally be to take the following steps **after** you marry:

i)   Elect for one of the properties to be your main residence
ii)   Put that property into joint names while it is your main residence
iii)   A short time later, elect the other property as your main residence
iv)   Put that other property into joint names whilst it is your main residence

See Section 6.22 regarding how to make main residence elections.

Steps (i) to (iv) can be completed within a relatively short period (say a month), but it is important that both properties continue to be used as your private residences up until the point they are put into joint names.

By putting each property into joint names whilst it is your main residence, you will each be entitled to the same periods of PPR exemption on both properties. This will tend to be beneficial where each member of the couple has a property which they have used as their main residence prior to the marriage.

Remember, however, as explained in Section 8.4, that the transferee will not be entitled to private letting relief in respect of any earlier periods of letting by the transferor.

Hence, the technique described above may not be the best strategy where a property has been rented out in the past; or indeed in any other case where it has not been the current owner's main residence throughout their ownership to date.

In these more complex cases, the best outcome will depend on a number of factors and the principles set out in Section 8.4 should be borne in mind.

Divorce and Separation

Once you get separated or divorced your married status for CGT purposes ends. 'Separated' means either legally separated under a court order or separated in circumstances which are likely to be permanent. The good news is that, once again, you will be able to have your own individual main residence for PPR relief purposes.

Alternatively, if you have not claimed any PPR relief on another property in the interim, nor made any main residence election in favour of another property, your former marital home may continue to be exempt as long as your ex-spouse continues to use it as their main residence. This extension to the PPR exemption only applies in the case of a subsequent transfer of the former marital home, or a share in it, to the former spouse, as part of a financial settlement.

8.6 HAVE YOUR CAKE AND EAT IT

Income Tax savings can be generated by transferring investment property into either joint names with your spouse or the sole name of the spouse with the lower overall income. In the right circumstances, moving income from one spouse to another in this way could save a higher-rate taxpayer over £11,000 in Income Tax in 2017/18 alone. As we saw in Section 8.2, some taxpayers could even save up to £18,400.

As explained in Section 8.3, this form of tax planning is not effective unless beneficial title in the property is genuinely transferred. But not everyone trusts their spouse enough to hand over title to their property!

For Income Tax purposes, at least, there is a way to solve this dilemma. Where property is held jointly by a married couple, there is an automatic presumption, for Income Tax purposes, that the income arises in equal shares. This 50/50 split will continue to be applied unless and until the couple jointly elect for the income to be split in accordance with the true beneficial title in the property.

Hence, where a married property owner wants to save Income Tax on their rental profits without giving up too much of their title to the property, what they should do is:

- Transfer the property into joint names with their spouse, but
- Retain 99% of the beneficial ownership and transfer only 1%, and
- Simply never elect for the income to be split in accordance with the true beneficial title!

Conversely

Conversely, of course, there will be cases where the actual beneficial ownership split is preferable for tax purposes. In these cases, the election to split the income on an actual basis should usually be made. Beware though that, once made, this election is irreversible.

8.7 INHERITED PROPERTY

In Section 6.11 we looked at the base cost of inherited property and saw that this is generally based on the property's value at the date of the previous owner's death. In many cases, this is pretty much all there is to tell and the new owner is treated in every respect as if they had purchased the property on the date of the previous owner's death.

There are a few areas of complication, however. Firstly, there is the fact that during the period of administration the deceased's estate is treated as a separate legal person, rather like a trust.

Like trusts, estates pay CGT at the higher rates of 20% or 28% (except where entrepreneurs' relief is available). The estate has its own annual exemption equal to the amount given to individuals. The exemption applies for the tax year of death and the following two tax years.

If a property is sold by the deceased's estate, it is treated as if it had been acquired on the date of the deceased's death for its market value on that date. Where 75% or more of the sale proceeds are to go to one or more beneficiaries who occupied the property as their main residence at the time of the deceased's death, the PPR exemption will apply to any gain arising.

Transfers of property from the estate to the beneficiary are exempt from CGT. Once the transfer has taken place, the beneficiary is treated as if they had acquired the property (or the deceased's share of it) for its market value on the date of the deceased's death.

Secondly, where the new owner of the whole property was already a joint owner prior to the deceased's death, the calculation of PPR relief is based on their whole period of ownership (see Section 8.2). However, a surviving joint owner cannot claim private letting relief on the deceased's share of an inherited property in respect of lettings made prior to the deceased's death.

Widows, Widowers and Surviving Civil Partners

The position applying where property passes to a surviving spouse depends on whether the property was the couple's main residence at the time of the deceased's death and on whether the survivor was already a joint owner prior to that date.

If the property was **not** the couple's main residence at the time of the deceased's death and the survivor was **not** already a joint owner then they are simply treated as having acquired the property on the date of the deceased's death.

Where the survivor was already a joint owner prior to the deceased's death, and the property was **not** the couple's main residence at that time, then they are in the same position as any other surviving joint owner, as described above.

Where the property **was** the couple's main residence at the time of the deceased's death then, for the purposes of calculating PPR relief, the survivor will be treated as if they had owned the property from the earlier of:

a)   The date that they first acquired any interest in it, or
b)   The date that the deceased first acquired any interest in it

None of this alters the basic rule regarding the inherited property's base cost. It only acts to determine what **proportion** of the gain is covered by PPR relief.

The survivor is not eligible for any private letting relief in respect of a letting made by the deceased alone. Where the survivor had been a joint owner prior to the deceased's death, they are unable to claim private letting relief on the deceased's share of the property in respect of lettings made prior to the deceased's death.

If the couple were separated at the date of the deceased's death (see Section 8.5), the survivor is treated like an unmarried partner for all CGT purposes.

8.8   TAX-FREE PROPERTY TRANSFERS

As we have already seen, married couples are able to transfer property from one spouse to the other free from CGT. However, transfers of property, or shares in property, to other people, such as an unmarried partner or adult child, present us with a problem.

In principle, such a transfer must be treated as if the property, or property share, had been sold for its open market value. In many cases, this would produce a significant CGT liability. (There are some important exceptions of course: including the transferor's main residence and property used in the transferor's trading business.)

However, where a property owner makes a lifetime transfer of property into a trust, they may elect to 'hold over' the capital gain arising. At a later date, the trust can then transfer the property to the intended recipient and the trustees may again elect to 'hold over' the gain. In this way, CGT may be avoided on both transfers.

The end result is that the transferee is treated as if they had purchased the property for the same price as the transferor.

However, they are **not** treated as if they acquired the property at the same time as the transferor. For all other CGT purposes the date of purchase is the date that the property is finally transferred out of the trust to the transferee.

This technique does not work where the trust is a 'settlor-interested trust' (see Section 6.11) and should not generally be used where PPR relief is available (see Section 6.19). Furthermore, 'hold over' relief is only available for CGT purposes and would not apply to a property classed as trading stock!

Transferring property to a trust has significant IHT implications. Problems can usually be avoided where the property is not worth in excess of £325,000 and the ultimate transfer to the transferee individual takes place within ten years. The tax-saving potential of this technique is examined in the Taxcafe.co.uk guide *'How to Save Inheritance Tax'*.

8.9   WHY 'LET TO BUY' BEATS 'BUY TO LET'

When a person lets out their existing home in order to fund the purchase of a new property, we call this 'Let to Buy'. From a tax perspective, 'Let to Buy' scores heavily over 'Buy to Let' for two main reasons:

- Both properties will attract PPR relief, and
- Equity in the former home can be released and used for any purpose whilst still attracting Income Tax relief on the interest arising

Example – Buy to Let
Gregor bought his current home in 2003 for £100,000 and in 2018 it is worth £200,000. Eventually, in 2028, he sells the property for £400,000. Naturally, it is fully exempt from CGT as it has been his main residence throughout his ownership.

Gregor buys a 'Buy-to-Let' property for £200,000 in 2018. This property is also sold for £400,000 in June 2028 when Gregor is a higher rate taxpayer. After his annual exemption for 2028/29 of £15,000 (say), Gregor has a taxable gain of £185,000 and a CGT bill, at 28%, of £51,800.

Example – Let to Buy
The situation is exactly as before except that, on acquisition of the second property in 2018, Gregor moves out of his former home, begins to rent it out and adopts the new property as his main residence.

Gregor's former home produces an overall gain of £300,000. Sixteen and a half years out of his total ownership period of 25 years is exempted by PPR relief. This represents the 15 years of occupation of the property as Gregor's main residence plus his last eighteen months of ownership. Gregor's PPR relief thus amounts to £198,000.

Gregor is also entitled to private letting relief of £40,000, bringing his gain down to £62,000 before his 2028/29 annual exemption of £15,000 (say). The taxable gain is thus a mere £47,000, giving him a CGT bill at 28% of just £13,160.

Gregor therefore saves £38,640 simply by moving house!

Added Benefits

In addition to Gregor's huge CGT saving, he could also save substantial amounts of Income Tax on his rental income by maximising the mortgage on his original home (see Section 4.4).

Gregor's Income Tax relief would be unaffected even if he used any additional borrowings for the deposit on his new home. Gregor might even manage to avoid the need to take out any mortgage on his new home, thus confining any risk to his rental property alone.

Note, however, that Gregor's Income Tax relief for his interest costs will be restricted from 2017/18 onwards and will be at basic rate only from 2020/21 (see Section 4.5). Hence, it may not necessarily be a good idea for him to maximise his borrowings in this way.

8.10   CLIMBING THE LADDER

In Chapter 6 we saw how far the PPR exemption can be extended. This can be used to great effect to enable a taxpayer to build up a property portfolio virtually free of any CGT. The basic method is best explained by way of example.

Example
Malcolm buys a small flat (Flat A) in July 2017. He moves in and it becomes his main residence. A year later, he buys another, larger, flat (Flat B). He does not immediately move into the new flat but spends a year renovating it. He moves into Flat B in July 2019, just before the anniversary of its purchase, and then starts renting out Flat A.

Malcolm now has two flats, both of which will be fully exempted by PPR relief until at least January 2021. Private letting relief may also further extend Flat A's tax-free status until July 2024 (depending on the ultimate sale price).

Example Continued
In July 2020, Malcolm buys a house (House C). Again, he does not move in immediately but spends a year renovating the house before moving in just before the anniversary of its purchase. He now starts renting out Flat B.

The Story So far (2021)

Flat A may be exempt from CGT until July 2024, Flat B will be fully exempted until at least January 2023, possibly until July 2027, and House C will be fully exempt until at least January 2023, possibly July 2025. All of this without even considering the annual exemption!

Eventually some of the earlier acquisitions will begin to be exposed to CGT. As illustrated in Chapter 6, however, this may take several years. When that point is reached, Malcolm can sell off the properties one at a time to make best use of his annual exemptions.

Potential Drawbacks

Many people have successfully followed a strategy similar to Malcolm's but there are one or two potential problems to be wary of. Firstly, HMRC has the power to overturn the PPR exemption if they perceive that the taxpayer is carrying on a trade of property development or is acquiring properties with the primary motive of realising a profit on their sale.

Secondly, as explained in Section 2.9, the gains arising on the disposal of property may now be treated as trading income if realising a profit on the property's disposal was one of the main purposes behind its acquisition.

Hence, Malcolm's strategy does carry some degree of risk. The longer he retains the properties after his original renovation and occupation periods, however, the more this risk will diminish.

Relying On the Principal Private Residence Exemption

In any planning scenario which places reliance on the PPR exemption, it is essential to ensure that the property or properties concerned genuinely become your private residence. There is no 'hard and fast' rule as to how long you must reside in a property to establish it as your private residence for CGT purposes. It is the quality of occupation that counts, not the length. Hence, it is recommended that you (and your spouse or partner and/or family, if applicable):

i)   Move into the property for a substantial period
ii)   Ensure that all relevant institutions (banks, utilities, HMRC, employers, etc) are notified
iii)   Inform family/friends
iv)   Furnish the property for permanent occupation
v)   Register on the electoral roll for that address
vi)   Do not advertise the property for sale or rent until after the expiry of a substantial period

It is not possible to provide a definitive view of what constitutes a 'substantial period'. What matters is that the property genuinely becomes your 'permanent home'. 'Permanent' means it is intended to be your residence, rather than a temporary abode. You must move into the property with no clear plans for moving out again.

As a rough guide only, you should plan your affairs on the basis that you will be residing in the property for at least a year, preferably two.

You may see some tax cases reported where taxpayers have successfully claimed the PPR exemption on a property which they occupied for much shorter periods. These cases may be helpful but they are very much dependent on their own specific circumstances. They cannot be regarded as setting a minimum occupation period which everyone can rely on.

As already stated, the question will ultimately be decided on quality of occupation, rather than length. Where you are looking to use the PPR exemption on a property, you must embark upon occupying that property wholeheartedly; a mere 'sham' occupation will not suffice.

Example
Harry bought his house in 1999 and has used it as his main residence ever since. In August 2017, the house is worth £400,000. Harry now decides to sell the house and realises that he can make more money if he has a swimming pool built. Harry and his family therefore move out of the house into a new home and he has the pool built at a cost of £30,000.

With its new swimming pool, Harry is able to sell the house for £500,000. He has therefore made an extra profit of £70,000 as a result of building the pool. Harry's extra profit of £70,000 will not be covered by his PPR exemption. It will, however, still be eligible for the annual exemption (£11,300), leaving Harry with a taxable gain of £58,900 and a CGT liability of up to £16,436.

In practice, Harry might be able to argue that some of the extra £70,000 profit was just down to getting a good offer, or was due to a general increase in property values over the period since work began on the pool. In other words, don't just accept that the whole of the extra gain is taxable: take other factors into account.

Many readers will be horrified by this last example but let me reassure you that HMRC generally only tends to use this power when major capital expenditure is blatantly carried out for no reason other than to make an extra profit on the sale of the property.

If Harry and his family had continued using the property after the pool was built and only sold it perhaps a year or two later, it is highly unlikely that there would have been any restriction to his PPR exemption. Hence, in general, homeowners can enhance the value of their property by making capital improvements and still retain their PPR exemption: as long as there is a reasonable delay between those improvements being carried out and the property being put up for sale.

In the more common situation where homeowners carry out minor renovation work in order to prepare a property for sale, there is not usually any restriction in their PPR relief.

Furthermore, in practice, HMRC will not restrict PPR relief simply because a homeowner has obtained planning permission for conversion or improvement work.

Practical Pointer
Where part of the PPR relief on a property is denied as a result of expenditure incurred specifically for the purpose of realising a profit on the sale of that property, the taxable gain arising remains subject to CGT and cannot be treated as a trading profit subject to Income Tax. The new rules applying to disposals after 4th July 2016 (see Section 2.9) have not altered this but the exemption only applies to the extent that the taxable gain would otherwise have qualified for PPR relief or private letting relief.

Home Conversions

Where a property undergoes extensive conversion work, it may no longer remain a single dwelling for tax purposes. This is what HMRC refers to as a 'Change of Use' and it has a far wider-ranging impact than merely letting out part of your home.

Example

David bought a large detached house for £360,000 in December 2005. He lived in the whole house for one year and then converted it into two separate, semi-detached, houses. He continued to live in one of these, but rented the other one out. The conversion work cost £60,000, bringing his total costs up to £420,000.

In December 2017, David sold both houses for £450,000 each, making a total gain of £480,000. David's gain must be apportioned between the two houses. As they each sold for the same price, it is reasonable to assume that the gain should be split equally between them (but see Section 5.2 for other allocation methods which might be used).

The £240,000 gain on the house which David retained as his own home will be fully covered by the PPR exemption. However, David's £240,000 gain on the other house will only be covered by the PPR exemption for one year out of his twelve years of ownership. His PPR exemption on this house thus amounts to only £20,000, leaving a taxable gain of £220,000 (before the annual exemption).

There are two very important differences here to the situation in Section 6.26 where part of the property was let out, both of which occur because the rented house is no longer part of the same dwelling:

i) The PPR exemption is not available for the last eighteen months of ownership
ii) No private letting relief is available

Tax Tip

David would have improved his position dramatically if he had spent some time living in the other semi-detached property after the conversion.

It may sometimes be more beneficial to treat the gains arising before and after the conversion as two separate gains. In David's case, this would have been preferable if the original property had already increased in value by more than £40,000 before the conversion. This gain would have been completely exempt and half of it would have related to the house which was subsequently rented out. Both approaches are equally acceptable and we will look at this alternative method in more detail later in this section.

Conversion for Sale

In our previous example, David did enough conversion work to create two new 'dwellings' and this radically altered the amount of PPR relief available. He did, however, retain both new properties long enough for them to remain capital assets in his hands under basic principles.

Where conversion work is carried out as a prelude to a sale, basic principles would usually dictate that the property has become trading stock. The profit arising on the development would then be treated as a trading profit and the principles examined in Chapter 5 would apply.

Nevertheless, there are situations where a homeowner may develop part of their property for sale and retain the more beneficial CGT treatment.

This is because HMRC cannot deem a former main residence to be trading stock unless they can show that the owner has a property development trade. Again, this position is unaltered by the new rules applying to disposals after 4th July 2016 (see Section 2.9), provided that the gain arising would have been fully exempt under PPR relief or private letting relief had the development not taken place.

This means that 'one-off' developments which homeowners carry out on their own property may sometimes continue to be subject to CGT instead of Income Tax.

Example

Spencer inherited a large house from his Uncle Charles in March 2012 when it was worth £1.2m. Spencer adopted the house as his main residence and lived there until September 2017, at which point it was worth £1.8m. Spencer then had the house converted into five flats at a total cost of £500,000.

Spencer moved into one of the flats and adopted it as his home. He then sold the other four flats for £650,000 each in March 2018. Spencer is a higher rate taxpayer and his CGT liability on the sale of the flats is calculated as follows:

	£
Sale proceeds (4 x £650,000)	*2,600,000*
Less:	
Value prior to conversion (4/5 x £1.8m)	*1,440,000*
Conversion costs (4/5 x £500,000)	*400,000*

Gain made on the development:	*760,000*
Less:	
Annual exemption	*11,300*

Taxable gain	*748,700*
	=========
CGT at 28%:	*£209,636*

For the sake of illustration, I have taken a very simplistic approach to the allocation of costs by assuming that the flats were all equal in size. In reality, a more sophisticated method will usually be appropriate, perhaps based on floor area or, better still, calculations prepared by a surveyor.

Spencer's capital gain is based on the extra value created as a result of the conversion. The property's previous increase in value before the conversion work began continues to be exempt because the whole property was his main residence during this period.

In this particular situation, Spencer does not appear to have a property development trade. His non-trading status is strengthened here by the fact that he had inherited the property. The situation might be different if he had purchased the property within one or two years before commencing the conversion work or had carried out any similar developments in the past. Furthermore, if Spencer already had a property development trade, it is likely this conversion would be seen as part of that business.

In practice, each situation has to be looked at on its own merits and HMRC will frequently argue that a trading activity exists.

If Spencer were deemed to have a property development trade, the gain of £760,000 made on the development would be taxed as a trading profit and could give rise to Income Tax of up to £344,100 and NI of somewhere between £15,200 and £17,763. (This maximum Income Tax cost arises if Spencer has other existing taxable income of £100,000 before taking the gain into account.)

Spencer's total tax liability could therefore be increased by up to £152,227.

Furthermore, if Spencer were treated as a developer, HMRC might also argue that the development profit of £190,000 on the flat which he retained should also be taxed as a trading profit, giving him a further tax bill of up to £89,300!

One drawback to treating the development profit as a capital gain is that Spencer cannot deduct any interest or other overheads: only direct costs. This seems a small price to pay in Spencer's case but, in some other cases, it may actually be more beneficial if the development is treated as a trading activity.

The New Residence

The flat Spencer retained for personal use has now become his main residence and will continue to be eligible for PPR relief. To see how this works in practice, let's return to the example.

Example Continued

Spencer moves out of the flat in September 2022 and then rents it out before eventually selling it in March 2026 for £1.04m. His CGT calculation is as follows:

	£
Sale proceeds	1,040,000
Less:	
Value when inherited (1/5 x £1.2m)	
240,000	
Conversion costs (1/5 x 500,000)	100,000

Capital Gain before reliefs	700,000
Less:	
PPR relief (£700,000 x 12/14*):	600,000
Private letting relief (maximum)	40,000

Gain before annual exemption	60,000
	======

* - March 2012 to September 2022 + last 18 months =12 years out of 14

The new flat is not the same 'dwelling' as the original house prior to the conversion work, but in our example they were both used as Spencer's main residence. He is therefore able to claim PPR relief on the appropriate proportion of the gain both before and after the conversion work.

The calculation set out above is not the only valid method. The law only requires a method which is 'just and reasonable'. An alternative method might be to view the gain on the first 'dwelling' from March 2012 to September 2017 as wholly exempt and then compute the gain on the second dwelling (the flat) as follows:

	£
Sale proceeds	1,040,000
Less:	
Value before conversion (1/5 x £1.8m)	
360,000	
Conversion costs (1/5 x 500,000)	100,000

Capital Gain before reliefs	580,000
Less:	
PPR relief (£580,000 x 6½/8½*):	443,529
Private letting relief (maximum)	40,000

Gain before annual exemption	96,471
	======

* - September 2017 to September 2022 + last 18 months = 6½ years out of 8½

This method produces a larger capital gain and is therefore likely to be favoured by HMRC. Nevertheless, the first method may also be regarded as 'just and reasonable'. At this point, I can only advise you to be aware of the alternative methods. Use the one that is best for you, but be prepared for an argument!

Lastly, there is also the possibility discussed above that the development gain on this flat may have been taxed already as a trading profit. In this case, the capital gain would be £390,000 (£1.04m - £650,000), PPR relief would be £292,500 (6/8ths), private letting relief would remain £40,000, and the gain before deducting Spencer's annual exemption would be £57,500.

If you're wondering why the PPR relief is 6/8ths in this last calculation when we used 6½ years out of 8½ in the previous one, it's because Spencer was able to treat the flat as his main residence from September 2017 in the earlier calculation (see Section 6.17), but would only be regarded as re-adopting it as a capital asset in March 2018 if it had been treated as trading stock during the development period.

8.13   SOMETHING IN THE GARDEN
(See Section 6.16 for general guidance on the application of the PPR exemption to gardens and grounds)

It's a common scenario: a taxpayer has a large garden, so they sell part of it off for property development. There are the right ways to do this and there are other ways, which are very, very wrong.

The Wrong Ways

DO NOT:
- Sell your house first before selling the development plot
- Fence the development plot off or otherwise separate it from the rest of your garden before selling it
- Use the development plot for any purpose other than your own private residential occupation immediately prior to the sale
- Allow the development plot to fall into disuse

Each of these will result in the complete loss of your PPR exemption for the development plot. Furthermore, do not assume that the plot is covered by the PPR exemption if the total area of your house and garden exceeds half a hectare.

Practical Pointer
Fencing off the plot alone may not necessarily lead to the loss of your PPR exemption on the plot; provided that the plot continues to be used for your own private residential occupation up to the point of sale. Nonetheless, there remains some doubt over this issue, so it is wise to avoid any separation of the plot from the rest of the garden prior to sale.

The Right Ways

First, the simple way: Carefully ensuring that you do not commit any of the cardinal sins described above, you simply sell off the plot of land. This sale will now enjoy the same PPR exemption as applies to your house itself. (If 90% of a gain on your house would have been exempt, then 90% of the gain on the plot will be exempt.)

The Other 'Right Way'

The only drawback to the simple way is that you do not get to participate in any of the profit on the development. But what if you hang on to the plot and develop it yourself?

Yes, at first this looks like we've gone the wrong way, but not if you then proceed to move into the new property and adopt it as your main residence. Your old house can safely be sold at any time up to eighteen months after the date you move out and still be covered by the PPR exemption.

The new house should be fully covered by the PPR exemption as long as you moved in within a year of the date that development started. As in Section 8.10, there are some potential dangers here, but the exemption should be available if you genuinely adopt the new house as your new main residence.

Wealth Warning 1
Although the new house will be covered by the PPR exemption, there is an argument that any gain on the land comprised in the development plot arising prior to the point that development commenced is not covered. For example, if the cost of the land were £12,000 (based on an allocation of the original house's purchase price) and it was worth £22,000 immediately prior to the commencement of the development, there would be a gain of £10,000 which was not covered by PPR relief. Such a small gain would probably be covered by the owner's annual exemption, but larger gains would lead to a CGT liability.

Wealth Warning 2
More worryingly, some commentators suggest that the gain on the new house would have to be calculated on a 'time apportionment' basis, with PPR relief only applying to the period of occupation. For example, if the land had originally cost £12,000 (as above) in 2007; the development had taken place in 2017 and cost £148,000; and the house was then occupied as a main residence until eventually being sold for £250,000 in 2022; the PPR relief would then be restricted to just £30,000, leaving a taxable gain of £60,000 (before the annual exemption).

At present, it is not clear which of the above interpretations is correct. Personally, however, I would argue strongly in favour of either full PPR exemption or the 'just and reasonable' allocation under 'Wealth Warning 1' above, as permitted by the relevant tax legislation.

What is beyond doubt is that if the newly developed property were sold straight away, this would give rise to a trading profit (see Chapter 5).

8.14   STUDENT LOANS

Each unmarried adult is entitled to have their own main private residence which is exempt from CGT.

Once your children reach the age of 18 therefore, it is possible to put some tax-free capital growth into their hands. (They do not actually have to be students by the way – it works just as well if they are in employment or even just living a life of leisure at your expense, as many teenagers seem to do!)

The basic method is fairly straightforward: all that you need to do is purchase a property in their name which they then move into and adopt as their main residence.

Financing can be achieved in a number of ways, but the important point is that they must have legal and beneficial title to the property. (Hence this simple technique should only be undertaken if you are prepared to pass wealth on to the children.)

The purchase of the property has possible IHT implications but these are avoided simply by surviving for seven years.

> **Wealth Warning**
> You should also be careful not to make any use of the property yourself, since, if you have provided the funds for its purchase, any subsequent occupation by you or your spouse may give rise to an Income Tax charge under the 'pre-owned assets' regime.

Keeping the Capital Growth Yourself

Alternatively, if you would prefer to keep the wealth yourself for the time being, you may want to use the trust method set out in the next section.

8.15   USING A TRUST FOR EXTRA PRINCIPAL PRIVATE RESIDENCE RELIEF

As explained in Section 6.19, a trust is exempt from CGT on a property occupied as a main residence by one of the trust's beneficiaries.

Although this exemption does not apply where a capital gain on a property has been held over on a transfer into the trust, there is no problem where the property is purchased by the trust in the first place (or is transferred to the trust with no hold over claim). Hence, it is possible to obtain PPR relief on an additional property using the following method:

i)   Set up a trust with another person (or persons) as the beneficiary (but not your spouse)
ii)   Purchase a residential property through the trust
iii)   The beneficiary adopts the property as their main residence (remember that, like everyone else, they can only have one main residence and the usual rules apply if they are married)

You retain the reversionary interest in the trust. This means that the trust assets will ultimately revert to you. As explained in Section 6.11, this means that the trust is a 'settlor-interested' trust and hold over relief is not available on any transfer of property into the trust. This is not a problem – you don't want hold over relief anyway!

Some years later, but within eighteen months of when the property ceases to be the beneficiary's main residence, the trust can either sell the property or transfer it to you. Either way, the gain arising will be exempt from CGT and you can either retain the property or enjoy the tax free sales proceeds.

Wealth Warnings
This method has potential IHT implications which are explained in detail in the Taxcafe.co.uk guide *'How to Save Inheritance Tax'*. In general, however, it is usually possible to avoid any problems by restricting the value of property held in the trust to no more than the amount of the IHT nil rate band (currently £325,000). A couple can effectively double this amount as long as they structure their investments carefully.

Once again, you should also be careful to ensure that neither you nor your spouse makes any use of the property whilst it is held by the trust as this may give rise to Income Tax charges under the 'pre-owned assets' regime.

8.16   PLANNING WITH ABSENCE PERIODS

In Section 6.18, we saw that there are some temporary periods of absence from a main residence which may still be included as a period of occupation for the purposes of PPR relief where certain conditions are met.

Where those conditions apply, it is only any period for which the owner actually **claims** PPR relief on another property that must be excluded.

This may sound like good news, but it may actually be disadvantageous in some cases. This is because, technically speaking, PPR relief is not actually **claimed**. Where the appropriate conditions are met, it applies automatically, leaving the property owner with no control over how it applies: or which property it applies to!

Example

In February 2010, Aisha bought a house in Sheffield for £80,000 and adopted it as her main residence. In August 2013, she was transferred to her employer's London branch, where she bought a flat for £350,000 and adopted it as her new main residence. She then began renting out her house in Sheffield. In August 2017, Aisha returned to Sheffield and resumed occupation of her original home. She then began to rent out her London property.

Later that year, Aisha decided to sell her Sheffield property and eventually sold it for £140,000 in February 2018, giving her a modest gain of £60,000.

Because Aisha has not claimed PPR relief on any other property for the period from August 2013 to August 2017, her Sheffield property is treated as her main residence for this period and is thus fully exempt from CGT.

BUT, the consequence of this is that her London property cannot be treated as her main residence for this period. This leaves this more expensive property fully exposed to CGT with no PPR relief or private letting relief available. When Aisha sells this property for £1m in 2022, her CGT bill could be up to £182,000!

To avoid this outcome, Aisha needs to make a PPR relief claim on her London property first: before any claim on her Sheffield property. She therefore needs to trigger a disposal of the London property before she sells the Sheffield property. She could do this by:

- Actually selling the property
- Transferring the property to a connected person (other than her spouse) (see Section 6.9 for a list of connected persons)
- Transferring the property into a company or a trust

Transfers of property into a company or trust give rise to many other tax implications which are examined in the Taxcafe.co.uk guides *'Using a Property Company to Save Tax'* and *'How to Save Inheritance Tax'*.

If the London property is disposed of before the Sheffield property then it will be treated as Aisha's main residence for the period from August 2013 to August 2017 and will be fully exempt from CGT (as she has sold it within less than eighteen months after the end of this period).

Meanwhile, the Sheffield property will no longer be treated as Aisha's main residence for this period. However, she will still be eligible for PPR relief for the first three and a half years of her ownership (when the property was her main residence) plus the last eighteen months. This exempts five years out of her total ownership period of eight years, giving her PPR relief of £37,500 (£60,000 x 5/8). She will also be eligible for private letting relief on the property, which will reduce her taxable gain to nil, leaving her with no CGT to pay.

As we can see, the temporary absence rules mean that there could be some periods where a property owner is potentially eligible for PPR relief on more than one property. The relief will automatically apply to the first property to be disposed of, so it is vitally important to ensure that the property attracting the most valuable relief is disposed of first!

Alternatively, in some cases, it may be sensible to simply avoid moving back into the original property so that the PPR relief entitlement on the more expensive property can be preserved. In our example, Aisha could have saved herself a lot of trouble if she had never moved back into the Sheffield property: and still had no CGT to pay on its sale.

8.17   FURNISHED HOLIDAY LETTINGS

Furnished holiday lettings enjoy the best of all worlds. They continue to be treated as investment properties whenever that is more beneficial, but get treated like a trade when many trading reliefs are up for grabs. They qualify as private residential accommodation, yet still get many of the advantages generally reserved for commercial property.

Even despite some recent changes, getting one of your properties to qualify as a furnished holiday let is the property tax equivalent of winning the lottery! (Albeit with the proviso that the winnings are not quite as great as they used to be and the chances of winning have been reduced!)

In essence, properties qualifying as 'furnished holiday lettings' enjoy a special tax regime, which includes many of the tax advantages usually only accorded to trading properties. At the same time, the profits derived from furnished holiday lettings are still treated as rental income.

The taxation benefits of qualifying furnished holiday lettings include the following:

- Entrepreneurs' relief
- Rollover relief on replacement of business assets
- Holdover relief for gifts
- Capital allowances for furniture, fixtures, fittings and integral features (see Section 4.9)
- No restriction on tax relief for interest and finance costs

- Despite its 'trading-style' advantages, NI should not usually be payable in respect of income from furnished holiday lets (but see Section 7.17)
- Non-UK residents investing in UK furnished holiday lettings will usually be exempt from CGT on gains arising up to 5th April 2015

The letting of holiday accommodation is, however, standard-rated for VAT purposes (whether or not the qualifying conditions set out below are met). The landlord must therefore register for VAT if gross annual income from UK holiday lettings exceeds £85,000. Foreign VAT registration will also often be required in respect of holiday lettings elsewhere within the European Union.

A furnished holiday letting business might also be exempt from IHT where the lettings are generally short-term and the owner (or their employees) was substantially involved with the holidaymakers' activities.

The available reliefs extend to any property used in a furnished holiday letting business. This will include not only the holiday accommodation itself but also any office premises from which the business is run.

Loss Relief

Losses arising in a furnished holiday letting business may only be carried forward for set off against future profits from the same furnished holiday letting business. For this purpose, all of a landlord's UK furnished holiday lettings are regarded as one business but any furnished holiday lettings elsewhere in the EEA are regarded as a different business. (All furnished holiday lettings within the EEA but outside the UK are regarded as the same business.)

Qualification

The qualification requirements for a furnished holiday letting are:

i) The property must be situated in the EEA (see Section 1.4)
ii) The property must be fully furnished (see below)
iii) It must be let out on a commercial basis with a view to the realisation of profits
iv) It must be available for commercial letting to the public generally for at least 210 days in a twelve-month period
v) It must be so let for at least 105 such days
vi) The property must not normally be in the same occupation for more than 31 consecutive days at any time during a period of at least seven months out of the same twelve-month period as that referred to in (iv) above

The twelve-month period in (iv) and (vi) above is normally the tax year. Where the property begins or ceases to be let out fully furnished during the tax year, however, then it is the first or last twelve months for which the property is let fully furnished (see below for the definition of 'fully furnished').

Landlords can elect for properties which qualified for the furnished holiday letting regime under the above criteria in the previous year to stay within the regime for up to two further tax years despite failing to meet the test under (v) above. In effect, this means that properties will generally only need to meet this test once every three years. The property will still need to meet all of the other tests, however, and the landlord must make genuine efforts to meet the test under (v) every year.

A taxpayer with more than one furnished holiday letting property may also use a system of averaging to determine whether they meet test (v). This extension cannot, however, be used in conjunction with the two year extension described above: properties must qualify in their own right before the two year extension can be claimed.

Other Qualification Issues

Whilst the property need not be in a recognised holiday area, the lettings should strictly be to holidaymakers and tourists in order to qualify.

Where a property qualifies as a furnished holiday let, it generally qualifies for the whole of each tax year: subject to the special rules for the years in which the fully furnished letting of the property commences or ceases, as described above.

Where, however, there is some other use of the property during the year, the CGT reliefs described above will be restricted accordingly. Nevertheless, it remains possible for the taxpayer and their family to use the property privately as a second home during the 'off season' and still fit within the rules described above.

The overall position must still fit in with rule (iii) above though and hence, in practice, the property must be made available for letting to third parties for a sufficiently large proportion of the year to give its owners a realistic expectation of profits.

The result of failing to meet this test would be the loss of furnished holiday letting status and hence the consequent loss of all the additional reliefs which that status provides.

Tax Tip
Preparing a credible business plan when you first acquire the property would provide valuable supporting evidence that you had a reasonable expectation of profit. A documented annual review of

the plan will also be useful, as the 'profit expectation' test must be met every year. A business plan will not help you, however, if it clearly bears no resemblance to your actual behaviour in respect of the property.

What Is a Fully Furnished Letting?

To be classed as a 'fully furnished letting', the landlord must provide sufficient furnishings so that the property is capable of 'normal residential use' without the tenant having to provide their own furnishings. Typically, this will include beds, chairs, tables, sofas, carpets or other floor coverings, curtains or blinds, and kitchen equipment.

The key phrase here is whether the property is capable of 'normal residential use' and the level of furnishings and equipment required must be considered in this context. In essence, the landlord must provide the tenant with some privacy, somewhere to sit, somewhere to sleep, somewhere to eat, and the facilities required to feed themselves.

Interaction with Other Reliefs

A property which qualifies as a furnished holiday let and which has also qualified as the owner's main residence at some time during their ownership, will be eligible for private letting relief. This produces a quite remarkable combination of tax reliefs.

Example
In Section 6.20 we met Bonnie who had a small cottage on Skye which, for ten years, she rented out as furnished holiday accommodation for 48 weeks each year and occupied herself for the remaining four weeks. The property also qualified as Bonnie's main residence (perhaps by election).

When, on 1st April 2018, Bonnie realised a capital gain of £104,000 on her sale of the property, we saw that she obtained PPR relief of £22,400 and private letting relief of £22,400, thus reducing her gain to just £59,200. But it doesn't end there!

Bonnie would then be entitled to entrepreneurs' relief (see below) on 48/52nds of this gain, i.e. £59,200 x 48/52 = £54,646.

This leaves only £4,554 exposed to CGT at the normal rate of either 18% or 28%. However, as Bonnie can allocate her annual exemption in the most beneficial way, she can exempt this amount altogether.

The taxable gain of £47,900 remaining after deducting her annual exemption of £11,300 is therefore wholly eligible for entrepreneurs' relief, giving Bonnie a CGT bill of just £4,790 (£47,900 x 10%), or a mere 4.6% of her total gain.

8.21   ENTERPRISE INVESTMENT SCHEME SHARES

CGT liabilities can be deferred by reinvesting some or all of a capital gain in Enterprise Investment Scheme shares. To obtain relief, the investment must take place within the period beginning a year before, and ending three years after, the date of the disposal which gave rise to the gain.

Furthermore, CGT reinvestment relief is still available even when the investor is connected with the company issuing the shares. Hence, it may even be possible to defer CGT on your property gains by investing in your own trading company!

Unfortunately, companies engaged in any form of property business are generally ineligible to issue Enterprise Investment Scheme shares.

Alternatively, products are available which enable taxpayers to utilise a 'portfolio' approach when investing in these intrinsically risky investments. This does not totally eliminate the risk, but it certainly improves the odds!

There is no limit on the amount which can be invested in Enterprise Investment Scheme shares for CGT deferral purposes.

Gains held over on reinvestment into Enterprise Investment Scheme shares become subject to CGT when those shares are sold.

Qualifying investments of up to £1m per year in Enterprise Investment Scheme shares issued by an unconnected company also carry an Income Tax credit of up to 30% of the amount invested. Investments may also be carried back to the previous tax year for Income Tax credit purposes.

Combining the Income Tax credit with the CGT deferral gives a potential for total tax savings of up to 58% of the amount invested.

8.22   SWEET SHOP COMPANIES

The 'sweet shop principle' is a method which enables property investors to defer CGT using Enterprise Investment Scheme shares. The idea is that you find a very simple, low risk trading business, like a sweet shop, which requires business premises. Then you set up 'Sweet Shop Company Limited' to run the shop. This company issues Enterprise Investment Scheme shares to you in exchange for the cash proceeds of a property sale. The company then uses this cash to buy its retail premises.

In this way, you are effectively able to roll over any capital gain into the purchase of the business premises, via the medium of the sweet shop company. This is probably the least risky way to secure a CGT deferral with Enterprise Investment Scheme shares.

It doesn't necessarily have to be a sweet shop, but it must not be any of the types of trade or business which are specifically excluded in the legislation and, as I explained in the last section, this covers most types of property business. Even hotels and guest houses are excluded.

8.23   THE SEED ENTERPRISE INVESTMENT SCHEME

The Seed Enterprise Investment Scheme provides Income Tax relief at 50% to individuals investing up to £100,000 per tax year in qualifying companies. Qualifying investments may also be carried back to the previous tax year for Income Tax relief purposes.

Capital gains which are reinvested in Seed Enterprise Investment Scheme shares are given a 50% exemption from CGT. This compares well with the Enterprise Investment Scheme, where capital gains are only deferred until the shares are sold, although half of the gain does remain exposed to CGT.

The combination of Income Tax and CGT reliefs provides the opportunity to obtain up to 64% tax relief on reinvested gains – leaving only a small part of the amount invested exposed to the inherent commercial risk of investing in small businesses.

Furthermore, since Income Tax loss relief would be available on 50% of the investment should the Seed Enterprise Investment Scheme company fail, the ultimate amount at risk may be as little as 16% for a higher rate taxpayer and just 13.5% for an additional rate taxpayer with annual income over £150,000.

Scheme Restrictions

There is a cumulative limit of £150,000 for the total amount raised by a company under the scheme. In fact, this limit actually applies to the **total** amount of state aid received by the company, **including** the value of shares issued under the scheme.

The main drawback, however, is that the scheme is targeted at new, small, 'start-up companies'. Broadly speaking, this means that the company issuing the shares must have:

- Total assets no more than £200,000 (before issuing the shares)
- Less than 25 employees (or full-time equivalents)
- Been in business for no more than two years (and not carried on any other business previously)

Investors must not be employees of the issuing company (but may be directors) and, together with their 'associates', must not hold, nor be entitled to acquire, an interest of more than 30% in the company's share capital. 'Associates' for this purpose include the investor's spouse, parents, grandparents, children, grandchildren, trusts set up by the investor or any of these relatives, and business partners of the investor.

There are many, many, further restrictions, including the fact that the company must be carrying on a qualifying trade or research and development, so professional advice is essential!

8.24 THE TENDER TRAP: THE BENEFITS AND PITFALLS OF RE-MORTGAGING (A.K.A 'EQUITY RELEASE')

"What, no tax at all? That's amazing! Well, thanks a lot, that's wonderful news." This is the kind of reaction I often get when people ask me about the tax consequences of re-mortgaging their properties, or 'equity release', as it is often called.

The situation is a pretty common one. You have a property which has risen significantly in value since you bought it. Rather than sell the property, you can realise the 'profit' from this growth in value by re-mortgaging and thus obtain the cash value of your equity by different means.

Initially, this is a good way of avoiding tax on the growth in value of your investment properties, but there are some long-term dangers inherent in this strategy which could ultimately prove to be your downfall if you are not prepared for them.

The combination of the initial benefits of re-mortgaging and the potential long-term pitfalls of the strategy is what leads me to call it 'The Tender Trap'. It's tender because of its initial benefits, but it can prove to be a costly trap from which it is difficult to escape. More about the trap later; to begin with, let's look at the benefits.

Example Part 1
Steve is a higher rate taxpayer. He has a buy-to-let property in Essex which has grown significantly in value since he bought it for £25,000 in 1998. In fact, by March 2018, the property is valued at £125,000. However, Steve feels that property values in Essex are unlikely to show any significant increase in the foreseeable future and he now wishes to invest in some new developments in Newcastle.

In order to pursue his new investment opportunity in Newcastle, Steve will need to 'cash in' his equity in his Essex property. Initially he considers selling the Essex property, but is horrified to learn that he would have a CGT bill of £28,000 (he has already used his annual exemption).

Instead of selling the property, therefore, Steve decides to re-mortgage it. His new mortgage is at 75% of current value, £93,750. Hence, after repaying his original mortgage of £20,000, Steve has freed up £73,750 of equity value in cash. What's more, he still has the rental income from his original property.

Initial Benefits

CGT can generally only be charged where there is a disposal of an asset. If you sell a property, you have made a disposal and hence there will usually be CGT to pay.

When you re-mortgage a property, however, you have not actually made any disposal, as you still own the property. Hence, although you will have realised some of your capital, you cannot be charged any CGT.

Although, in our example, Steve did this for investment purposes, this CGT benefit remains equally true whatever your reason for re-mortgaging a property.

Example, Part 2
Steve uses the £73,750 which he generated by re-mortgaging to provide the bulk of the funds for three deposits of £25,000 on some new properties in Newcastle costing £100,000 each. He takes out a 75% mortgage on each property.

If we assume that the net yield on each of Steve's four properties after all costs except interest is 6% then his total profit before interest for 2018/19 will be £25,500. If we also assume that Steve pays 4% interest on all of his mortgages, his total interest cost will be £12,750. 50%, or £6,375, of this may be deducted from his rental income, leaving him with a taxable profit of £19,125. The tax on this, at 40%, amounts to £7,650, from which he can deduct basic rate relief on the remaining £6,375 of his interest, leaving him with a final Income Tax liability of £6,375.

Another Benefit

At this stage, we can see that Steve is also enjoying a second benefit: Income Tax relief for all of the interest on his new mortgage over his Essex property.

Where the funds generated by re-mortgaging an existing property are used to purchase new investment properties, the interest on the new borrowings can be claimed against the income from the new properties. This applies even if the re-mortgaged property is the borrower's own home. The interest relief remains available as long as the funds are invested for business purposes.

Sometimes, however, the borrower will re-mortgage a property for other reasons – perhaps simply to provide living expenses. Whilst this will still produce the CGT benefit described above, only interest on borrowings against a rental property up to the value of the property when first rented out (plus other capital invested in the business) will be eligible for Income Tax relief under these circumstances (see Section 4.4 for further details).

Furthermore, it is vital to remember that Income Tax relief for interest paid by residential landlords is now being restricted and will be at basic rate only by 2020/21 (see Section 4.5 for details).

Hence, whilst re-mortgaging will continue to provide some Income Tax benefits, it is important to weigh up the additional costs arising and consider the future viability of your property business based on getting tax relief at just 20%: even when those costs meet the criteria set out in Section 4.4.

Example, Part 3

By March 2021, each of Steve's properties has increased in value by 20%. He has re-mortgaged each of them up to 75% of their current value, generating a further £63,750 of tax-free equity in the process. He has used this to provide the bulk of the funds for two deposits of £32,000 on some new properties in Manchester costing £128,000 each. As before, he takes out a 75% mortgage on each new property.

At this stage, Steve's portfolio is worth a total of £766,000 and he has total borrowings of £574,500 (75%). Let us also assume that his income from other sources amounts to £80,000.

Making the same assumption on yield as before, Steve will have total rental profits before interest of £45,960 for 2021/22. This will give him total taxable income of £125,960, meaning that he will lose his personal allowance (see Section 3.3).

If we again assume that Steve pays 4% interest on all of his mortgages, his total interest cost for 2021/22 will be £22,980. This will attract Income Tax relief at basic rate only. Steve's Income Tax liability on his rental income is thus as follows:

Profit before interest: £45,960 x 40% =	*£18,384*
Lost personal allowance: £12,800(say) x 40% =	*£5,120*
Less:	
Interest relief: £22,980 x 20% =	*(£4,596)*

	£18,908
	======

At this stage, Steve is scraping by in income terms, making a profit after tax of just £4,072 (£45,960 − £22,980 − £18,908) on a portfolio worth £766,000. Nonetheless, he has enjoyed substantial capital growth and has total equity of £191,500.

But he is extremely vulnerable to any changes in market conditions. If his rental yield fell to 5%, he would be left with a profit after tax of just £936. A 2% increase in interest rates would leave him with an annual profit of £11,490 and an Income Tax bill of £16,610: giving him an annual deficit of £5,120. If both of these things happened, he would have an annual deficit of £8,256!

And we still haven't looked at 'the trap'!

The Trap

CGT is based on the difference between sales proceeds and purchase cost. Hence, in order to calculate the capital gain arising when you sell a property, you deduct the original cost of the property from your sale proceeds.

What you **do not** deduct in your capital gains calculation is the outstanding amount of the mortgage over the property!

Naturally, if you have used additional borrowings to make improvements to the property, then these costs may also be deducted from sale proceeds. However, where your additional borrowings have been spent, given away, or used to invest in other properties, you will have a liability to the lender without a corresponding deduction in your capital gains calculation. This is what creates the trap and we will go back to Steve to see it in action.

Example, Part 4
In April 2022, there is a sudden downturn in the property market with property values typically falling by around 15%. Steve runs into some financial difficulty and decides that he needs to sell one of his properties. The rental yield on his original Essex property has been pretty poor lately, so he sells this property for £127,500.

Steve's borrowings against this property now amount to £112,500 (75% of the property's value before the downturn), so he realises net proceeds of only £15,000 (even before any sale expenses). However, as Steve's original cost for the property was only £25,000, he realises a capital gain of £102,500. His CGT bill at 28% could therefore be up to £28,700. Even if he has his annual exemption of (say) £13,000 available, he would still have £25,060 to pay.

*After tax, Steve's sale of the Essex property will therefore actually generate an overall net **cost!***

Responsible Borrowing

As we can see, pursuing a strategy of constantly re-mortgaging your properties may seem like a great way to realise tax-free equity, but it can have disastrous consequences in the long run.

To avoid falling into this 'tender trap', investors need to borrow responsibly, taking account of their potential CGT liabilities, the restrictions in Income Tax relief for interest, and the impact of changes in market conditions.

In Conclusion

Using a re-mortgaging strategy to build your property portfolio can have significant CGT benefits. Realising your equity through additional borrowings is more tax efficient than selling properties when you intend to reinvest the proceeds in your portfolio.

However, the restrictions in Income Tax relief for interest mean that this strategy is not as beneficial as it used to be and high levels of borrowing will leave you extremely vulnerable to changes in market conditions.

Furthermore, a trap awaits the unwary and can, in the most extreme cases, put the taxpayer in a quite untenable position!

8.25   NON-DOMICILED INVESTORS

A UK resident but non-UK domiciled taxpayer may opt to only pay UK tax on income or capital gains from foreign properties if and when these sums are remitted back to the UK. This is known as the 'remittance basis'.

However, any adult resident in the UK for seven or more of the previous nine UK tax years who opts to use the remittance basis must pay an annual charge (known as the 'Remittance Basis Charge') unless their total unremitted overseas income and gains for the year are less than £2,000.

The charge for 2017/18 is £30,000. This increases to £60,000 for an adult resident in the UK for 12 or more of the last 14 UK tax years.

Hence, non-UK domiciled taxpayers who are long-term UK residents generally have to either pay tax in full on their overseas income and capital gains or face a heavy annual charge.

Taxpayers paying the Remittance Basis Charge are also subject to CGT at the higher rates of 20% or 28% on any capital gains which remain taxable, regardless of the level of their income (except where entrepreneurs' relief applies).

Furthermore, all UK resident taxpayers claiming the remittance basis lose entitlement to their personal allowance and CGT annual exemption if they have unremitted overseas income and gains of £2,000 or more. The effective cost of these further punitive measures in 2017/18 alone could be up to £7,764.

For some taxpayers, the total annual cost of claiming the 'remittance basis' could be almost £70,000!

Even so, some non-UK domiciled individuals may still be able to make considerable tax savings by investing in foreign property and retaining their income and gains from that property overseas.

Tax Tip
Individuals claiming the remittance basis may claim exemption from UK tax on any funds remitted to the UK for the purpose of making commercial investments in qualifying businesses. The detailed rules for this exemption are highly complex, so anyone hoping to benefit should seek professional advice.

Deemed Domicile

Under current Government proposals (yet to be enacted), from 2017/18 onwards, any individual resident in the UK for 15 or more of the past 20 UK tax years will be deemed to be UK domiciled for all UK tax purposes.

Individuals with a UK domicile of origin who have acquired a non-UK domicile of choice, but who later return to the UK, will also be treated as UK domiciled for any year in which they are UK resident from 2017/18 onwards.

Those falling foul of the 15 year rule may still claim the remittance basis to exempt them from CGT on the element of any gain on overseas property arising before 5th April 2017. The Remittance Basis Charge will still apply, however, and will be increased to £90,000 if they have been UK resident for 17 or more of the last 20 UK tax years.

Apart from this, anyone deemed to be UK domiciled under these provisions will be unable to claim the remittance basis.

8.26 USING LEASE PREMIUMS TO GENERATE TAX-FREE RECEIPTS

As we saw in Section 6.34, the granting at a premium of a lease of between two and fifty years' duration gives rise to a capital receipt equal to 2% of that premium for each whole year that the lease exceeds one year. For example, 12% of the premium charged for a seven-year lease will be treated as a capital disposal. Clever investors might consider this a good way to use their annual CGT exemption.

Example
Bob owns a small workshop which Terry wants to lease for 20 years. If Bob charges a premium of £29,737, 38% of this (£11,300) will be treated as a capital disposal. If Bob has no other gains this year, his 2017/18 annual

exemption will cover any capital gain, meaning that £11,300 of the premium is received tax free. Bob and Terry then simply negotiate a level of rent which takes suitable account of the premium Terry has paid.

To keep this example simple, I have ignored any base cost which Bob has in the workshop. (See Section 6.34 for more details.)

8.27   THE RENTAL LOSS – CAPITAL GAIN DILEMMA

Some investors have found themselves with rental losses carried forward which they are unable to set against capital gains arising on the same properties.

If the rental losses are likely to be used against other rental income in the foreseeable future (see Sections 4.12 and 4.15 for details) then all well and good: this will save Income Tax at 20%, 40% or even more.

In fact, any foreseeable Income Tax saving is probably better than a maximum CGT saving at 28% at some uncertain date in the future when the property is sold. However, where it seems unlikely that rental losses will ever be relieved against future rental income, securing CGT relief at up to 28% for some of your expenditure could be your best option.

It is worth bearing this in mind before claiming expenses for Income Tax purposes. Many costs are quite clearly revenue in nature but, in a few borderline cases, it may be worth considering whether treating the expense as a capital improvement may actually be better in the long run.

As we saw in Section 4.7, any renovation costs incurred on a new rental property which cannot be claimed for Income Tax purposes will be allowed for CGT purposes. Hence, it will sometimes be wise to resist the impulse to claim as much as possible at this stage.

Renovation costs which simply increase the amount of carried forward rental losses are of dubious benefit when there is no foreseeable relief for those losses and it may be better to secure some CGT relief instead by classifying costs as capital improvements whenever it is reasonable to do so.

More Tax-Free Lease Premiums

In the previous section, we saw how it was possible to use lease premiums to generate tax free income. Lease premiums also provide a further opportunity for tax-free income when the investor has rental losses brought forward.

As explained in Section 4.14, a proportion of any premium for a short lease of no more than 50 years' duration is treated as income.

Hence, where an investor has rental losses brought forward, they could consider granting short leases at a premium instead of selling their property.

The rental losses brought forward can then be set off against part of the lease premium received, leaving a much smaller sum exposed to CGT.

This strategy is generally only worth considering when the investor has a large amount of rental losses available which are unlikely to be relieved against rental income in the foreseeable future, or which are likely to provide future Income Tax relief at no more than 20%.

The effective rate of Income Tax relief for many residential landlords' rental losses in the future is likely to be just 20% (see Section 4.12).

8.28   WINDING DOWN GRACEFULLY

As discussed in the previous section, some property investors have built up large amounts of rental losses. A simple way to ensure that you utilise your rental losses is to wind down your property business slowly over a number of years.

As you sell properties and use the proceeds to repay borrowings on your remaining portfolio, you will slowly increase your profit levels as your interest costs reduce. However, because of the rental losses you have accumulated in the past, you may be able to enjoy many years of tax free rental profits as you wind your business down and prepare for retirement.

> **Wealth Warning**
> Due to the changes to Income Tax relief for interest, brought forward rental losses may not always last as long as you might think (see Section 4.12 for an illustration of this in action). Despite this, the 'winding down gracefully' strategy will usually remain worthwhile. Even if you end up enjoying an effective rate of relief of just 20%, this is better than losing the benefit of your losses altogether.

Capital Gains Tax Benefits

The 'winding down gracefully' strategy is also a good way to save CGT. By selling your properties slowly, over many years, you will be able to utilise your annual exemption many times. In some cases, you may also benefit from the lower CGT rate applying to gains falling within your basic rate tax band each year.

Example Part 1

Bill and Kate have a portfolio of 20 jointly held residential rental properties. They have built their portfolio over many years; each property stands at a capital gain of £50,000 with the total capital gain on the whole portfolio amounting to £1m. They are currently both higher rate taxpayers but they are approaching retirement and now wish to close down their property business.

If they were to sell their entire portfolio straight away, they would be subject to CGT at 28% on their entire capital gains of £1m, less their two annual exemptions. They would therefore have a total CGT bill of £273,672 (£1m – 2 x £11,300 = £977,400 x 28%).

Instead of this, however, Bill and Kate decide to 'wind down gracefully'. They each retire before the end of the current tax year. This reduces their taxable income for 2018/19 to just £31,000 each.

They then start selling just one property each year and use the sale proceeds to both supplement their income and make a few investments elsewhere. In the first year, 2018/19, they each make a gain of £25,000 (£50,000/2) which is reduced to £13,400 each by their annual exemptions of £11,600 (say). As they each have more than £13,400 of their basic rate band available, they will pay CGT at just 18%, i.e. £2,412 (£13,400 x 18%), or £4,824 in total.

Their taxable income will change over the next 19 years due to a combination of many factors, including:

- Restrictions in interest relief (see Section 4.5)
- Reduction in rental income due to sale of properties
- Increases in yield from remaining properties
- Income from investments purchased with property sale proceeds
- Beginning to receive their state pensions

However, we will assume for the sake of illustration that they are able to keep their income at a level which means their basic rate bands continue to cover their taxable gains each year.

We will also make the fairly conservative assumption that the CGT annual exemption increases by just £300 each year. This means that, over the 20 year period they are selling off their properties, the annual exemption averages £14,450. Their taxable gains may therefore be summarised as follows:

	£
Total capital gains	1,000,000
Annual exemptions (2 x 20 x £14,450)	578,000

Taxable gains	422,000
	========

The total CGT payable at 18% is therefore just £75,960, meaning that Bill and Kate have saved almost £200,000! (£273,672 – £75,960 = £197,712 saved)

Is This Realistic?

Yes: I have a computer model which factors in the changes in Bill and Kate's taxable income as listed above and which shows that their taxable gains still remain within the basic rate band each year. This is based on a number of assumptions which are set out below.

Whilst I am confident that my assumptions are reasonable, not everyone's results will work out the same as Bill and Kate's. Nonetheless, out of a saving of almost £200,000, over £155,000 of this is due to using 40 annual exemptions instead of just two and this saving would still be available even if the couple were higher rate taxpayers.

One important factor I did ignore is the fact that there will probably be considerable capital growth in Bill and Kate's properties over the next 20 years. I did this in order to make a fair comparison between the CGT arising on an immediate sale and the tax arising on the same sale proceeds spread out over a longer period.

In effect, we can say that Bill and Kate have saved almost £200,000 on their **existing** capital gains.

However, if we make one further assumption: that the value of Bill and Kate's properties increases by 5% each year, we can make a more realistic comparison.

Example Part 2
Based on the assumptions set out below, Bill and Kate's net proceeds on an immediate sale would be £601,328 (£1.75m less CGT of £273,672 and borrowings of £875,000).

Their total sale proceeds under the winding down gracefully strategy (one sale per year) would be £3,037,935 and their CGT bills would total £374,172. After repaying their borrowings, they would be left with a net sum of £1,788,763.

Winding down gracefully would therefore leave Bill and Kate **almost £1.2 Million Pounds better off** in cash terms!

But the value of cash received in 20 years' time is not the same as receiving that cash today. So, let's discount Bill and Kate's future receipts at a rate of, say, 2.5% per year to see if they are really better off.

On this basis, we get a 'present value' for Bill and Kate's future net proceeds of £1,320,172, meaning that, even taking the time value of money into account, they are still over £700,000 better off in the end. (And that's not even including all the rental income they will have received over the next 20 years.)

Wealth Warning

The above example is based on the assumption that CGT rates will not increase in the future. There is no guarantee that such increases will not occur. If tax rates increase significantly, investors like Bill and Kate could be better off selling the majority of their portfolio now.

Even under these circumstances, it may still make sense for investors with rental losses brought forward to retain some property in order to utilise those losses. As we saw in Section 4.12, however, only one property needs to be retained to preserve the benefit of rental losses.

Assumptions Made in the 'Bill and Kate' Example

i)   Bill and Kate both begin to receive their state pensions in October 2024
ii)   Their state pension entitlement is based on a current value of £8,000 each, increased by 2.5% each year
iii)   The higher rate tax threshold will rise to £50,000 in roughly equal steps from 2018/19 to 2020/21 and then increase by 2.5% each year thereafter. (George Osborne promised that it would increase to at least £50,000 by 2020/21, although your guess is as good as mine as to whether we can still rely on that promise!)
iv)   The CGT annual exemption increases by £300 each year in Part 1 of the example
v)   The CGT annual exemption increases by 2.5% each year in Part 2 of the example
vi)   Each property has a current value of £87,500. This equates to a total of £1.75m for the 20 properties in the portfolio
vii)   Each property has a mortgage equal to 50% of its current value, with interest payable at 3%. Total mortgages at the outset are thus £875,000
viii)   The properties currently yield net profits before interest (but after all other allowable costs) equal to 4.5% of current value
ix)   Rental profits before interest increase by 5% each year from 2019/20 onwards
x)   25% of net sale proceeds after tax are invested. The investments grow at 5% per annum and yield annual income equal to 2.5% of value
xi)   Properties grow in value at the rate of 5% per year (Part 2 only)
xii)   Bill and Kate have no other income after 2017/18 apart from their rental income, income from investments per (x) above and state pensions per (ii) above
xiii)   There are no changes in CGT rates (see 'Wealth Warning' above!)

8.29   ROLLOVER RELIEF

The capital gain arising on the sale of a property used in your own trading business may be rolled over into the purchase of a new trading property within the period beginning one year before, and ending three years after, the date of disposal of the original property.

This effectively defers any CGT liability on the original property until such time as the new property is sold.

Property qualifying under the furnished holiday letting regime is treated as trading property for the purposes of this relief (see Section 8.17 for further details).

Full relief is available only if the old property was used exclusively for 'trading purposes' throughout your ownership, or at least since 31st March 1982, if it was acquired earlier. Furthermore, for rollover relief purposes, it is the sale **proceeds** of the old property which must be reinvested and not merely the capital gain. Any shortfall in the amount reinvested is deducted from the amount of gain eligible for rollover.

If there is less than full trading use of the property then an appropriate proportion of the gain arising may be rolled over.

Example
Stavros sells an office building in March 2018 for £600,000, realising a capital gain of £240,000. He has owned the building since March 2008 and, up until March 2013 he rented all of it out to tenants. From March 2013 until the date of sale he used two thirds of the building as his own premises from which he ran a property development business.

Stavros is therefore eligible to roll over £80,000 (£240,000 x 5/10 x 2/3) of his capital gain into the purchase of new trading premises. The eligible amount has been restricted by reference to both the time the property was used for trading purposes and the proportion of the property used for trading purposes.

In August 2018, Stavros buys a small gift shop in Cornwall for £180,000 and begins to use it as his own trading premises.

Stavros is therefore able to claim rollover relief of £60,000. He cannot claim the full £80,000 which was eligible for rollover, because he has only reinvested £180,000 out of the £200,000 qualifying portion of his sale proceeds (£600,000 x 5/10 x 2/3 = £200,000).

The new qualifying property does not need to be in the same trade or even the same kind of trade. It could even be a qualifying furnished holiday let.

There is no minimum period for which the new property needs to be used for trading purposes, although it must be acquired with the intention of using it for trading purposes.

In our example, Stavros could run the gift shop for, say, two years and then convert it into residential property. His CGT rollover relief would not be clawed back, although he would have a reduced base cost for the property when he eventually came to sell it.

Tax Tip

Where you have a capital gain eligible for rollover relief, it is only necessary to use the replacement property for trading purposes for a limited period. This might include initially running the new property as a guest house or qualifying furnished holiday let before later converting to long-term letting or even adopting it as your own home.

What Kinds of Investment Properties Can Qualify?

Rollover relief is generally only available to property investors for:

- Furnished holiday lettings (see Section 8.17)
- The trading premises of a property development, property dealing or property management business
- Property where the owner provides significant additional services

The latter case would generally require a level of services akin to a guest house, although the owner need not reside there themselves.

Gains on other rental properties may be eligible for rollover relief in certain limited circumstances, such as a compulsory purchase of commercial property, or residential property purchased by a tenant under the Leasehold Reform Act 1967.

8.30   USING YOUR BASIC RATE BAND TO SAVE CAPITAL GAINS TAX

The rate of CGT applying to most gains depends on the level of your taxable income for the relevant tax year.

At current rates, savings of up to £3,350 can be achieved by ensuring that your capital gains fall into a tax year in which you have a lower level of income. This saving represents the difference between the rates of CGT applying to gains falling into the current basic rate band of £33,500 (10% or 18%) and the rates applying once the basic rate band has been exhausted (20% or 28%).

Where you are also able to utilise your annual CGT exemption, the total saving available could be up to £6,514 (£3,350 + £11,300 x 28%).

How Can Property Investors Use These Savings?

We have already seen one example of how property investors may be able to use these savings in Section 8.28, where a property investor couple were pursuing a strategy of 'winding down gracefully'. This could typically arise where the investors have retired from previous employment or self-employment and are now living off modest pensions plus their rental income.

Even small investors with only one or two properties may be able to make significant CGT savings by waiting until they retire before selling their properties.

Example
Edwina has a residential investment property which will yield a capital gain of £60,000 when she sells it. She has a salary of £40,000 in 2017/18 but is due to retire on 31st March 2018. She is also currently making a rental profit of £1,000 per month.

If Edwina was to sell her property shortly before 5th April 2018, she would be subject to CGT at 28% on a gain of £48,700 (£60,000 less her annual exemption of £11,300), giving her a bill of £13,636.

If, however, she was to delay her sale until 6th April 2018, or shortly afterwards, she would pay CGT at just 18% on the first £34,800 of her taxable gain, thus reducing her tax bill to just £10,072 (see notes below).

Notes to the Example
i)   The basic rate band for 2018/19 has been estimated at £34,800
ii)   The annual exemption for 2018/19 has been estimated at £11,600
iii)   I have assumed that Edwina's total income for 2018/19 will be less than her personal allowance. A retiring taxpayer can usually achieve this by deferring their pension entitlement. Even if Edwina had some investment income which used up part of her basic rate band, she would still make a considerable saving by waiting until after she retires to sell her property
iv)   I have also assumed that CGT rates will remain the same in 2018/19
v)   Remember that the date of sale for CGT purposes is the date on which there is an unconditional sales contract (see Section 6.6)

The example also demonstrates the fact that selling an investment property early in a tax year means that there is less income from that property to use up your basic rate band, thus potentially producing a CGT saving.

There are many other situations where property investors may be able to reduce their CGT liability by selling property in a tax year in which their taxable income is at a lower level. Examples include:

- Self-employed taxpayers making large capital allowances claims
- Employed taxpayers on career breaks
- Company owners who are able to refrain from taking income out of their company that year
- Furnished holiday letting landlords with large capital allowances claims
- Investors reducing their taxable income by making tax-advantaged investments, such as investment bonds

Remember, however, that there is no guarantee that CGT rates will not be increased in the future.

Extending the Basic Rate Band

The basic rate band can currently be extended through the payment of pension contributions or gift aid donations. Whilst it is generally more beneficial to use this as a means to save Income Tax, it can also be used to save CGT. Furthermore, where a property owner is unlikely to ever have income in excess of the higher rate tax threshold, this may be their best opportunity to make tax savings through these payments.

Example Revisited
In Section 6.4, we met Boudicca who had a taxable gain of £38,000. She had taxable income of £30,000, leaving £15,000 of her basic rate band available which reduced her CGT bill to £9,140.

Let us now assume that Boudicca makes a net pension contribution of £2,880 in March 2018. This is grossed up for the basic rate tax relief given at source and is treated as a 'gross' pension contribution of £3,600, thus extending Boudicca's basic rate band to £37,100 (£33,500 + £3,600) and giving her a higher rate tax threshold of £48,600 (£45,000 + £3,600).

This means that there is now £18,600 (£48,600 – £30,000) of Boudicca's basic rate band available and her CGT calculation will be as follows:

£18,600 x 18% =	*£3,348*
£19,400 x 28% =	*£5,432*
Total	*£8,780*

Boudicca's pension contribution has saved her £360 in CGT.

Combining the tax relief of £720 given at source with her £360 CGT saving gives Boudicca a total benefit of £1,080: increasing the value of her net pension contribution by 37.5%.

A gross pension contribution of £3,600 (or £2,880 net) is the maximum for which an individual with no taxable earnings is able to obtain tax relief. 'Earnings' for this purpose means employment income or self-employment or partnership trading income.

Those with earnings of more than £3,600 can generally obtain tax relief for gross contributions up to the lower of £40,000 or the total amount of their earnings for the year.

8.31 AVOIDING THE HIGH INCOME CHILD BENEFIT CHARGE

Many parents are now suffering the draconian HICBC on income between £50,000 and £60,000. This creates the truly horrendous tax rates set out in the table in Section 3.3. Some property investor couples may, however, be able to avoid the HICBC by redistributing their income.

Example
Salvatore and Cherilyn are a married couple with a portfolio of rental properties yielding total annual profits of £90,000. Cherilyn owns more properties than Salvatore, so she receives £60,000 of this profit.

The couple also have three young children and are therefore eligible to claim £2,501 per year in Child Benefit (at current rates). However, Cherilyn's profit share means that she will effectively have to repay the Child Benefit by way of an additional Income Tax charge of £2,501.

The answer to this problem is simple: Cherilyn should transfer some of her properties to Salvatore. If, as a result, Cherilyn's share of the couple's profits is reduced to £50,000 or less, she will not be subject to the HICBC – thus saving the couple £2,501 per year (at current rates).

Ideally, it would generally be best if the couple owned all their properties jointly. They would then have profits of £45,000 each. Not only would they avoid the HICBC, they would also make further savings by making full use of Salvatore's basic rate tax band.

In short, many couples can avoid some or all of the HICBC by evening up, or equalising, their income – and the easiest way to do that is to own all their properties jointly.

One of the consequences of the restrictions on Income Tax relief for interest paid by residential landlords is that many more property investor couples are likely to be caught by the HICBC in the future. All of the advice given above remains sound, but these couples will need to reduce their taxable 'profit' under the new rules set out in Section 4.5 to £50,000 per person, or less, in order to avoid the HICBC.

Unmarried Couples

For unmarried couples, the solution is not so simple, as a direct transfer of properties from one partner to the other, or into joint names, will generally lead to a CGT charge. This can often be avoided, however, by using the technique set out in Section 8.8.

Joint Income over £100,000

A couple with total joint taxable income over £100,000 may not be able to avoid the HICBC altogether but, if your total joint taxable income is less than £120,000, you could still minimise the overall impact by equalising your income as discussed above. Alternatively, you could avoid the HICBC by transferring properties into a trust or a company. These strategies have many further tax implications and require professional advice.

8.32 PARTNERSHIP PROBLEMS

Some of the legal background to property partnerships was covered in Section 2.14. Most of the tax rules outlined throughout this guide apply equally to partnerships, including any individual members of corporate or limited partnerships.

> **Wealth Warning**
> Profit shares attributed to a member of a partnership which is not subject to UK Income Tax (typically a company) may, under certain circumstances, be allocated to the individual members of the partnership for tax purposes.

In many ways, a property partnership simply combines joint ownership with a more sophisticated profit sharing agreement. However, a partnership is considerably more flexible, as, subject to the terms of the partnership agreement, partners may join, leave or change their profit share at any time.

Each partner is taxed on his or her share of rental income, trading profits or capital gains, as allocated according to the partnership agreement (subject to the 'Wealth Warning' above).

There are, however, restrictions on any 'non-active' partners claiming relief for their share of partnership trading losses. Broadly speaking, a partner is usually classed as 'non-active' if they spend an average of less than ten hours per week engaged in the partnership's trading activities.

Firstly, the total cumulative amount of loss which a non-active partner may claim is restricted to the amount of capital which they have invested in the partnership. Capital contributions may be excluded if the investment was made primarily to secure extra loss relief.

Secondly, there is an annual limit of £25,000 on claims for partnership trading loss relief by non-active partners. This limit applies to the total claims made by any individual each tax year in respect of all partnerships in which they are a non-active partner and any trade in which they are a so-called 'non-active sole trader' (see Section 5.12).

The restriction of relief for partnership trading losses is of particular concern to 'husband and wife' property trading partnerships where one spouse is not actively involved. Getting the less active spouse to work in the business for at least ten hours a week may therefore be advisable.

Interest Relief

Partnerships investing in residential rental property are subject to the same restrictions on tax relief for interest and finance costs as individuals (see Section 4.5).

A partner who borrows funds to invest in the partnership is entitled to tax relief for the interest on those borrowings but this, again, is subject to the restrictions set out in Section 4.5 (to the extent that the partnership is investing in residential rental property) and also to the tax relief 'cap' explained in Section 3.11.

Stamp Duty Land Tax

A major drawback to property investment partnerships is the danger of incurring SDLT charges at frequent intervals. SDLT is payable whenever a partner:

a) Introduces property into a partnership,
b) Takes property out of a partnership, or
c) Changes their profit share

SDLT may also be charged on partners withdrawing capital from a partnership within three years of introducing property.

Example Part 1
Dave has been in a property investment partnership with four friends, Dozy, Beaky, Mick and Tich, for several years. The five friends each have a 20% profit share. Dave would now like to retire and wishes to leave the partnership. The partners agree that, by way of consideration for giving up his partnership share, Dave should take the property known as 'Dee Towers' with him. Dee Towers is an office building worth £1m.

Dave already had a 20% share in Dee Towers through the partnership, so he is treated as acquiring an 80% share, worth £800,000, when he leaves. He will therefore face a SDLT charge of £29,500! (See Section 7.5)

Example Part 2
A short time later, Mick inherits £1m from his great aunt Shirley. He decides that he would like to invest this in the partnership. At the same time, Tich has decided that he would like to retire and wishes to sell his partnership share. Mick therefore buys Tich's 25% partnership share for £1m, thus increasing his own share from 25% to 50%.

Immediately prior to Mick's new investment, the partnership had a commercial property portfolio with a total gross value of £20m and borrowings of £16m. Whilst the partnership's net assets are only £4m, the SDLT charge is based on the property portfolio's gross value.

Mick has increased his profit share from 25% to 50%. He is therefore treated as having acquired a 25% interest in commercial property worth £20m. Hence, Mick will be faced with a SDLT bill of £239,500! (See Section 7.5)

By and large, therefore, anyone using a property investment partnership should try to get their profit shares right in the first place and do their utmost to avoid changing them at a later stage.

Note, however, that a straightforward cash investment into the partnership will not incur any SDLT charge if there is no change in the partnership profit shares. Hence, if Mick had simply put £1m into the partnership, rather than buying out Tich's share, he could have avoided the SDLT charge.

Note also that the amount which Mick paid for Tich's share has no bearing on the amount of SDLT payable which is based instead on the gross value of the partnership's property portfolio. It is worth contrasting this with the position which would have existed if the five friends had set up a property investment company instead.

Subject to some anti-avoidance rules, the shares in a property investment company can change hands for a Stamp Duty charge of only 0.5%: which represents a considerable saving compared to the rates which often apply to property investment partnerships. Furthermore, the charge on company shares would be based on the actual consideration paid for those shares and not on the gross value of the underlying properties.

Example Revisited

As above, Mick is investing £1m in a property investment business which owns a property portfolio with a gross value of £20m but has net assets of only £4m. This time, however, he is purchasing shares in a property investment company. His Stamp Duty liability will therefore be just £5,000.

The lesson here is clear – if you and your colleagues are likely to change profit shares with any degree of frequency whatsoever, a company is likely to be much better than a partnership.

Other Partnerships Holding Property

There is no SDLT charge on the purchase of profit share in most trading partnerships, including a property management partnership. Sadly, however, this relaxation does not apply to property investment, property development or property dealing partnerships.

The other charges described above continue to apply to all partnerships.

Wealth Warning

HMRC interprets the SDLT rules for partnerships as applying not only to property held by the partnership, but also to property held by an individual partner for use in the partnership business.

Land and Buildings Transaction Tax

Partnerships investing in property in Scotland will be subject to LBTT on those properties rather than SDLT. Most of the principles outlined above continue to apply, although the rates are different (see Section 7.20).

The position for purchasing shares in a property investment company is not affected by the location of the company's properties. Hence, in 'Example Revisited', Mick would still have paid Stamp Duty of £5,000 if the company's properties had been in Scotland.

The Annual Investment Allowance

In most cases, the AIA is available to partnerships in the same way as any other business entity (see Section 3.10). However, where one or more of the members of the partnership is a company, the AIA will not be available.

8.33   LIMITED LIABILITY PARTNERSHIPS

Like a Scottish partnership, a limited liability partnership ('LLP'), is a legal person and may own property directly. All of the rules described in the previous section apply equally to LLPs, subject to the points set out below.

Interest on funds borrowed to invest in, or lend to, a property investment LLP is not eligible for any Income Tax relief.

An LLP is not eligible to claim the AIA.

Members of an LLP whose profit share is mostly fixed without reference to the overall performance of the business may, under certain circumstances, be treated as employees for Income Tax and NI purposes.

8.34   EMIGRATION

As explained in Sections 2.15 and 6.3, non-UK residents are not generally liable to UK CGT on commercial property or on overseas property. They are liable for UK CGT on UK residential property: but only on the part of any gain arising after 5th April 2015.

Hence, there are still opportunities to make significant CGT savings by emigrating. However, merely going on a world cruise for a year will not be sufficient, as it is usually necessary to become non-UK resident for more than five years in order to avoid paying UK CGT in full on all your capital gains.

The Taxcafe.co.uk guide *'Tax Free Capital Gains'* includes detailed guidance on how to successfully achieve, and maintain, non-UK resident status through emigration. The guide also provides a detailed examination of the UK CGT regime applying to non-UK residents, together with advice on how non-UK residents can avoid, or at least reduce, UK CGT through numerous tax-planning strategies.

In this section, I will just provide a brief overview of what is required to successfully achieve non-UK resident status for CGT purposes and the benefits arising. The main points worth noting are:

- Emigration must generally be permanent, or at least long-term (a period of more than five years is usually required)
- Disposals should be deferred until non-UK resident
- Limited return visits to the UK are permitted but these are subject to some very complex rules which can be extremely restrictive
- Resuming UK residence before the expiry of the required period may result in substantial CGT liabilities
- It is essential to ensure that there is no risk of inadvertently becoming liable for some form of capital taxation elsewhere. (There's no point 'jumping out of the frying pan into the fire!')

Emigration to avoid UK CGT is a strategy which is generally only worth contemplating when the stakes are high. Naturally, therefore, detailed professional advice is always essential. The following example illustrates the broad outline of what is involved.

Example
Eleanor has been a highly successful property investor for many years. By April 2015, she has a UK residential property portfolio worth £12m and would face potential CGT liabilities of over £2m if she were to sell it. She also has some commercial property investments which would give rise to a further £1m of CGT if she disposed of them.

Eleanor therefore decides to emigrate and, on 3rd April 2018, she flies to Utopia where she settles down to a new life.

During the 2018/19 UK tax year, Eleanor sells all her UK properties. She is fully exempt from any UK CGT on her commercial properties as she is a non-UK resident.

Her UK residential property portfolio sells for a total of £13m. As a non-UK resident, she is only liable for UK CGT on the portfolio's increase in value after

5th April 2015: £1m. Hence, she has a UK CGT bill of just £280,000 (£1m x 28%).

(I have ignored the annual exemption for the sake of illustration and assumed that Eleanor is a higher rate taxpayer for UK Income Tax purposes.)

Eventually, Eleanor decides that she wants to return home and, on 8th April 2023, she comes back to the UK to live. As Eleanor was non-UK resident for over five years, she will remain exempt from UK CGT on the remaining, more substantial, part of the capital gains realised in 2018/19.

In this example, emigrating has saved Eleanor more than £3m in UK CGT: all of the tax which would have arisen on her commercial properties and all of the tax which would have arisen on her UK residential properties if she had sold them for their market value on 5th April 2015.

Remember, however, that Utopia does not exist. Real countries have their own tax systems and may potentially tax immigrants like Eleanor on their UK capital gains. It is therefore always essential to take detailed local professional advice in the destination country.

8.35 YEAR END TAX PLANNING

Rental Income

For individuals with rental income, it is generally necessary to draw up accounts for the tax year, rather than for any other accounting period. Hence, for these property businesses, 5th April is usually twice as important since, not only is it the end of the tax year, but it is generally also the end of their accounting period.

Where I refer in this section to 'your year end', those with property rental businesses should therefore generally read this as meaning 5th April.

Property Trades

As we saw in Chapter 5, those with property trades may choose their own accounting date. Where I refer in this section to 'your year end', those with property trades should read this as meaning their own accounting date, rather than the tax year end.

The Tax Year End

Where I refer to 'the tax year end' this means 5th April whatever kind of business you have!

Timing Is Everything

For most property businesses the 'accruals' basis will apply, meaning income and expenditure must be recognised when it arises or is incurred, rather than when it is received or paid. Hence, whenever you need to make some business expenditure in the near future, it may make sense to ensure that it takes place by your year end, in order to get tax relief in an earlier year, rather than having to wait another twelve months.

Obviously, this does not mean it is worth incurring expenditure just for the sake of it. It is seldom wise to make uncommercial decisions purely for tax reasons! What it does mean is that it can often be worth accelerating some of the expenditure, which is going to be taking place in any case, so that it falls into an earlier accounting year.

Conversely, those who are basic rate taxpayers this year, but expect to be higher rate taxpayers next year, may be better off by delaying business expenditure so that it falls into next year and provides tax relief at 40% instead of just 20%.

Furthermore, in some cases, those expecting total taxable income between £100,000 and £123,600, or over £150,000, next year may also be better off by delaying business expenditure so that it falls into that year and provides tax relief at 45% or 60% (see Section 3.3 and Appendix A). The same may apply to some of those who expect to be subject to the HICBC next year (see Section 3.3).

Businesses on a Cash Basis

For businesses operating on a cash basis (see Sections 4.18 and 5.13) the tax-planning objective will usually be to accelerate the actual *payment* of any necessary expenditure to before the accounting year end.

Landlords on the cash basis might also do well to consider setting the due dates for rent receivable to fall shortly after the tax year end.

Any property traders using the cash basis may want to consider deferring sales until after their accounting year end where possible.

As before, the position may differ if the taxpayer expects a higher level of total taxable income next year.

Capital Allowances

Where capital allowances are available (see Section 3.10 for details), the full allowance is usually given for the year in which the expenditure is incurred. Where expenditure is eligible for capital allowances, therefore, consider making your purchase by your year end.

However, where you have already incurred qualifying expenditure in excess of the AIA (see Section 3.10) this year, it may be more beneficial to defer any further expenditure in order to get full tax relief for it in your next accounting period rather than a writing down allowance of just 8% or 18%.

Note that any assets bought on Hire Purchase must actually be brought into use in the business by your year end to qualify for capital allowances.

Cars

Some capital allowances may be available on a car which you use in your property business. The allowance is usually restricted by reference to the private use of the car, but nevertheless it is worth noting that:

- A balancing allowance is usually available on the sale of an old car previously used in your property business, and
- A full year's allowance will be given on any new car brought into use in the business by your year end

Hence, both sales of old cars and purchases of new cars before your year end will often save tax where the vehicles are used in your property business.

Beware, however, that sales of old cars can sometimes give rise to a balancing charge (although a balancing allowance is far more common).

Employees' Bonuses

If you have any employees in your property business, it may be worth considering whether you wish to pay any of them a bonus before your year end. However, bonuses are only worth thinking about from a tax-planning point of view if either:

a) You were going to pay them anyway, or
b) The employee is your spouse, partner or other family member.

Those with a spouse, partner or other family member working in their business may also wish to ensure that these employees receive sufficient salary by the tax year end to utilise their personal allowances.

Appendix A

UK Tax Rates and Allowances: 2016/17 to 2018/19

	Rates	2016/17 £	2017/18 £	2018/19 £
Income Tax				
Personal allowance		11,000	11,500	11,800(2)
Basic rate band (3)	20%	32,000	33,500	34,800(2)
Higher rate/Threshold (3)	40%	43,000	45,000	46,600(2)
Personal allowance withdrawal				
Effective rate/From	60%	100,000	100,000	100,000(2)
To		122,000	123,000	123,600(2)
Additional rate/Threshold	45%	150,000	150,000	150,000(2)
Starting rate band (4)	0%	5,000	5,000	5,000(2)
Personal savings allowance (5)		1,000	1,000	1,000(2)
Dividend allowance		5,000	5,000	2,000
Marriage allowance (6)		1,100	1,150	1,180(2)
National Insurance				
Threshold	9%/12%	8,060(7)	8,164	8,372(1)
Upper earnings limit	2%	43,000	45,000	46,600(2)
Employment allowance		3,000	3,000	3,000(2)
Pension Contributions				
Annual allowance		40,000	40,000	40,000(2)
Lifetime allowance		1m	1m	1.025m(1)
Capital Gains Tax				
Annual exemption		11,100	11,300	11,600(1)
Inheritance Tax				
Nil rate band		325,000	325,000	325,000
Main residence nil rate band		n/a	100,000	125,000
Annual Exemption		3,000	3,000	3,000
Corporation Tax Rate		20%	19%	19%
VAT Threshold		83,000	85,000	88,000(1)

Notes

1. Estimated, based on CPI inflation at 2.5%
2. Assumed/estimated based on announcements to date
3. Reduced basic rate band and higher rate threshold apply for Scottish taxpayers from 2017/18 (see Section 7.22)
4. Applies to interest and savings income only
5. Halved for higher rate taxpayers; not available to additional rate taxpayers
6. Available where neither spouse pays higher rate tax
7. Secondary threshold for employers was £8,112 in 2016/17. Thresholds aligned thereafter

Short Leases

(See Section 6.34)

Proportion of the original cost of a lease of 50 or more years' duration allowed as a deduction for CGT purposes on a disposal of that lease.

Years Remaining	%	Years Remaining	%
50	100	25	81.100
49	99.657	24	79.622
48	99.289	23	78.055
47	98.902	22	76.399
46	98.490	21	74.635
45	98.059	20	72.770
44	97.595	19	70.791
43	97.107	18	68.697
42	96.593	17	66.470
41	96.041	16	64.116
40	95.457	15	61.617
39	94.842	14	58.971
38	94.189	13	56.167
37	93.497	12	53.191
36	92.761	11	50.038
35	91.981	10	46.695
34	91.156	9	43.154
33	90.280	8	39.399
32	89.354	7	35.414
31	88.371	6	31.195
30	87.330	5	26.722
29	86.226	4	21.983
28	85.053	3	16.959
27	83.816	2	11.629
26	82.496	1	5.983

Appendix C

Abbreviations Used in this Guide

ADS	Additional Dwelling Supplement
AIA	Annual Investment Allowance
ATED	The Annual Tax on Enveloped Dwellings
CGT	Capital Gains Tax
CIS	Construction Industry Scheme
EEA	European Economic Area
GAAR	General Anti-Abuse Rule
HICBC	High Income Child Benefit Charge
HMRC	HM Revenue and Customs
IHT	Inheritance Tax
LBTT	Land and Buildings Transaction Tax
LLP	Limited Liability Partnership
MTD	Making Tax Digital
NI	National Insurance
PAYE	Pay As You Earn
PPR	Principal Private Residence
SDLT	Stamp Duty Land Tax
SIPP	Self-Invested Personal Pension Scheme
UK	United Kingdom
UTR	Unique Taxpayer Reference
VAT	Value Added Tax

Lightning Source UK Ltd.
Milton Keynes UK
UKOW06f0605030917
308453UK00003B/33/P